D0772371

Governing Ideas

A volume in the series

Cornell Studies in Political Economy

EDITED BY PETER J. KATZENSTEIN

A full list of titles in the series appears at the end of the book.

NATIONAL UNIVERSITY
LIBRARY   SAN DIEGO

Governing Ideas

STRATEGIES FOR INNOVATION IN FRANCE AND GERMANY

J. NICHOLAS ZIEGLER

CORNELL UNIVERSITY PRESS

Ithaca and London

Copyright © 1997 by Cornell University

All rights reserved. Except for brief quotations in a review, this book, or parts thereof, must not be reproduced in any form without permission in writing from the publisher. For information, address Cornell University Press, Sage House, 512 East State Street, Ithaca, New York 14850.

First published 1997 by Cornell University Press
First printing, Cornell Paperbacks, 1997

Printed in the United States of America

Cornell University Press strives to utilize environmentally responsible suppliers and materials to the fullest extent possible in the publishing of its books. Such materials include vegetable-based, low-VOC inks and acid-free papers that are also either recycled, totally chlorine-free, or partly composed of nonwood fibers.

Library of Congress Cataloging-in-Publication Data

Ziegler, J. Nicholas
    Governing ideas : strategies for innovation in France and Germany
/ J. Nicholas Ziegler.
        p.   cm. — (Cornell studies in political economy)
    Includes index.
    ISBN 0-8014-3311-8 (alk. paper). — ISBN 0-8014-8371-9 (pbk. : alk. paper)
    1. Technological innovations—Economic aspects—France.
  2. Technological innovations—Economic aspects—Germany.
  3. Technology and state—France.   4. Technology and state—Germany.
  I. Title. II. Series.
  HC280.T4Z54   1997
  338'.064'0943—dc21   97-7144

Cloth printing   10 9 8 7 6 5 4 3 2 1

Contents

Preface | vii

1. Technology and the Politics of Knowledge-Based Competition | 1

2. Professional Identities and Policy Strategies | 17

3. Digitizing the Public Telephone Network: Telecommunications | 40

4. Retooling the Industrial Plant: Machine Tools | 91

5. Searching for Industrial Sovereignty: Semiconductors | 157

6. Conclusion | 197

Notes | 211

Index | 247

Preface

This book asks why different countries approach the challenges of economic competition so differently. It seeks an answer by examining public policies for promoting technological advance in France and Germany. Few spheres of human activity have become so intimately linked in practice, and so frequently separated in theory, as politics and technology. Since economic competition hinges increasingly on the use of knowledge, political leaders have come to see technological innovation as an ever more attractive source of growth. Yet, the ways in which technology policies alter the distribution of knowledge remain much less clear or predictable than the ways in which other policies alter the distribution of material resources.

My original goal in comparing French and German technology policies was to illuminate the impact of politics on the ability of industrial firms to apply scientific knowledge to the tasks of product development and process innovation. France and Germany seemed excellent cases for such a comparison. Political leaders in both countries took an active role in economic development, but they did so with the aid of very different political institutions and policy instruments. In conducting fieldwork—interviewing officials and managers, reading trade journals, visiting production sites—I soon learned that my emphasis on the formal legal institutions of government failed to capture much of the story. The strategies and plans developed by policymakers might well follow hypotheses derived from the literature on comparative politics. But the realization and modification of those policies over time were strongly affected by knowledge-bearing groups—especially scientists, engineers, technicians, and skilled workers—and by the way these groups conceived of their roles in public efforts at innovation. In the course of my research,

I therefore focused increasingly on the links between policymakers and these other knowledge-bearing elites.

From this research and subsequent analysis, I argue that public strategies for innovation are decisively shaped by knowledge-bearing groups that view alternative policies largely in terms of their compatibility with established jurisdictions and professional self-images. This approach differs from most perspectives on public policy, which explain government action either through the relative power of domestic interest groups or through the structure of particular public agencies. These approaches tend to view policy challenges as given and policy consequences as self-evident. My approach, by contrast, asks why policymaking elites in different countries define policy tasks in such distinctive ways, and why other knowledge-bearing elites perceive their roles in implementing these policies so differently in different countries.

In answering these questions, this book makes three basic points. First, I argue that the advanced economies are shifting steadily from scale-based competition to knowledge-based competition. One result is that the distinctive approaches to technology observed in different countries result not so much from explicit national "strategies" or predetermined "trajectories" as from longstanding and persistent relations between policymakers and knowledge-bearing elites. The prerogatives, prestige hierarchies, and informal codes of conduct that govern these relations are rooted in historical processes by which expert occupations achieve public recognition.

Second, by emphasizing the importance of historically produced occupational identities, I call for a broadened understanding of the comparative analysis of institutions. I argue that the main schools of analysis, which see institutions as frameworks of recognized rules or as organizational structures defined by control over material resources, are incomplete. These forms of institutional analysis rest on the clarity of utilitarian calculations made by autonomous actors. But many important domains of government action—of which technology policy is a key example— are characterized by such uncertainty that it is difficult for interest groups or other actors to anticipate their consequences. In these cases, contending actors continue to struggle over policies and institutions, but the struggles are motivated as much by conflicting identities as by conflicting interests. Along with the other approaches, we need a concept of institutional order that helps to illuminate the interplay of interests and identities.

Third, the close links between occupational identities and institutional forms illuminate the staying power of the distinctive national approaches to technology documented in this book. Even in times of economic internationalization, institutions for research and development make knowledge available to firms in patterned ways. These mechanisms for the diffusion of knowledge, in turn, make it more rational for firms in different countries to pursue some innovation strategies rather than others. Since these mechanisms rest on the identities of certain occupational groups, they cannot be changed by legislative acts that alter the rules of the game or by shifts in the nature of resource dependencies among organizations. This does not mean that institutions for science and technology are immutable, but it does mean that they change slowly through an incremental process of interaction between formal rules and the inherited identities of knowledge-bearing elites. This approach to processes of competitive adjustment has significant implications for practical policy approaches, as well as future research.

This book is the product of a lengthy itinerary, intellectual as well as geographic, during which I received help from numerous individuals and institutions. One of the pleasures of finishing it is the opportunity to thank them.

I have benefited enormously from the intellectual environment of Cambridge, Massachusetts, which served as my home base for the project. The book began in the Department of Government at Harvard University and was entirely revised at the Sloan School of Management at the Massachusetts Institute of Technology. A number of people at both institutions have, through their assistance and their own writings, provided guidance of a kind that goes far beyond the references in any text. Peter Hall has supported my work from the outset with his unparalleled blend of enthusiasm and clarity. Other exemplary teachers and scholars who have influenced this project include Suzanne Berger, Harvey Brooks, Stanley Hoffmann, Richard Locke, Charles Maier, Gene Skolnikoff, and Ray Vernon.

During my years at Harvard, I received particularly important advice and encouragement from Sam Huntington, Joseph Nye, Robert Putnam, and the late Judith Shklar. Office space and subsequent support were provided by the Center for International Affairs and the Center for European Studies, where Abigail Collins and Guido Goldman generously encouraged my efforts.

During my further work on this project, colleagues at MIT have helped in many ways. The insights I gained at the Sloan School enabled me to understand my findings from entirely new perspectives. I particularly thank Michael Cusumano, Mauro Guillén, Rebecca Henderson, Tom

Kochan, Don Lessard, Willie Ocasio, Paul Osterman, Ed Roberts, Eleanor Westney, and Joanne Yates. My neighbors in the Political Science Department at MIT who provided constructive criticism and encouragement at key points include Ken Oye, Richard Samuels, Harvey Sapolsky, and Steve van Evera. I am also indebted to many students, including Phyllis Dininio, Jeff Furman, Andreas Gast, Gunnar Trumbull, and Rebecca Weil, for their research assistance as well as the challenging questions they asked.

In Europe, I received logistical and intellectual support from several sources. In Germany, I began fieldwork at the Deutsche Gesellschaft für Auswärtige Politik in Bonn. At a crucial juncture in the research, affiliation with the Max-Planck-Institut für Gesellschaftsforschung in Cologne allowed me to conduct important additional interviews. I am grateful to Renate Mayntz for inviting me to the Institute, and to Fritz Scharpf and Wolfgang Streeck for their hospitality on subsequent visits. In Paris, I received guidance from Jean-Jacques Salomon and Geneviève Schmeder at the Program in Science, Technologie, at Société of the Conservatoire National d'Arts et Métiers. Additional guidance in both countries was provided by François d'Alançon, Henri de Bresson, Élie Cohen, Henry Ergas, Beate Lindeman, Ingo Kolboom, Deborah Seward, Christiane Reichhardt, and Hans Vorländer.

In addition to those named above, many friends and scholars on both sides of the Atlantic took time from their own work to comment on the argument in one form or another: Chris Allen, Martin Baethge, Lewis Branscomb, Frank Dobbin, Aaron Friedberg, Edgar Grande, Steve Graubard, Jürgen Häusler, Ellen Immergut, Ethan Kapstein, Horst Kern, Jonah Levy, Charles Sabel, Anno Saxenian, F.-M. Scherer, David Soskice, Kathleen Thelen, Lowell Turner, David Vogel, Douglas Webber, Steve Weber, and John Zysman all helped me to make this a better book. Peter Katzenstein provided valuable advice at too many points to recount. Gary Herrigel's independence of mind made him a steadfast source of intellectual companionship.

Margaret Weir is in a category of her own. I'm not sure how she always managed to pose her unerring questions in the guise of cheerful encouragement, but by doing so she made all my tasks easier in this project as in others.

Financial support for research and writing came from the following foundations and grant programs: the Krupp program of the Center for European Studies at Harvard University, the Social Science Research Council, the Ford Foundation program in European Societies and Western Security, the MacArthur Foundation program in International Security, the Center for Science and International Affairs at Harvard University, the Dean's Fund at the Sloan School, the Friedrich-Ebert Stiftung in Bonn, and the Max-Planck-Institut für Gesellschaftsforschung in Cologne.

I received a different but no less important kind of aid from the scores of busy civil servants, elected officials, scientists, engineers, and company officials who consented to interviews. Given the potential sensitivity of the questions I asked, I have not identified interview subjects by name. In most cases, the interviews provided information that was corroborated by written sources; where interviews were the main source for information central to the argument, I have cited them in the notes, indicating the organization and date for each. Although the subjects' contributions therefore remain anonymous, such contributions are central to empirical research of this kind, and I hope my interview subjects will find my analysis faithful to the complexities of their experience.

For their remarkable humor and efficiency, I am grateful to Roger Haydon, Barbara Salazar, and Kay Scheuer at Cornell University Press.

Finally, I thank my parents, Pat and Jerry Ziegler, who first taught me the rewards of intellectual engagement and the value of informed citizenship. I dedicate the book to them.

J. NICHOLAS ZIEGLER

Cambridge, Massachusetts

Governing Ideas

CHAPTER ONE

Technology and the Politics of Knowledge-Based Competition

This book examines political strategies for promoting technological change in industry. Public policies to promote technology are ubiquitous and highly contentious. Periodically during the 1970s and 1980s, public officials in many countries seized upon industrial technology for its potential in bolstering economic performance. Faced with relentless pressures in the industrializing countries for higher living standards and anxious concerns in the advanced countries for continuing industrial competitiveness, political leaders tried to shape technological change to serve competitive performance. Entire societies adopted technological capability as one of the main indices for evaluating their political leadership and for comparing themselves to others.

Most studies of technology policy are couched in terms of government intervention and market outcomes. Proponents of an activist role for government typically argue that political interventions can provide essential support for critical industries if those interventions are intelligently planned and implemented. Opponents argue that government-supported technology projects are likely to be captured by industry interest groups in ways that preclude efficient management. In both views, the options are debated largely in terms of more government or less government.[1]

This book argues that the dichotomy between government intervention and laissez-faire is far too crude to illuminate the many mechanisms by which governments shape technological advance. Whether through specifically targeted programs or generally available public goods, politically allocated resources are necessarily part of the environment for innovation. Equally important, the terms of debate about the government's role in technology also vary dramatically from country to country. The terms of debate themselves matter because they inform the precise mechanisms by which public resources are distributed—often with decisive consequences for innovative performance.

The perspective I advance in this book centers neither on state agencies nor on market forces but rather on the links among different types of knowledge-bearing elites. Knowledge-bearing elites are those occupational groups whose livelihood and status depend on their use of specialized or expert knowledge. The knowledge-bearing elites most directly involved in public policies for industrial innovation include public administrators, scientists, engineers, and technically trained workers. These groups have grown in importance because industrial competition has shifted dramatically in recent decades from reliance on advantages of scale toward an emphasis on the use of specialized knowledge. This shift puts increasing importance on technological innovation and on the ability to combine the different types of knowledge that, together, may lead to innovation. The groups that carry this knowledge may be spread across state agencies and private organizations very differently in different countries. We therefore need some way to characterize and analyze the political interactions among them. I argue that these knowledge-bearing groups engage in an ongoing competition for influence, which I call "the politics of competence." This politics of competence, I contend, hinges on the professional authority that these groups exercise as well as on the material resources that they command.

By focusing on the politics of competence, my perspective differs from other approaches in several ways. First, since knowledge-bearing groups span public and private sectors, my approach emphasizes the relations among these groups as much as the structure of the organizations in which they work. Second, because some of the key groups involved in technological change are specific to particular industrial sectors, I investigate sectoral variations as well as cross-national variations. By focusing on groups that span the public-private boundary and by remaining sensitive to sectoral variation, my approach avoids the stark opposition between state capacities and market forces that characterizes most previous works that treat public strategies for innovation.

The tendency to look at technology policies in the dichotomous terms of state-versus-market is especially pronounced in the United States. Since policy debate relies heavily on comparisons between the United States and other countries, it implicitly establishes domestic institutions in the United States as the reference point. Some authors invoke U.S.

institutions as the standard for "fair" competition. Others belittle the effectiveness of U.S. institutions and exaggerate the virtues of other versions of capitalism. By uncritically elevating a single variant of capitalism to an ideal type, however, both views reinforce the misleading view that entire countries are either more or less suited to promoting innovation.

The approach taken in this book instead emphasizes the distinctive strengths and weaknesses of different countries in different industries. In order to illuminate the great variety of ways in which public policies shape processes of technological change, I compare two countries, France and Germany, where the central government has long played an accepted role in economic development. Specifically, I examine three industries that were central to the efforts of French and German policymakers to raise their countries' level of technology: telecommunications switching equipment, machine tools, and semiconductors.

The substantive importance of these cases needs little explanation. France and Germany are the largest industrial democracies after the United States and Japan. As two of Europe's second-wave industrial economies in the nineteenth century, they formed a variety of institutional arrangements and policy instruments for promoting industry. Their experience in recent decades therefore provides essential evidence for a more robust theory of the ways in which public policy and business competition are linked. The three sectors compared in this book are central to any country's ability to master the so-called information revolution. For comparative purposes, these industries display a range of sector-specific examples that illuminate public efforts to promote industrial change.

These three cross-national industry comparisons yield no simple pattern of success or failure. If anything, the observed patterns differ sharply from the expected outcomes. For the first few decades of the postwar period, France was viewed as the exemplary case of a country capable of promoting growth through political action. Germany was, by contrast, considered a country where centralized economic institutions dominated a fragmented federal state.[2] One implication of these views—accepted by many French and German citizens—was that France far outperformed Germany in technology-intensive industries. In the 1980s, however, the consensus began to change. Suddenly, Germany began to be viewed as having a remarkable capacity for adjusting to changing markets and technologies. French firms meanwhile were criticized for rigid internal organization and undue dependence on public policies such as competitive currency devaluation. At the same time, Japanese competitive strengths, which had previously been likened to France's political capacities, began to appear more similar to the German pattern of industrial networks and strong currency.[3]

The outcomes analyzed in this book suggest that neither contrast is accurate. Rather, each country relied on remarkably consistent policy approaches—which, however, had very different consequences in different sectors. The configuration of knowledge-bearing elites in France enabled large, "mission-oriented" efforts to develop specific technologies for particular public goals. By contrast, the configuration of knowledge-bearing groups in Germany encouraged "diffusion-oriented" efforts to promote the adoption of existing technologies through entire branches of the national economy.

In practice, French policymakers could readily mobilize the knowledge necessary for upgrading the country's telecommunications infrastructure. Yet they found it extraordinarily difficult—and ultimately impossible—to strengthen the competitive performance of the country's machine tool sector. And in the semiconductor sector, French policymakers found that they could maintain a domestic production capability only by joining forces with non-French firms. In Germany the outcomes were almost the mirror opposite. German policymakers had great difficulty upgrading the German phone system. Yet they devised a range of policies that substantially improved the competitive capabilities of the machine tool sector. In supporting the semiconductor industry, German officials encouraged cooperation between national and non-national producers, but without diluting national ownership in the way their French counterparts had done.

These findings strongly support the central empirical claim of this study, that different countries have characteristic strengths and weaknesses in matters of technology. My explanation for these strengths and weaknesses centers on the growth of knowledge-based competition and the way different countries respond to it. Since the challenges of knowledge-based growth stem from changes in the international economy, an understanding of the international context is crucial.

CONTOURS OF THE POLICY CHALLENGE: THE INTERNATIONAL CONTEXT

The shift from scale-based to knowledge-based competition is only one of three main underlying changes in the world economy since World War II. The origins of this shift extend back considerably earlier than the postwar period. Technology and the knowledge embodied in it were central to industrial capitalism from the outset. Already in the early nineteenth century, power machinery had enabled the growth of factory manufacture. By the end of the nineteenth century, large firms had begun to routinize the accumulation of knowledge in corporate research laboratories. The use of knowledge became even more important in industrial strategies roughly two decades after World War II, when firms and governments began to seek growth much more through innovation than through expanding supplies of labor and capital. The consequences of this shift emerged in conjunction with two other major changes in the institutional arrangements for international economic competition: the end of the Cold War and the relative decline of the United States in world affairs.

The end of the Cold War was the most visible of these underlying changes, because it removed the polar opposition between market economies and centrally planned economies. Far from signaling the end of international tensions, however, the downfall of communism in 1989 presented a set of new challenges for the institutions of market exchange and political democracy.[4] The opposition between command economies and market economies was replaced by a new competition among the capitalist economies themselves. Political authorities had already begun experimenting with a range of new governance mechanisms that were neither purely market-driven nor purely hierarchical. Networks, associations, and regions became more prominent—both as analytic constructs and as practical forms for coordinating economic production.[5] Much as it showed that existing doctrines of military security were inadequate, the end of the Cold War also confirmed the need for reassessing categories for analyzing economic institutions.

The second major shift in international arrangements since the settlement of World War II was the relative decline in American power. Even as it was winning the Cold War, the United States was losing its position of dominance in the world economy. In the first two postwar decades, the United States clearly had sufficient power to provide the collective goods—the reserve currency, the capital, the market demand, and much of the technology—that drove postwar economic development around the globe.[6]

By providing these public goods, the United States acted as hegemonic leader of the West; it possessed both the ability and the self-interest to pay to costs of maintaining an open world economy.[7] Power was not, however, the sole determinant of U.S. leadership in the early postwar decades. In constructing institutions for an open economy in the 1950s

5

and 1960s, U.S. negotiators sought adherence to the norms of free trade in international commerce while accepting considerable diversity in the domestic institutions of its trading partners. European governments in particular, whose adherence to market principles hinged on delicate political bargains in the immediate postwar years, retained their own particular institutions for redistributing the costs of economic change among different domestic groups. Postwar planners accepted the argument, made famous by Karl Polanyi, that the rules of market exchange were "embedded" in the institutions of different countries. For this reason, John Ruggie has applied to the postwar international economic regime the term "embedded liberalism," designating a set of rules that combined economic liberalism in foreign economic policies and welfarist interventionism in domestic policies.[8]

As the decline in relative U.S. power made its leadership of the free-trade system more difficult and less attractive, the compromise of embedded liberalism came under pressure.[9] Conflicts over monetary and trade policy became especially apparent. More generally, however, the particular domestic arrangements of different countries seemed to be providing sources of competitive advantage in international markets. Managers and political leaders alike began to look overseas, not only to Japan, but also to France and Germany, for possible lessons. Overall, the United States was less able than in earlier decades to support the norms of embedded liberalism. Policy asymmetries that had previously been managed within the framework of embedded liberalism emerged as suddenly more contentious. Like the end of the Cold War, the decline in relative U.S. power elevated differences in the domestic political arrangements of the industrial democracies to a much greater level of prominence than they had had earlier.

These two changes in the structure of the international system meant that the shift toward knowledge-based competition began amidst considerable institutional experimentation. Today, the changing nature of international competition is unmistakable. Numerous lines of inquiry indicate that knowledge has become an increasingly important determinant in the competitive performance of both firms and countries as a whole. In the 1960s, Raymond Vernon pointed out how multinational enterprises used technological innovation to gain advantages that went beyond simple factor endowments.[10] More recently, theories of strategic management have focused increasingly on internal resources, especially technological skill and human knowledge.[11] Growth theorists have refined the treatment of educational levels and inventive activities in models of endogenous growth.[12] Similarly, debates on the sources of national competitive advantage have stressed workforce qualifications, scientific knowledge, and other intangible factors.[13]

This shift from scale-based to knowledge-driven competition contributed to the relative decline of the United States in ways that complicated the crisis of embedded liberalism. An important source of power for liberal hegemons was the ability to dominate markets for high-value goods. The United States achieved such superiority largely through the technology it had accumulated during World War II. Since one of the characteristics of capitalism is to cultivate new markets by diffusing technology and the rules of market exchange, it was not surprising that U.S.-based firms gradually lost their monopolistic hold on many kinds of technology after 1945. The diffusion of technology thus led to a predictable decline in relative American economic power.[14]

Yet the diffusion of technology further undermined the country's ability to act as hegemon because it occurred just as knowledge-based advantages were becoming more important in economic competition and as control over raw materials and traditional factors of production were becoming less important. That is, U.S. firms were losing their monopolistic position in many technologies just as technology was growing as a source of economic power, and traditional factors of production—namely, land, labor, and capital—were declining.

The shift toward knowledge-based competition also complicated the crisis of embedded liberalism for another reason. In scale-based competition, managers seek to combine traditional factors of production in order to position the firm effectively in a range of product markets. In knowledge-based competition, the managerial task is to assemble heterogenous resources that cannot be easily replicated by other firms.[15] Management scholars generally view these resources as being created and maintained within the firm. It is quite clear, however, that heterogenous resources and firm-level capabilities often depend on the way managers combine assets within the firm and resources available outside the firm. In knowledge-based competition, therefore, the managerial task often depends on resources supplied by other institutions in the firm's environment. This approach to management brings knowledge-producing institutions into the realm of political scrutiny. Thus, during the shift to knowledge-based competition, arrangements for technology development—supplier chains, university-industry relations, committees for technical standards, industrial research consortia and networks—are increasingly viewed as sources of market advantage that may require political management. Like changes in the structure of the international system, this change in competitive conditions also accentuates institutional asymmetries that had posed few difficulties among the industrial democracies under the compromise of embedded liberalism.

Together these three shifts in the world economy transformed the institutional arrangements that had emerged after World War II. In the postcommunist era, institutions for economic governance are being revised at all levels of analysis, from the organization of the firm to the nature of the international economy. At the level of state-society relations, the great ideological oppositions between liberalism, socialism, and fascism are losing their sway over world politics. These ideologies are not simply disappearing, however, as predicated by earlier work on the end of ideologies. They are instead being redefined by struggles over alternative forms of organization, some new and some revived from earlier periods.

Most of these alternative forms entail less centralized and more malleable mechanisms for making collective decisions. They do not represent grand images for entire societies and world politics but rather new forms of association and governance for economic production. The old categories of political economy were designed to illuminate strategies for resolving the problem of scarcity, while the new categories need to illuminate alternative strategies for using knowledge to strengthen the capabilities of firms and countries in international competition.

The problem of technology policy is one of the central policy issues in this broad transformation of the institutional foundations for economic life. Yet, we cannot simply discard the old categories of analysis and trumpet the arrival of a new set of paradigms. Precisely because the compromise of embedded liberalism allowed considerable diversity in domestic structures, it masked the workings of distinctive national arrangements whose significance for technology-based competition became apparent only in the 1980s and 1990s. In this book I criticize the old categories and move toward new categories by using empirical case studies to analyze the links between politics and industrial competition. Accordingly, it is important to begin by examining the existing perspectives on comparative politics.

DEFINING THE PROBLEM OF TECHNOLOGY POLICY

Despite their importance to the changing terms of international competition, technology policies do not fit easily into the prevailing frameworks of comparative political science. Part of the problem is that none of the available perspectives explain the range of sectoral outcomes produced by public policies for technology in France and Germany. More generally, however, public policies for promoting innovation pose a problem for comparative politics because politics and technology represent such different spheres of human endeavor.

The main perspectives in comparative politics focus on the age-old political tasks of exercising power, brokering interests, and negotiating compromise. The realm of technology, by contrast, concerns such problems as establishing technical parameters, exercising expertise, and fulfilling performance standards. Politics is commonly defined as the process of adjudicating conflict, and technology is commonly defined as the process of applying scientific knowledge to practical human purposes. If we accept these rough definitions, then technology policy represents political action at the boundary of intellectual and economic life.[16]

Precisely because it links the disparate spheres of politics and scientific knowledge, technology policy poses a challenge for analysis. Although technology is far from synonymous with science, attitudes toward technology are closely tied to prevailing conceptions of science. And science, in turn, has goals that differ dramatically from the instrumental purposes of politics. In its effort to provide a unified explanation of the natural world, science is much more than an instrumental activity. More than any other field of endeavor, science represents the norms of rational inquiry that are central to the modern worldview.[17]

The norms of scientific inquiry can be found in all industrialized democracies. Yet, the autonomy and internal integrity of the scientific process do not necessarily extend to the institutions that finance it or apply its results. The few comparative studies available show that countries display characteristic policy approaches in their strategies for supporting science and technology and that policy elites can define these approaches very differently, even in countries that occupy quite similar positions in the international economy.[18] The point of comparing public strategies for technological advance is therefore not to question the internal integrity of the scientific process or its underlying epistemology, but rather to examine how administrative and technical elites in different countries think about the task of bringing scientific knowledge to bear on industrial change.

Liberal Perspectives

Liberalism is the indispensable starting point for studies of politics and technology. Emerging in seventeenth-century England, liberalism is the political doctrine that arose simultaneously with both parliamentary democracy and organized scientific inquiry. Based on classical works in English political philosophy, liberalism holds that public policies ought to be determined by the aggregated preferences of individuals. This relationship does not always in fact obtain, but in well-functioning liberal democracies, the preferences of the electorate should guide political leaders, and changes in preferences should be articulated by political parties, debated in electoral contests, and eventually reflected by changes in public policies.

This view of politics implies a limited central state where popular sovereignty is moderated by the institutions of representative government. Such a view emphasizes the power of those who represent social interests—elected legislators and lobbyists for organized social interest groups. When confronted with problems of a highly scientific or technical nature, this view of politics faces two particular difficulties usually known as the dangers of interest-group "capture" and technocracy.

The problem of interest-group capture becomes especially pronounced in pluralist forms of liberal democracy, where interest groups form freely to seek those policies that best serve their needs. In matters of science and technology, pluralists justify government support for basic research on the grounds of market failure. Since market incentives will lead private firms to underinvest in research and development because of the tendency for benefits to flow to customers and competitors, some government support for basic R&D is consistent with the liberal view of the limited state.[19] When the line between basic research and commercial development is blurred, however, this perspective provides less help in determining the public interest. Commercialization projects are supported by the interest groups who will most directly benefit, often making it difficult to determine which projects are entirely captured by particular interest groups and which projects genuinely serve a larger or more public interest.[20]

The problem of technocracy is another example of the difficulty in defining the public interest. Since broad segments of the electorate cannot judge the pros and cons of highly technical issues, they cannot knowledgeably formulate their own preferences. In such cases, pluralist democracies need mechanisms for keeping political leaders both well informed by experts and accountable to the larger electorate.

Not surprisingly, authors in the pluralist tradition have sought to resolve both problems by clarifying relations among different groups. In an analysis that remains one of the most useful, Don Price argued that expertise and accountability can be reconciled by reinforcing the demarcations between professional groups on a "spectrum from truth to power." Price delineated a continuum of expert groups from pure scientists to the applied-science professionals such as doctors and engineers, to administrators and, finally, to elected politicians. In clarifying these distinctions Price was not trying to impose a functional segregation of tasks but rather to point to an existing gradient from the freedom granted to scientists to the political responsibility demanded of elected figures.[21]

Although Price's synthesis continues to illuminate the tensions between science and public policy in the United States, it cannot be easily applied to other societies. As Price himself noted, the affinities between science and parliamentary democracy grew out of particular circumstances in seventeenth-century England: the Puritan rebellion against royal authority early in the century was followed by a quite distinct movement to establish science as one basis of a more open and secular form of public life.[22] Countries whose political institutions did not build on these historical affinities developed quite different linkages between science and politics. As explained in the next chapter, knowledge-bearing elites in continental Europe did not follow the same "associational" path to self-regulating professional status that they did in Britain, or later, in the United States. On the contrary, their members were certified and licensed by the state.[23] In such circumstances, state agencies were much more deeply engaged in sustaining scientific knowledge and technical expertise than Price's analysis suggested. While Price's emphasis on relations among expert groups is central to my argument in this book, his spectrum from truth to power cannot be used for comparative analysis without devoting much more attention to the state's role in generating and applying expertise. This task is one of the goals of the chapters that follow.

Statist Perspectives

In response to the pluralist view of public policy, which sees it as the result of shifting societal pressures, many scholars turned their attention to the institutional bases of politics.[24] As a corrective to pluralism's emphasis on societal change, these authors centered their analysis on bureaucracy, law, statecraft and other attributes of state power.

Writers in this strand of institutionalist analysis relied on Alexander Gerschenkron and Max Weber as guides for analyzing the institutional levers that enabled the state to orchestrate and impose long-term strategies of development.[25] Gerschenkron provided the concept of economic backwardness, showing how late-industrializing countries developed the type of centralized institutions that were needed to raise capital for rapid industrialization. Max Weber's work, which provided a multifaceted approach to comparative historical analysis, was adopted by the state-centered strands of institutionalist analysis largely for its explication of rational-legal forms of authority.[26]

Many formulations of this revived interest in state institutions relied on the concept of state "capacities." Building on Gerschenkron's historical analysis, Peter Katzenstein constructed a typology of "strong" and "weak" states, based on the centralization and differentiation of state and society. A related approach was John Zysman's thesis that different financial institutions provided states with more or less ability to intervene in processes of industrial change.[27] By distinguishing between systems based on administered credit and those based on equity markets, Zysman showed how public policymakers in countries such as Japan and France had more ability than their counterparts in the United States or Britain to direct capital to those sectors that they expected to contribute disproportionately or "strategically" to the national economy.

This state-centered view of politics emphasized the power of public officials—often in the form of a professional civil service—to impose long-term strategies without following the preferences of political parties or particular interest groups. As Theda Skocpol argued, the state's ability to retain "loyal and skilled officials" had long been part of the "sinews of state power."[28] By examining the avenues and sequences by which expertise entered the policy debate, Skocpol and Margaret Weir showed how policy was produced through a historical process in which actors at each point reacted to a legacy of previous policies.[29] Using a similar approach, Peter Hall argued that policymaking could be best understood as a case of social learning in which the state accumulated experience and expertise over time.[30]

In pointing toward "historically evolved interrelationships between states and knowledge-bearing occupations," this approach is particularly important to my argument. Yet, in tracing these relationships, the state-centered approach emphasizes "specific organizational structures the presence or absence of which seems critical to the ability of state authorities to undertake given tasks."[31] By emphasizing the structural characteristics of state power, this form of institutionalist analysis often obscures variations in ability of public cadres to mobilize technical elites in particular industrial settings. The concepts of state "strength" or state "capacity" imply that a government's ability to impose policy strategies is a function of the state's internal organization rather than of the policy sector or target in question. Yet subsequent studies have found that even highly centralized states are obliged to rely on external networks in important cases.[32] In more technical areas, such as environmental regulation and energy sourcing, the processes of bargaining and securing consent are crucial to the state's ability to implement policies effectively.[33] Of the cases analyzed in this book, the state-centered approach helps explain the success of French policymakers in telecommunications but offers little insight into the obstacles they confronted in the equally strategic sectors of machine tools or semiconductors. Attention to the instruments of state power is essential in comparing technology policies, but it needs to be supplemented with a finer-grained analysis of relations between public officials and particular technical elites.

Neocorporatist Perspectives

The limitations of pluralist and state-centered approaches led to a focus on the institutions by which interests are aggregated and represented in the political arena. The principal example of this approach was neocorporatist theory. Rather than accept the pluralist assumption that individuals freely shifted their preferences, the neocorporatist literature argued that individuals in many countries could register their preferences only through large and relatively fixed groups.

According to this view, many central issues of public policy are decided through direct negotiations among organized groups rather than through the electoral and legislative processes emphasized by pluralist theories.[34] This view of politics placed great weight on the power of centralized interest groups, represented by peak associations for management and organized labor. In fact, tripartite bargaining among representatives of management, organized labor, and the state appeared in several European countries in the 1970s as governments responded to the inflationary repercussions of the oil price shocks. Such neocorporatist mechanisms were especially helpful in explaining how policymakers in certain countries obtained wage restraint from labor in return for full-employment macroeconomic policies.[35]

For science and technology policies, however, the concept of neocorporatist bargaining has certain limits. Like the liberal and state-institutionalist perspectives summarized above, neocorporatist analysis is much more sensitive to variations across countries than across sectors within a single country. Since the problems of industrial development varied so much from sector to sector, it is difficult to see how a single pattern of bargaining among the main interest groups could be applied to all sectors within a given country. Among the cases I have examined in this book, interest group bargaining explains much about labor-management cooperation in the German metalworking industry, but offers few insights into German policies in telecommunications or semiconductors.[36]

More generally, by defining occupational groups strictly as economic interest groups, the neocorporatist literature neglects the questions of status, self-image, and the other non-material characteristics that shape the identities of those knowledge-bearing occupations most involved in technology policy. The historical literature on corporative organization shows that craft and trade groups often maintain their solidaristic forms of group identification through long periods of terrific political and institutional change.[37] The symbolic and ideational elements of occupational identity can be as important to policymakers, scientists, and engineers as particular bargaining imperatives. Much of this book seeks to show how the issues of occupational identity that shape the collective strategies of production workers also shape the many ways in which administrative and technical elites try to influence official strategies for technological change.

THE POLITICS OF COMPETENCE

This book builds on all three of these approaches in explaining the divergent outcomes of public efforts to promote technological change in industry. It does so by focusing primarily on the relationships among administrative and technical elites. In particular, I argue that the strengths and weaknesses displayed by different countries in promoting technology can be explained only through longstanding links between different kinds of knowledge-bearing elites. I draw on the liberal-pluralist view that relations among groups are central, but I also assert that these relations are rooted in institutional histories. Therefore I employ the institutionalist insight that state power helps define group relations, although here I deny the strong form of the state-centered argument, which suggests that group interests are determined by their position in a state-dominated institutional landscape. In addition, I agree with the neocorporatist view that organized occupations comprise critical interlocutors for political leaders, but I question whether these groups must be defined solely in terms of economic interest.

The argument is elaborated through the cases, but can be characterized in brief. If policymakers are to promote technology, they must identify and apply those types of knowledge that are pertinent to a particular industrial problem. Though they need not execute these tasks themselves, they must be able to mobilize the specialists—including scientists, engineers, and skilled workers—who can execute them. These occupational groups are the key resources necessary to achieve public policy goals in technology. For this reason, the institutional distribution of technical knowledge imposes real constraints on the strategies and instruments that policymakers can employ toward any policy goal.

Yet, the problem for analysis is not as simple as inferring a range of possible policies from the existing distribution of trained personnel across private and public organizations. The institutional distribution of technical knowledge is more than an objective constraint on policy; it is also a historical artifact that reflects deeply ingrained ideas about the proper relationship between expertise and political power. Put less abstractly, technical elites are not just raw material which policymakers or managers can deploy in response to changing conditions. As members of professional groups, they define their career aspirations according to historically derived commitments and prestige hierarchies rather than strictly material rewards. The prestige and legitimacy accorded to professional groups are in practice inseparable from histories of institution-building in which negotiations with political authorities often play a major role. In this sense, policymakers and managers work within a legacy of past bargains among professional and political elites every time they need to train, recruit, or deploy technically skilled personnel. Policy depends in often overlooked ways on the self-images and prestige hierarchies that inform relationships among administrative and technical elites.

By stressing relations among occupational elites, this argument extends institutionalist perspectives to public strategies for technological change. At the same time, by stressing the symbolic stakes at issue in the way professional elites contribute to policy, I seek to broaden the scope of institutional analysis. Most institutionalist accounts in political science put primary emphasis on the structural characteristics of institutions. By portraying institutional arrangements as reward matrices within which actors choose among alternative courses of action, they assume that these actors are motivated by a clear conception of their self-interest. Such a view understates the importance of institutions as repositories of the beliefs, values, historical memories, judgments and customs that comprise part of the larger cultural context. Yet these cultural factors become especially important when people confront tasks characterized by great uncertainty or ambiguity. Since most efforts to promote technological change involve just these qualities, technical elites often rely on custom as well as professional judgment. Professional elites have a general interest in adapting their methods to new problems, but they also have reasons for defining those problems in ways that emphasize their own time-honored claims to competence and authority. Once knowledge and judgment are tempered by custom, then institutional dynamics need to be seen within their larger cultural context—that is to say, within the religious, political, scientific, and other norms that groups invoke to advance their place in public life.

This book relies frequently on organizational analysis—both for describing industries and for comparing relationships among administrative and technical elites. The positions occupied by these elites in a political economy largely determine their access to political decisions and their control over public resources. Yet, their positions within the structure do not tell us how professional elites will perceive their interests or use their influence. To explain any group's political strategies, we also need to ask how its members are identified, recruited and socialized. These are the processes that provide insight into inherited beliefs, self-images and goals. Since public efforts to promote technological change are formulated and executed almost exclusively by members of administrative and technical elites, the possibilities for industrial change can only be understood through explanations that address their views. The central analytic claim of this study is that we need to go beyond purely structural analysis of institutions and to examine the beliefs, norms, and self-images of the elites that inhabit those institutions if we want to explain both sectoral and national variation in policy efforts to promote technological advance.

Such an argument must fulfill several requirements. First, it must advance a plausible claim that the ideational predispositions of elites cannot be entirely inferred from their organizational setting. Such a view would necessarily differ from those models of organization that treat ideas either as irrelevant or as reflections of organizational structure. Second, the argument must provide a brief historical overview of the formation of French and German elites, without which it is impossible to show what kind of ideational predispositions these groups bring to organizational life. Third, such an argument must show how these predispositions could enter into relations between a superordinate authority such as the state and subordinate organizations such as business enterprises. That is, the argument must show how these ideational factors enter into policy formulation and implementation, and how they lead to different results across sectors.

CHAPTER TWO

Professional Identities
and Policy Strategies

Technology policy is not made in a vacuum. Policies for promoting innovation seek to accumulate and apply technical knowledge to politically designated goals. To accomplish these tasks, policymakers negotiate with social interest groups, much as they do in formulating other types of public policy. In matters of technology, however, public officials must also take particular account of the existing distribution of knowledge, which they seek to mobilize and at times to alter. Knowledge resides in organizations, but it is the beliefs and self-images of the professional elites within these organizations that animate knowledge. Accordingly, in promoting technological change, policymakers need to fashion policy strategies that are consistent with the self-images of the knowledge-bearing groups they seek to involve in pursuit of their policy goals.

KNOWLEDGE, ORGANIZATIONS, AND INSTITUTIONS

Technical knowledge falls into several categories—scientific learning, engineering knowledge, technical expertise, skill, and practical know-how—all of which can be used by economic actors.[1] Nevertheless knowledge cannot be adequately understood by analogy to other standard economic input factors that can be purchased and deployed on the basis of cost. Instead, knowledge resides in persons, who—with rare exceptions—work in organizations and belong to networks both within and without their main place of work. To be sure, a great deal of labor-market behavior can be explained through parsimonious models of human capital, with employees selling their skills and knowledge to those organizations that offer the highest compensation. Those people whose work involves a high degree of technical knowledge, however, tend to seek out institutions that provide privileges—especially prestige, proximity to colleagues, and autonomy—that they consider critical to their ability to use their knowledge. Because these choices make some employers considerably more desirable than others, the distribution of technical knowledge is best understood as part of a broader institutional order for science and technology.

By emphasizing the explanatory significance of this institutional order, I argue that we must look beyond organizational structure if we wish to explain policy outcomes. This concept of institutional order is rooted in the works of Max Weber, Philip Selznick, and Clifford Geertz. In their different ways, all of these writers saw social action in terms of two equally important goals—a search for meaning and a search for control over material resources. The irreducibility of both goals meant that most issues in human affairs required the use of structural analysis and interpretive analysis together. It was Philip Selznick who applied these insights to the distinction between organizations and institutions. According to Selznick and his followers, organizations are static entities described by "organigrams," job descriptions, spans of control, and means-end relations that can be adjusted to meet the technical requirements of the organization's goals. In contrast to organizations, institutions are more than mere tools because they have symbolic significance. Institutions are "infuse[d] with value beyond the technical requirements of the task at hand." Institutions embody particular ideas and ways of doing things. As Selznick puts it, people identify with and fight over institutions.[2]

This concept of institutional order can be applied to all organizations in a political economy—from government bureaucracies to central banks or local chambers of commerce. The part of an institutional order that shapes the distribution of technical expertise can be called the professional order for science and technology. This professional order concerns policy in two analytically distinct ways—one objective, the other symbolic.

In the objective sense, the professional order for science and technology includes the certified organizations and procedures that produce the "raw material" for policy efforts. This side of the professional order has several elements. First, it consists of those expert occupations that are defined by explicit licensing, accreditation, or delegation of power from the state. Second it includes the organizations responsible for scientific research and technical training—schools, universities, government agencies, national labs, industrial firms, and professional associations. Third, it includes the administrative procedures for giving certain expert groups regular access to public decision making. And fourth, it rests on the formal selection mechanisms for recruitment into its component occupations. Through these four elements, the professional order for science and technology shapes the human resources available to policymakers. In so doing, it imposes very real constraints on policy strategies and instruments.

In the second, symbolic, sense, however, the professional order for science and technology imposes equally significant ideational constraints on policymakers. It does so through the beliefs and self-images that together make up the implicit outlooks or "worldviews" of its constituent occupational groups. Worldviews are not complete or perfectly logical sets of beliefs to which all members of an occupation subscribe; they are, however, persistent sets of self-images, specialized vocabularies, and moral commitments that help the members of a given craft or expert occupation to recognize one another and to interpret their place in the world.[3]

The worldviews elaborated by knowledge-bearing occupations consist of postures toward the external world as well as ways of thinking about their own work. First, most expert occupations have some collective sense of mission based on public needs to which their knowledge is directed. Second, such occupations typically elaborate a collective view, often contested, toward the state and their relation to it. Third, scientific and technical elites define and defend principles of research practice and technology development. Finally, like other professions, each expert group tends to have its own shared sense of the proper mix of abstract and practical knowledge necessary for its job. These beliefs and self-images impose constraints on public policies because they inform the strategies that appeal to policymakers and delimit the range of policy instruments acceptable to target groups. As a result, it is not organizational structure alone but the interplay of organizational structure and the worldviews of different occupational groups that explains the evolution of technology policies.

This approach to institutional order shows how to combine the historical institutionalists' emphasis on state power with the sociological institutionalists' more interpretive approach that follows Selznick's work. Historical institutionalists show how large organizational structures are created amidst the key turning points in a society's development. Sociological institutionalists are more concerned with the way organizations, once created, adapt to incremental change. As Charles Perrow summarizes this sociological perspective, "institutionalization is the process of organic growth, wherein the organization adapts to the strivings of internal groups and the values of the external society."[4] More recent variants of this view replace the concepts of ethical norms and value orientations with the concepts of cognitive norms, classifications, and repertoires of action.[5] But, like their predecessors, the more recent sociological institutionalists advance the view that the formal or technical characteristics of organizations do not alone capture their origins, adaptability, or durability. By drawing on several variants of sociological institutionalism, I argue that the emergence of a larger institutional order is an inherently political process in which organizational tools are imbued with the visions and self-images of those groups that succeed in establishing larger social missions and purposes.

This concept of institutional order is quite different from the economic approaches that emphasize efficiency and the maximization of wealth. One such approach grew out of Oliver Williamson's efforts to explain the many cases where economic transactions are removed from the market. According to Williamson, many transactions are best conducted through anonymous market mechanisms. Other transactions are characterized by traits—uncertainty, recurrence, and asset specificity—which make them susceptible to more efficient control through hierarchical forms of organization. By analyzing the way these characteristics affect behavior, Williamson seeks to explain a range of organizational solutions—or "governance structures"—for economic life.[6]

Another economic approach to institutions grew out of the analysis of property rights. This approach also seeks to explain the boundaries of firms and their internal incentive structures but by focusing on ownership regimes rather than on transaction costs. The property-rights approach offers rich insights into a range of nonstandard contracting problems, especially those created by relationship-specific investment in different types of assets.[7] While the transaction-cost and property-rights approaches often lead to different insights into business-government relations, they both imply that organizational forms are selected on the basis of their efficiency. It is this efficiency assumption that distinguishes them from more historical or sociological types of institutionalist analysis.

The sociological critique of economic approaches agrees that governance structures and incentive structures are important, but claims that they are not completely generated by the characteristics of transactions or property rights. According to the sociological view, economic relations are "embedded" in a context of social relations.[8] This book advances the view that technology-promotion policies are embedded not only in a set of social relations but also in a set of beliefs and occupational self-images which validate those relations. If transaction costs and incentive structures apply to technology innovation, then one of their central attributes—namely human-asset specificity—is inseparable from a range of context-specific factors that shape the professional order for science and technology.

It is precisely these context-specific factors that require interpretive analysis. Both individually and collectively, human beings attach meaning to the organizations in which they work, and these meanings vary in ways that cannot be inferred from the structure of the organizations themselves. In recent years, other scholars have found interpretive approaches especially important for studying the politics of labor law, regional adjustment, and industrial policy.[9] This book claims that public strategies for industrial change in an era of knowledge-based competition require a similar interpretive approach for understanding the political interactions of knowledge-bearing elites.

ELITES, PROFESSIONS, AND OCCUPATIONAL WORLDVIEWS

Elites play a particular role in institutions because they generate the ideas that dominate the symbolic aspect of any institutional order. Not surprisingly, Philip Selznick emphasizes the autonomy of elites as one source of an institution's adaptive capacity. This view diverges from Herbert Simon's concept of bounded rationality, which implies that organizations impose cognitive limits on all subgroups. Writing about the ideal-typical organization, Simon and coauthor James March observe that "the categories and schemes of classification it employs are reified, and become for members of the organization, attributes of the world rather than mere conventions."[10] By contrast, Selznick's "theory of elite autonomy" suggests that the logical arrangement of functional specialties cannot be the sole criterion for designing organizations.[11] Selznick's followers have adopted some of Herbert Simon's concepts, but have given considerably more weight to the external sources of ideas in organizational life.[12] Combining these different strands of thinking, James March and coauthor Johan Olsen argue in a later synthesis of organizational theory that institutions are shaped by a "logic of appropriateness" as much as by a "logic of consequences."[13]

In light of this logic of appropriateness, the economic approach to institutions is powerful but incomplete. To understand the professional order of science and technology, we need to look further into the way professional groups are formed, how their ideational predispositions are generated, and why those predispositions are sometimes sustained, and sometimes modified, by organizational structures.

The professions have been a central concern in postwar sociology and have attracted a mixture of optimistic supporters and cynical critics. In the 1950s and 1960s, scholars fastened upon the professions as occupations that mitigated or softened the impersonal, rational-legal character of organizational life.[14] According to this view, the professions have been characterized not only by a high degree of systematic knowledge, but also by a primary orientation toward community interest, a code of ethics internalized through socialization, and a system of rewards based on "symbols of work achievement" that are "ends in themselves" rather than "means to some end of individual self-interest."[15] Because professionals are expected to use their knowledge in a disinterested way to serve their clients, they exemplify a pronounced form of trust in modern societies.[16]

In most of these respects, earlier writers believed the professions differed from other occupations in degree rather than in kind. These writers saw an ongoing "competition for status" among occupations that had already gained professional recognition and those occupations that sought such recognition.[17] More recently, Andrew Abbott reinforced this view, finding that almost all expert groups passed through a certain sequence of conflicts and internal changes as they gained professional status. While the sequence was similar in all cases of professionalization, the timing of the changes and the scope of jurisdiction gained by each group was not dictated by any formula.[18] On the contrary, the prestige and legitimacy given to different professional groups resulted from complex histories of intergroup competition and institution building, which Magali Larson called their "professionalization projects."[19]

A group's professionalization project differed from the development of other occupational groups at the point at which it obtained public recognition. According to some writers, precisely because the unusual autonomy enjoyed by the professions was "ultimately secured by the grace of the state," it was artificial.[20] This view had its critical explanatory power mainly in Britain and the United States, where an "associational" or spontaneous pattern of professional formation gave many professions a high degree of self-regulation. In these countries, professions frequently advanced jurisdictional claims in "public" arenas such as the mass media and educational institutions.[21] In the countries of Continental Europe, on the other hand, the role of the central state in professional development was much more pronounced. In these countries, the question for comparative analysis was precisely how deeply the state became involved in the origins and the subsequent definition of different professional groups.[22]

As a consequence of these different histories, the English term, "profession," has no perfect translation in French or German. This is one reason that the term "knowledge-bearing elites" is sometimes more precise. As long as we recognize that there are different pathways through which groups gain public recognition, however, the term "profession" can be used. In this use, it implies a type of influence that is decisive in many policy areas. By virtue of their public recognition, professions are able to require longer schooling for their members, to demand more organization autonomy on the job, to devote more resources to interorganizational networks, and to secure access to public policy decisions more regularly than other occupational groups.

There is, accordingly, no abstract or trans-historical logic that determines the degree or form of "professional" recognition granted to particular occupations. It is true that law and medicine are accorded high autonomy in most societies. Parallels of this sort are, however, hardly sufficient to show that occupational prestige hierarchies are "invariant in all complex societies," or that "this must be so as a consequence of inherent features of the division of labor as it exists in all societies."[23] On the contrary, political authorities may support the normative claims of contending occupations quite differently in different countries. French observers have consistently remarked on the influence of lawyers in the United States, within as well as outside the government.[24] English and American observers, by contrast, are frequently surprised by the political access granted to engineering degree holders in France.[25] At this level of discrimination, the hierarchies by which occupations are ranked vary considerably from country to country and can only be explained as a product of national histories.

This view presents the professions as occupational elites that have won positions of political privilege in an ongoing competition to define and impose their values on certain areas of social life. Understood this way, the professions are key groups in the transmission of the larger culture. Not only do their own practices have symbolic weight, but they are granted more autonomy than other occupational groups to think reflectively about the values and purposes of their work. As Everett Hughes put it, professional elites claim a mandate to think for the rest of society about such issues: "Every profession considers itself the proper body to set the terms in which some aspect of society, life or nature is to be thought of, and to define the general lines, or even the details, of public policy concerning it."[26] The occupations granted professional status are those with the greatest influence in defining boundaries among different spheres of endeavor and claiming competence within their chosen sphere.

For this reason, national variations in occupational prestige matter greatly. By ranking professional elites, occupational hierarchies indicate which types of knowledge are considered important enough to provide ordering principles for the whole of society. In France, where engineering degree holders have extensive access to political decisions, the implication is that human affairs can be ordered through excellence in the application of principles of natural science. In the United States, where lawyers have more access than engineers, the implication is that human affairs can be better ordered through awareness of legal claims and the precedents that have been used to resolve them in the past.

These occupational relations are anchored in organizational hierarchies and privileges, but they also reflect the worldviews of knowledge-bearing occupations refined through the process of jurisdictional competition. Through professionalization and competition, professions develop a repertoire of jurisdictional claims. These jurisdictional claims provide programs for policy actions as well as frames of reference to legitimize those programs.[27]

Professional groups continually revise their jurisdictional claims. Interestingly, however, the underlying vocabulary for professional worldviews in a particular country is surprisingly persistent. As Andrew Abbott puts it, "the legitimating values involved in professional social structures vary strikingly from country to country, a variation that indeed surpasses their variation over time within a given country."[28] These values are resistant to change because, while claims to new or expanded jurisdiction can be advanced through negotiation, they also have to be compatible with the symbolic resources that each profession has invoked in the past.

The values, programs of action, and frames of reference that comprise a profession's worldview are distinct from but closely linked to the substance of that group's expertise. Much as craftworkers have convictions about the quality of the materials and processes they use, expert occupations follow conventions about the mix of abstract and practical knowledge appropriate to their work. These conventions are very apparent among the professions involved in science and technology. For scientists, whose work involves the continual replacement of existing knowledge with new findings, the movement toward increasingly abstract formulations is a characteristic strategy for maintaining professional standing.[29] Engineers are very different. Since their work involves the application of scientific knowledge to a broad and continually growing range of practical spheres, different engineering subspecialties settle on different mixes of abstract and problem-specific knowledge.[30] Public officials similarly arrive at characteristic blends of academic knowledge and political intuition. In economic policy, these ingredients typically form a "prism through which" policymakers see "the economy and their role within it."[31]

Taken together, these programs for action, frames of reference, and other aspects of occupational worldviews provide a way of analyzing the cultural self-understandings of the different groups involved in public life. By linking these worldviews to particular occupations, this approach establishes one way of bringing cultural factors into political and economic analysis. By emphasizing specific occupational groups, this approach strives to avoid the blanket generalizations about "national character" that often deter political scientists from cultural analysis.[32] Since occupational worldviews provide a cultural toolbox for social action, they can be linked quite closely to the political efforts of particular groups.[33] Such collective visions and self-images are difficult to delimit. Through careful empirical work, however, they can be documented, linked to identifiable social groups, and analyzed in terms of their consequences for strategies of industrial change.

In examining the occupational worldviews that shape technology policy, this book makes three types of comparisons: across countries, over time, and across industrial sectors. Since ideas and organizational forms are mutually reinforcing, it is difficult to separate them through static comparisons. One author has expressed the point by comparing game theory and historical approaches as follows: "That institutions and ideas are locked in a relation of mutual dependence is, in fact, one of the central notions underlying the game-theoretic analysis of institutions. From a static point of view, it is both unimportant and impossible to untangle the causal relation between these elements. From the standpoint of historical analysis, however, the causal connection between ideas and institutions is a central explanatory issue."[34] Of course, the web of organization and ideas is not seamless. A range of writings suggests three analytic "openings" which allow investigators to examine the links between organization and ideas in useful ways.

First, even if we acknowledge that organizational form and ideational predispositions are tightly linked, we can use focused comparisons to examine institutions across different cultural contexts. Such comparisons help identify the specific mechanisms by which ideas or assumptions legitimize similar institutions in different countries. Stanley Hoffmann has argued for the place of cultural factors in political analysis in much these same terms: ". . .after all structural explanations have been offered (especially when the structures are quite comparable to those of other countries), there remains something specific and irreducible to the other explanations; 'culture' quite properly comes in there—if only to show how, precisely because of its resilience and strength, it sometimes can distort institutions that were supposed to foster a different mode of conduct."[35] This approach requires assessing structural similarities across national contexts in order to show how differences in outcome may be traceable to beliefs, values, and self-images. This approach is powerful because it is simple. It has the disadvantage of treating culture as a residual factor, yet since ideas and attitudes are so difficult to document, this approach is often the only one possible.

Occasionally, however, clear differences in the ideas and attitudes of contending groups will allow for more direct analysis of the cultural components. Such an analysis entails asking how the groups within a particular institution attempt to define that institution's mission in ways that serve their own goals. These goals sometimes reflect non-material interests in promoting justice, peace or other social values. Such interests are of course difficult to prove, because it may be impossible to gain reliable access to the actors' motivations. Often, however, the lag between organizational and ideational change is illuminating. Even as circumstances and organizational needs change, the ideals that carry political salience remain sticky or culturally constrained. Through comparison, it is therefore often possible to show that appeals to certain ideals work better in one polity than in another.[36]

A third analytic comes from comparing ideas that legitimize the central or most prestigious institutions of the society. There may always be a tension between those ideas that legitimize the ruling institutions and those that legitimize the peripheral institutions. Reigning ideas have, by definition, a greater normative content than ideas articulated by peripheral groups, because these groups are closely tied to sectoral institutions and their ideas are informed by the problems of that particular sector.[37] This tension is crucial in technology promotion policies, where the normative notions are usually articulated by policymakers in the central ministries, while sectoral views more closely reflect the existing distribution of qualified specialists in a particular industrial setting.

Accordingly, there is also a social dimension in the link between those who formulate policy and those who implement it. The outlooks of the technical elites involved in policy implementation emerge from idiosyncratic and often unexamined historical experiences. The outlooks of these groups vary not only from country to country but also from sector to sector. They are therefore investigated in the empirical chapters that follow. The outlooks of central administrative elites who formulate policy are largely constant across sectors. Their outlooks can be well understood by examining the socialization and recruitment processes that give these elites their identity. These processes are well documented in sociological and historical literatures and are therefore more accessible. Their examination is the task of the next section.

PROFESSIONAL ORDERS FOR SCIENCE AND TECHNOLOGY

The professional order for science and technology includes the organizations responsible for research and training as well as the ideas and practices of the many groups that inhabit those organizations. At any given point in time, it represents those norms and practices that have won out over alternatives. Since institutions for science and technology generate both the resources for and the constraints on technology policy, certain aspects of their historical emergence are indispensable to the argument.

The values and practices embodied in an institutional order in one historical period will not necessarily be functionally adapted in subsequent periods to the tasks that confront policymakers. According to the argument advanced here, underlying assumptions about the state's role in promoting science and technology grow out of institutional arrangements that can be traced back many decades and sometimes even centuries. Three sets of questions regarding this historical process are important for an understanding of patterns in technology policy. First, what was the relationship between political authority and the scientific community at the time it gained recognition in a particular society? In particular, how did political authorities and scientific leaders understand and justify the relationship between the state and the scientific enterprise? Second, which scientific or technical occupations are granted political access? What types of knowledge are considered important in the state's realization of its own goals? Third, what kind of hierarchy characterizes different levels of scientific and technical work? Were the links among the different elites permeable or closed? The answers to these questions are very different for France and Germany, and in each case they are different from answers that have often been based on studies of seventeenth-century England and the United States.

France—an Order of State-Created Elites

In France, social investment for science and technology has been channeled toward a group of "state-created elites" since the seventeenth century.[38] France founded its Académie des Sciences in 1666. The restricted membership and activities of the Académie helped maintain royal control over the scientific enterprise. Whereas England's Royal Society, according to the sociologist Joseph Ben-David, "was an independent corporation based on mixed membership including amateurs and politicians of science as well as scientists of outstanding accomplishments, the Académie was a sort of elevated scientific civil service composed only of a small number of scientists of high reputation." Science was supported to serve the military and economic purposes of the absolutist monarchy rather than to serve any broader social or intellectual agenda.[39]

The principle of state support for public purposes continued through the upheavals of the eighteenth century. Three notable institutions— the Ecole des Ponts et Chaussées, the Ecole du Génie Militaire at Mézières, and the Ecole des Mines—were founded during the Ancien Régime to provide civil and military engineers for royal purposes. In 1794, shortly after the Revolution, the Ecole Polytechnique took over the training of military officers and became the prototype for the *grandes écoles*. Also founded in 1794 were the Ecole Normale Supérieure for philosophy and the natural sciences and the Conservatoire National des Arts et Métiers for practical arts and trades. If the leaders of the Revolution had conceived of national education as a "duty of the state toward is citizens,"[40] Napoleon saw education as serving the interests and the moral stature of the State. This rationale was already clear in the training that was offered by the grandes écoles for military officers, civil engineers, and other direct servants of the state. When Napoleon created an Imperial University to train physicians, lawyers and other professionals, the same principle was applied. The state sought to preserve a monopoly on higher education.

The desire for a reservoir of highly trained public servants at the elite level also entailed the suppression of those organizations best suited to train people in the practical and industrial arts, namely guilds and trade associations. Such intermediary associations were prohibited in June 1791 by the Le Chapelier Decree, which expressed revolutionary suspicion of particular interests in principle. Although this legal prohibition was gradually loosened in the later nineteenth century, by then it had become part of France's political culture and industrial life.

In the later nineteenth century, an orientation to learning based on deductive reasoning seems to have become established in the state-sponsored institutions. This result seems paradoxical in a century where the main motivation for educational reform came from the practical concerns of industry. The deductive bent is, however, consistently mentioned by historians of the period. The bastion of this educational orientation was the Ecole Polytechnique, whose status under the Ministry of War gave it great prestige. Despite concerted pressure by republican reformers at the end of the century to make it more utilitarian, the Polytechnique managed, with a few concessions, to keep its entrance requirements in the classics and its curriculum steeped in "the deductive approach to knowledge."[41] Institutions established to serve industry adopted similar methods, much to the chagrin of the country's emergent metalworking industry who regarded their graduates with considerable doubt and suspicion.[42] One result was that the tasks of industrial training were accomplished largely within the firms. With little official support or coordination, industrial training was left largely to freely contracting employers and apprentices—a situation which led some observers in the last third of the nineteenth century to speak of a crisis in vocational education.[43]

Despite the far-reaching changes experienced by French polity and society through the Second World War, the essential features of elaborate training for elite cadres and weak investment in intermediate and elementary skills persisted in the postwar period. If anything, the educational system remained the one institution where older attitudes and styles "reigned supreme."[44] The system of state-created elites was consolidated in 1945 by the foundation of the Ecole Nationale d'Administration (ENA). In theory, ENA was supposed to end the fraternal recruitment practices by which the alumni of the older grandes écoles had colonized the *grands corps,* as the elite administrative services within the French state were known.[45] In practice the top graduates from ENA and the Ecole Polytechnique predictably acquired the best places in the elite services. The *polytechniciens* maintained their dominance in the more technical Corps des Mines, Corps des Ponts et Chaussées, and Corps d'Armements, while the so-called enarques (the ENA graduates) took the lion's share of the less technical administrative services.[46] In comparison to the universities, which were legally required to accept any applicant who passed the *baccalauréat,* the grandes écoles maintained their prestige through the privilege of selecting students through highly competitive exams. During vehement debates on educational reform—particularly concerning the *loi Faure* in 1968 and the *loi Savary* in the early 1980s—the grandes écoles tenaciously and successfully fought to preserve the right to impose their own stringent entrance requirements.[47]

The educational system that supports the order of state-created elites has important consequences. The stratification consistently and explicitly favors the deductive orientation best exemplified by the Ecole Polytechnique. This deductive orientation does not characterize all of the more than 150 smaller *écoles d'ingénieurs* that are the majority of the grandes écoles,[48] but it is clearly the basis of *polyvalence*. Although rarely defined, this term is used to refer to a highly admired set of intellectual skills that are supposed to enable a person to apply rigorous thought to a broad range of problem-solving situations. Through the generations, the ideal of *polyvalence* has been raised to the status of an unquestioned virtue or ideology in France.[49] The prestige hierarchy among these schools is explicit, inasmuch as the selectivity of the leading schools is one of their primary assets. The most prestigious of the grandes écoles d'ingénieurs—the Polytechnique, Mines, and Ponts et Chaussées—test mathematics and physics almost exclusively on their entrance examinations. As a result, these subjects dominate any secondary school curriculum that is geared to preparing students for the particularly difficult examinations.[50] According to the social historian Terry Shinn, who has studied the biographies of over one thousand polytechnicians since the early nineteenth century, this rigorous socialization inculcates a "deductive epistemological style" that continues throughout the graduate's subsequent career. This claim seems to be supported by members of the elite technical corps, who frequently remark that their suitability for the leading positions in business and government rests on their general aptitudes for synthesizing and analyzing information rather than on any specialized skills.[51]

By maintaining theoretical engineering training as one of the primary routes to political power, the system of state-created elites effectively supports the rationale of state-directed utilitarianism for basic research. Until very recently, most of the grandes écoles supported only nominal research activities while the universities were geared to teaching the large numbers of students entitled by their baccalauréat to further education.[52] Fundamental inquiry has been mainly conducted under the umbrella of the Centre National de Recherche Scientifique (CNRS), founded in 1939 to compensate for the weakness of the universities. Though the CNRS is occasionally described in the terms used by Michael Polanyi as a "republic of science," state support means that it is inescapably subject to centralized coordination and evaluation in terms of its contribution to larger social goals.[53] In the 1980s, centralized coordination of all CNRS institutes was encouraged under the banner of "pluridisciplinary" research programs, while autonomous agenda-setting was decried as "balkanization."[54] In 1982, reforms introduced to encourage utilization of CNRS research results were explained by a top official under the label of "*néo-colbertisme.*"[55]

A major part of the research effort is conducted through mission-oriented bodies that operate under direct ministry supervision. The most notable include the Commissariat à l'Energie Atomique (CEA), founded in 1945; the Institut National de la Recherche Agronomique (INRA), reestablished after the war in 1946; the Centre National d'E-tudes Spatiales (CNES), founded in 1962; the Institut National pour la Santé et la Recherche Médicale (INSERM), founded in 1964; the Centre National pour l'Exploitation des Océans (CNEXO) and the Institut de Recherche d'Informatique et d'Automatique (IRIA), created in 1967.[56]

A final feature of the order of state-created elites is a deep split between the elaborate, competitive classroom training of those in the grandes écoles and the much less effective programs for practical vocational education. As Marc Maurice, François Sellier, and Jean-Jacques Sylvestre show in detail, the basic programs in vocational training have usually served as terminal certificates rather than as bases for further training and career advancement. In the 1960s and 1970s, vocational training served as a consolation at any point where a student did not survive progressively competitive academic schooling.[57] The implication is that vocational training in practical skills is not a path to career advancement. There were several attempts in the 1970s and 1980s to establish technically oriented alternatives to the traditional baccalauréat and to provide special university departments for technical studies (*instituts universitaires de technologie,* or IUT) which lead to the *diplôme universitaire de technologie* (DUT). These technical tracks attracted growing numbers of students, but they only slightly altered the impermeable boundaries that separate levels in a hierarchy that favors training in deductive methods.[58] A student's progress in academic programs largely determined the level at which he or she entered, and usually stayed, in the hierarchy of vocational certification. The institutional arena for educational competition and social advancement remained decisively oriented in favor of theoretical training at the older, state-sponsored schools.

31

Germany—an Order of State-Certified Occupations

If France's investment in scientific and technical training is focused on a cohesive group of state-created elites, Germany's efforts have long been directed toward a much broader range of state-certified occupations. Unlike the French elites, trained in state institutions for state service, the German professions (*Berufe*) emerged from the older guilds and orders and were granted considerable powers of self-governance.

The robustness of corporative forms of organization in Germany can be traced to many sources, from the nature of German Protestantism to the proliferation of local political jurisdictions. Leonard Krieger argues that the German concept of freedom was—in contrast to the English concept of liberty—linked to the sovereignty of the community through which the individual was protected against subjugation by external authorities.[59] Such a concept of freedom provides no axiomatic grounds for individual claims to liberty against arbitrary government; nor does it encourage the freedom of scientific inquiry as an individual right against claims of the community or the corporate body within which inquiry is performed.

While their sources are far more complex than can be analyzed here, the principles of self-governance *Selbstverwaltung* and social autonomy (*soziale Autonomie*) were consolidated through decisions made in the early nineteenth century. Reacting to Napoleon's victory at Jena in 1806, the Prussian reformers Baron von Stein and Prince von Hardenberg sought to revitalize the state bureaucracy through a conscious mixture of imitation and rejection of the French example. The difference between France's state-created elites and Germany's state-certified professions was clearest in the famous university reforms designed by the influential Minister of Education Wilhelm von Humboldt. Most universities had already received extensive corporative privileges from local principalities that pre-dated Prussia's steady ascendance in northern Germany. Under the combined efforts of Humboldt, Stein, and Hardenberg, the privileges of hereditary social elites were tempered by the newer professional status groups (*Berufstände*) and learned individuals (*Gebildete*) who entered the state hierarchy in growing numbers.[60] After founding the University of Berlin, Humboldt described the relationship between learning and government as follows: "The state must not ever demand from the university that which would serve its purposes directly, but should hold to the conviction that when the universities fulfill their true aims, they will also thereby serve the state in its purposes, and from a far higher point of view."[61] The principle of autonomy was articulated in direct contrast to the Napoleonic model of a state-controlled educational system.[62]

The same principles of social autonomy and self-governance which applied to the universities also supported forms of economic organization that encouraged non-elite training. Liberal ideas of free trade and commerce were consciously mixed with the older traditions of subnational authorities. In direct contrast to the French experience, the old guilds and craft associations were given legal recognition as public-law corporate bodies (*Kammerrecht*).[63] Through the nineteenth century, craft organizations fought to maintain their control over apprenticeships and entry to the craft professions. In 1897, they were given the exclusive right to set standards and administer examinations for entry to the trades. One of the results was a comprehensive system of industrial apprenticeships that supplemented private practical training with collectively financed professional schooling through the *dual System*.[64]

The difference between state-created elites and state-certified occupations was clearest in the case of the engineers. Although France's Ecole Polytechnique was the envy of several German technical experts in the early nineteenth century, such an institution was hard to imagine in the German context.[65] The engineering profession emerged from the industrial growth of nineteenth-century society much more spontaneously in Germany than in France, and took clear form only in 1856, with the founding of the Association of German Engineers (Verein Deutscher Ingenieure, or VDI). By the time engineers were able to lobby for influence in public affairs, other professional groups had preempted the privileges available from state recognition. The prestige of state support went not to the technical schools but to the universities, and Berlin began to replace Paris as the center for world science after 1830.[66] Positions in the civil service were largely controlled by jurists and graduates from the faculties of history or classics, who vigorously defended their competence against incipient claims from the engineers.

Largely barred by other professional groups from positions in the civil service, German engineers used their technical competence to secure recognition as outside advisors to the Prussian state in technical matters. The engineering association described its aim as a "cordial cooperation among the mental powers of German technology" which would serve the general interest of German industry.[67] Within a few decades, the VDI addressed one of the major issues in industrial technology—the safety requirements of steam-boilers (*Dampfkesselkontrollfrage*). Although the VDI could not persuade the Prussian bureaucracy to admit engineers to public service, it steadily consolidated its

33

position as the main "parapublic" institution responsible for advising the young German state on technical aspects of industry safety.[68] Through their participation in the Dampfkessel-Überwachungs-Vereine (DÜV), the engineers also asserted a role in monitoring industrial compliance with the regulations that were based on their recommendations.[69]

The place of engineers in nineteenth-century Germany gave practical science a far stronger social base than it had in France. On the one hand, engineers were an upwardly mobile group drawn from diverse origins.[70] They therefore sought status through advanced certification. The Technische Hochschulen emulated the ideal of classical education (*Bildung*) by deepening the theoretical aspect of their curriculum. On the other hand, the engineers knew that German industry was their primary constituency.[71] Unlike the elite French engineers, whose position depended on their ability to defend a monopoly over certain state offices, German engineers had to adapt their expertise to changing problems.

In contrast to the deductive epistemological style that took root in France, an "ethos of qualification" characterized Germany's hierarchy of technical occupations and has continued into the postwar period.[72] As a result of this ethos of qualification, each technical occupation in Germany enjoyed more autonomy within its particular sphere of recognized expertise than did its counterpart in France. The German state had the power to support particular occupations by according them exclusive state recognition, but once having granted them recognition, in the postwar period it was required, practically and often legally, to consult with representatives of these occupational groups. Unlike the French state, the German state was therefore not the supreme or the only embodiment of competence. Rather the state was expected to secure qualified advice and thereby to ensure that public policy was consistent with expert consensus.

This ethos of qualification was probably least evident at the level of university education, where a series of reforms gave the federal government steadily more control in university finance, admissions, and governance. Although the image of the Humboldtian university was "constantly invoked by both the proponents and the opponents of reform," there was general agreement that the autonomy of the university had been tempered.[73]

The nature of engineering training in Germany shows how the ethos of qualification promoted a mixture of theoretical and practical learning which differed from the French notion of "polyvalence." In the postwar period, the higher technical schools (*Technische Hochschulen*) have been allowed to call themselves technical universities (*Technische Universitäten*) and their graduates (*Diplom Ingenieure*) receive a full science-based education. Since the nineteenth century, industrialists have also promoted an engineering degree (*graduierter Ingenieur*) which skilled workers and technicians can obtain through part-time or continuing attendance at nonuniversity engineering schools (*Ingenieurschulen,* now usually known as *Fachhochschulen*).[74] Detailed case studies indicate a fruitful tension between these two types of engineers that is markedly different from the highly formalized relations that Michel Crozier reported among technical professionals in French firms.[75]

The contrast with France is clearest, however, at the level of basic and intermediate vocational education. The *dual System* carefully mixes book-learning in occupational schools with practical training at the workplace. The curricula (particularly the articulation of workplace training and classroom work) are laboriously negotiated at the local level by the firms and the schools, while the standard requirements for examination and certification are approved at the federal level by representatives of employers and trade unions.[76] In the 1960s, almost 70 percent of all West German sixteen-year-olds opted for some kind of industrial or office apprenticeship, while only 18 percent did so in France. Advancement to higher levels of skill and competence is frequent in Germany. From the viewpoint of the individual, the occupational hierarchy in Germany is much more permeable—or as some scholars have called it, "dynamic"—than in France.[77] From the viewpoint of employers, the system provides a continuous spectrum of competence from practical to theoretical—a configuration which contrasts markedly with the stark disjunction in France between the general education of the grandes écoles and the plant-specific skills taught through on-the-job occupational training.

These different histories have produced distinct professional orders for science and technology. As the historical institutionalists suggest, these institutional arrangements are rooted in the major turning points of a society's political and economic development. In France, the sequence of state formation followed by industrialization meant that the engineering profession emerged within the state. As a result, the professional identity of French engineers rested heavily on their ability to reserve public service positions for themselves and dominate the decision-making process. In Germany, the fact that industrialization had begun before a unified national policy was consolidated meant that the engineering profession was based almost entirely in industry. As a result, German engineers gained public recognition through advising the state rather than through staffing it themselves.

These patterns were not, however, locked immutably in place. Instead they were sustained by organizational forms and ideational justifications that reinforced each other. This combination of organizations and ideas shaped the "social reproduction of technical personnel" in particular ways.[78] France's order of state-created elites was reproduced through an impermeable hierarchy of occupations whose upper levels embodied the deductive epistemological style that helped them to monopolize positions of public trust. Germany's order of state-certified professions was reproduced through a much more permeable hierarchy of occupations characterized by an ethos of qualification at all levels. Both the ideational and the organizational aspects of these professional orders need to be understood in order to explain the making of policy.

Policy: Formulation and Implementation

Policymaking is the art of matching the resources at hand to the desired end. In the case of technology policy, the primary resources—technically trained experts—are produced by the institutional arrangements already described. To compare how policymakers mobilize these resources, we need some way of categorizing policy strategies and instruments.

All states employ a range of policies to promote technological advance. The most conspicuous cases are large-scale efforts to produce specific technologies or systems needed by state agencies to fulfill their particular missions. Such efforts exemplify "mission-oriented" strategies.[79] Mission-oriented strategies typically aim at weapons systems, transportation infrastructure, or (in some countries) medical technologies. The instruments used to implement such strategies vary in detail, but include large, centrally coordinated projects with line-item financing and some degree of organizational autonomy from other government business.

At the other end of the spectrum are "diffusion-oriented" strategies, which aim at the dissemination of technological capabilities through a broad cross-section of the economy or population. Such efforts typically aim at strengthening human resources and public information resources. The instruments for implementing such policies may include tax credits (especially for research and development and certain equipment investment), student loan programs, other educational programs, public data banks, and many instances where the state helps establish industrial standards and norms.

Needless to say, different tasks call for different strategies and instruments. Enhancing research and development tax credits might assist
the aerospace industry a great deal, but it would not be a good way to
produce a space vehicle. At the opposite extreme, establishing a national
center for space studies might draw advanced engineering students to
specialize in aerospace engineering, but it would not be a good way to
support a country's scientific establishment in general.

If policymaking were a strictly technical matter, then policymakers
would seek the mix of instruments most appropriate to the particular
challenge. Such an approach would lead policymakers in all countries
to formulate similar policies for similar problems. Of course, there
would be considerable adjustment across countries as policymakers took
account of country-specific resources, but aside from these adjustments,
policies in different countries formulated to fit the same problem would
look similar.

The professional order that generates the human resources for technology policy also sustains a framework of ideas in which policymakers
work. This framework includes analytic beliefs about the way the world
functions. These beliefs are, in turn, reinforced by an ethos or set of
ethical values that justify particular forms of action. Using somewhat
different terminology, Peter Hall calls this interpretive framework a
"policy paradigm." As he notes, such a paradigm is "embedded in the
very terminology through which policymakers communicate about their
work, and it is influential precisely because so much of it is taken for
granted and unamenable to scrutiny as a whole."[80] As a result, the ideas
held by policymakers are not limited to explicit doctrines. They also
include informal conventions or unarticulated predispositions to define
problems in certain ways. Accordingly, implicit assumptions as well as
analytic beliefs help to shape the contours of technology policies in
important ways.

Technology policies also depend on the sector in question. Producing
automobiles, garments, aircraft, and digital watches will pose different
problems and require different solutions. Even as they grapple with the
difficulties of particular industries, however, policymakers in a given
country display characteristic approaches in the way they define sector-
specific problems and fashion solutions to them. We may not observe
exactly the same solutions proposed for all sectors in a given country;
according to the argument made here, however, we should observe
analogous differences across countries in the solutions proposed for
any given sector. Put more concretely, German policymakers are not
likely to formulate exactly the same types of programs to promote

37

semiconductors, telecommunications, and machine tools as their French counterparts, but they are likely to propose programs for all three sectors that differ from the French programs in analogous ways.

In the first instance, these nationally specific approaches to technology policy express the beliefs and values that inform existing institutional arrangements. They can be observed mainly in the process of policy formulation, where the central elites have the greatest impact. Of course, the relationship between institutions and policies is not completely characterized by the determining power of institutional arrangements over the beliefs and attitudes of policymakers. If the professional order for science and technology were a binding blueprint for the way policymakers think about ways of promoting expertise, the result would be a perfect replication of institutions and policies from one generation to the next.

As the concept of policy legacies reminds us, however, current policy is also partly a reaction to previous experience. Each iteration of policy formulation is informed by past successes or failures. The basis for learning better policy strategies lies in the link between formulation and implementation. There is no guarantee that policy strategies formulated on the basis of received wisdom can be implemented in all industrial sectors. If policymakers blindly apply received formulas to new challenges, several problems may arise. They may rely on customary industrial partners, at the risk of subsidizing private agendas as much as achieving public objectives. They may find that certain types of expertise cannot be mobilized for problems that the professional elites consider uninteresting. Or they may even find that their strategies assume a kind of expertise that does not exist.

Such cases, where the administrative elite's inherited outlook generates strategies that cannot be implemented, are especially interesting. They show whether public officials can break away from customary ways of thinking about policy and, if so, whether they can identify and mobilize the expertise needed to implement new approaches.

In such cases, the networks between administrators who formulate policy and technical elites who implement policy become crucial. Technology policy requires the bringing of disparate resources to bear on very specific problems that are peculiar to given industrial sectors. Rarely do state administrators have the specific expertise needed to judge when, how, and to what degree such resources should be applied to a particular industry's problems. Unless they have access and regularized links to the various occupational groups who know a particular industry, administrators can hardly hope to tailor their programs to deal with the obstacles and frictions that accompany their effort to effect change.

The cases compared in the following chapters show how French and German policymakers attempted to deal with three very different challenges. The challenge in telecommunications was to develop the complex and expensive infrastructural technology required for digital telephone exchanges and to install them in existing public telephone networks. The challenge in the machine tool sector was to disseminate a better understood combination of technology and skill through a widely dispersed industrial landscape of small and medium-sized firms. The challenge in the semiconductor sector was the greatest of all; it involved producing or importing specific types of expertise that were not available within either country and constructing an institutional setting in which national development teams could generate a self-sustaining process of technical learning. In each case, policy efforts were shaped by organizational structures but also by the beliefs, outlooks, and self-images of the occupational elites who populated those structures.

CHAPTER THREE

Digitizing the Public Telephone Network: Telecommunications

This chapter compares French and German policies for technological change in the telecommunications sector.[1] Specifically I compare policy efforts to promote the transition from electromechanical to digital technologies in public telephone exchanges. These policies were crucial to efforts in both countries to build on the initial decades of postwar reconstruction. The telephone system, a relatively low priority through the 1960s, emerged in the 1970s and 1980s as the foundation for a dramatically enhanced communications infrastructure.

The comparison between French and German policies is revealing. Despite striking similarities in the administrative and industrial organizations that were involved, the experiences of these two countries in modernizing their telecommunications networks were virtually mirror images of one another. The French telecommunications authority successfully encouraged the early development of a French digital exchange, the E-10, but was unable to parlay its early advantage into sustained leadership in international markets. The German Bundespost was, by contrast, extremely slow in moving to digital switching technology, but its traditional national supplier, Siemens, made up its early disadvantage and subsequently solidified its place as a leading competitor in international markets.

These differences were neither incidental nor inconsequential. Important segments of the political elite made telecommunications a high priority. By the end of the 1970s, the sector had emerged as one of the few arenas where European firms were serious candidates for high-technology leadership. In France, the famous Nora-Minc report recommended a national effort to make France the third electronic power in the world by combining telecommunications and data processing. In Germany, the telecommunications industry also came to be seen as a pivotal sector in efforts to modernize the entire German economy.[2]

This chapter begins the argument, elaborated in comparing policy toward the machine-tool and semiconductor sectors, that public agencies are constrained in their ability to promote technological advance by the professional order that governs the distribution of expertise in a particular country. In particular, some countries are better able to implement "mission-oriented" strategies for promoting technological advance, while others are better positioned to conduct "diffusion-oriented" strategies.[3]

The comparison of telecommunications policy in France and Germany shows that such differences exist even in sectors where the organizational structure of the state agencies and firms is similar. In both France and Germany, the development of public telephone switches naturally suggested a mission-oriented policy. The technology entailed large, lumpy investments, which were directly necessary for the fulfillment of a public agency's central mission—the provision of telephone service. The type of innovation involved—a radical jump to entirely new designs and components—also seemed to require the concentration of resources provided by the mission-oriented approach. Despite these similarities in objectives, public authorities in the two countries relied on quite different time frames and methods in mobilizing resources to promote technological innovation in the public phone network.

In France, the telecommunications industry became an exemplary case of the *grand projet*.[4] As in other *grands projets* ("large-scale projects"), the state played the dominant role. It conducted R&D in a public research installation, financed a commercial prototype, and provided a market through public procurement. This recipe had been successfully used for nuclear power technologies, oil exploration, and rail transport. In the 1970s, it was to be applied to telecommunications as well. The recipe for the *grand projet* had not, however, invariably produced success. Conspicuous failures had occurred in computers and supersonic aerospace. A crucial element in the more successful cases was provided by specialists in the civil service whose technical competence was adequate to monitor and link the various phases.

In the telecommunications sector, the technical community was formed from the corps of public communications specialists, the *ingénieurs des télécommunications*. These ingénieurs des télécommunications used the national research laboratories as a base to advance their position within the French telecommunications authority, the PTT. They started working on fully digital telephone exchanges in the mid-1960s—somewhat later than American engineers at Bell Laboratories, but well before anyone had installed working models. Indeed, the French were among the first to install small digital exchanges in the early 1970s, and their research led enabled them to begin large-scale production of the new technologies in 1977, once expert opinion decided they were economical.

By early the 1980s, France had one of the most fully digitized telephone networks in the world. Equal access to communications services stood as a symbol of popular democracy, and successful experiments with new services gave the country another mark of technical distinction along with its earlier achievements in nuclear power, oil exploration, and aerospace.

By contrast, Germany's civil servants were in no position to dictate the timing or the specifications for renovating the public telephone system. They relied heavily on private-sector consortia, led by Siemens, to develop network materiel. Without an independent development capacity, the German Bundespost had less familiarity with digital technologies. An intermediate technology, the semi-electronic switch, became seriously delayed in development in the mid 1970s. Not until twelve years later did Siemens and the Bundespost abandon the project, at which point Siemens devoted its research efforts to the fully computerized exchanges that were favored in the international marketplace. Beneath the technical issues lay basic political questions. The public's interest in alternative development options was effectively tied to one firm's efforts to develop the new technology. Siemens recouped its technological position quite quickly but, through the 1970s and into the 1980s, allowed the Federal Republic to lag behind its neighbors.

THE ORGANIZATIONAL CHALLENGE

The organizational arrangements for governing the French and German telecommunications industries exhibited far greater similarity than other sectors involving technological innovation. In both countries, the telephone system was run through a traditional public administration which combined a legal monopoly on postal and telecommunications services. Since these services had long been regarded as essential features of a well-governed society in both countries, the competent authorities had been granted considerable autonomy to fulfill their missions. Both the French PTT and the German Bundespost had to bargain with other ministries to obtain funds. Within the constraints set by their budgets, however, both agencies enjoyed great discretion in planning investment programs and setting operational goals.

In addition to bargaining with other state agencies to obtain investment funds, the telecommunications authorities were obliged to bargain with the industrial firms from whom they purchased equipment. Through such purchases, the PTT and the Bundespost were among the largest procuring agencies in their countries. As such, they had a number of different objectives. First, they sought a price in line with world market prices. Second, they wanted up-to-date technology. Third, in maintaining and modernizing the public network, they could only use equipment which was compatible with the existing network. Fourth, they were under considerable (often binding) pressure to buy from suppliers with domestic fabrication facilities. The compromises among these objectives created a dilemma: The first and second objectives necessitated as much competition as possible among a range of potential suppliers, whereas the third and fourth objectives tended toward the cultivation of longstanding and therefore privileged relations with particular suppliers.

The trade-offs that characterized telecommunications procurement in the 1970s and 1980s provided an interesting case study for economic perspectives on organization. According to the transaction-cost approach, these purchasing decisions exhibited precisely those conditions—uncertainty, frequency, and asset specificity—that led to nonstandard contracting. Under these conditions, the buyer could not both benefit from privileged relations with particular suppliers and enjoy equal access to a wide range of anonymous suppliers. The property-rights approach also suggested the significance of relationship-specific assets. As soon as a seller invested resources in assets that could only be used to produce customized goods, the seller had both a unique ability and a unique need to sell those goods to the customer who could use them. Whether the assets in question involved plant location, dedicated physical assets, or specialized human assets, they introduced a new element into contractual relations.[5]

The case of European telecommunications does not precisely fit these economic approaches, which deal with problems of individual firms. Nonetheless, these approaches help to clarify the structural similarities in French and German arrangements for telecommunications procurement. Both the PTT and the Bundespost had to rely on relationship-specific investments made by equipment suppliers in the human resources that were required for developing customized equipment. Since

43

these development teams had to meet the constraint of "backward compatibility," which required that any equipment added to a public phone system be compatible with the existing network, suppliers had to devote scarce resources to design or adapt a proprietary product to network-specific uses. As the supplier's installation teams worked with the network authorities, they engaged in "learning by doing" and gained a great deal of transaction-specific specialized training. Any manufacturer who accumulated this practical know-how was well positioned to execute further contracts with the same buyer; by the same token, if the buyer offered no further contracts, much of this practical knowledge was too specific to be redeployed to other jobs. An inverse dilemma was created for the public purchaser. Future equipment could be more conveniently purchased from a supplier who knew the system. If the authorities became locked into any particular supplier's technology, however, opportunities for competitive bidding and pricing could disappear.[6]

These considerations suggested that the French PTT and the German Bundespost should have concluded very similar kinds of relationships with their main equipment suppliers. Indeed, both French and German policymakers responded to the trade-offs between longstanding supplier relations and competitive bidding, but they did so in quite different ways.

The French Context

The convention of state control over telecommunications in France had historical roots in national security. As early as 1793, the Committee on Public Safety established a semaphore optical relay, the world's first telegraph system, to transmit news between Paris and the revolutionary armies. Through a halting process that lasted until the mid–nineteenth century, the state-operated system was again made available to the public.[7] In 1879, the telegraph administration and postal service were combined in a Ministry of Posts and Telegraph. In 1889, after a decade of rather unsatisfactory operation by a private concessionary (the Société Générale des Téléphones) the nascent telephone system was brought under the ministry's direct management control. In 1925, the ministry became formally known as the Ministry of Posts, Telegraph, and Telephone (PTT).[8]

For the first three decades of the postwar period, the PTT presided over one of the oldest and most limited phone systems among the industrialized countries. This situation resulted from the low priority it was accorded. The PTT was one of the largest—but also one of the sleepiest—public agencies in France. In 1941 the Vichy regime significantly changed the overall organization of state-business relations, and operational responsibility for communications was divided into three directorates: one for the postal service, one for telecommunications, and one for financial services. By the late 1960s, the postal service employed 160,000 persons, while the telecommunications authority, employed only 110,000. Although the DGT ran a surplus which helped finance the postal division's losses, the latter's size enabled it to dominate the ministry's overall policies and its more specific functions concerning personnel, finances, and buildings.[9]

In addition through the 1960s, the DGT was subordinate to the two administrative bodies that controlled the entire range of economic policy in France: the Ministry of Finance and the Planning Commission. The Ministry of Finance emerged during the early postwar period as the gatekeeper of government spending, settling ultimate priorities in industrial policy. The DGT did not gain access to substantial capital resources until the late 1960s.[10] Before that time, its investments were strictly governed by the budgetary considerations of the Treasury officials in the Ministry of Finance. The Planning Commission took a longer-term perspective on industrial development than did the Ministry of Finance, but it favored other sectors such as building materials, steel, oil extraction, and automobiles over telecommunications.[11] The DGT was not much different from other state agencies involved in economic development. Its action was hampered much more by a lack of administrative clout within the state than by any lack of autonomy from social interest groups.

Aside from the budgetary limitations imposed by the Ministry of Finance, the DGT was relatively free of external pressures. No organized groups outside the DGT strongly supported development of the telephone network, but none strongly opposed it either. The Ministry of Industry, often considered business's main advocate within the French state, had little if any voice in telecommunications matters because they were considered a separate functional area to be regulated by the DGT in conjunction with the more powerful ministries of Finance and Defense. It is true that the PTT administration was sometimes folded into the Ministry of Industry, but it always had its own secretary of state with ministerial rank. The legislative Assembly and the political parties had even less influence over specific policy or investment decisions since specific budgetary decisions were worked out between the Ministry of Finance, the Planning Commission, and each specialized agency. Telephone users were extremely unorganized as an interest group.[12] Thus, the DGT's strongest ties to French society consisted of a set of longstanding relationships with its equipment suppliers.

Since the early twentieth century, the French state has relied on a combination of foreign and indigenous suppliers. This practice fostered an element of competitive bidding on major contracts. Yet, the need to accommodate the idiosyncratic features of the network led the authorities to keep doing business with those firms that committed research and production facilities to the French industry. These firms included the private concessionary, Société Générale des Téléphones (SGT), which had initially exploited the Bell telephone in France, as well as two foreign-based firms, the American ITT (International Telephone & Telegraph) and the Swedish firm Ericsson. The main suppliers quickly established stable market shares, on which they could then rely in planning their own investment and employment programs.

The first set of negotiations for switching equipment occurred in the 1920s, when automatic telephone exchanges of the rotary design became widely available. ITT was just establishing itself as one of the world's archetypal multinational firms. It quickly became France's dominant supplier of the new rotary exchanges through its subsidiaries, Le Matériel Téléphonique (LMT), acquired in 1920, and the Compagnie des Téléphones Thomson-Houston (later renamed Compagnie Générale des Constructions Téléphoniques, or CGCT), acquired amidst negotiations with the French PTT in 1926.[13] The two ITT subsidiaries won most of the orders for Paris and medium-sized cities, while the Swedish firm Ericsson, which in 1911 had established a French subsidiary (Société de Téléphone Ericsson, received most of the rest.[14]

The French Société Industrielle des Téléphones (SIT, the name given the Société Générale des Téléphones in 1895) received only 40 percent of the orders for rural automatic exchanges, while the small number of rural manual exchanges was split between SIT, the cooperative Association des Ouvriers en Instruments de Précision (AOIP), and a few other very small French firms. In sum, the ITT subsidiaries, LMT and CGCT, held between two-thirds and three-quarters of the market for public switching equipment. Ericsson received 22 percent of the market. The all-French suppliers were confined to the remaining markets for rural automatic exchanges and the thoroughly residual manual exchanges.

The advantages held by prior suppliers in subsequent contracts became especially apparent in the 1950s, when the old rotary exchanges were being replaced by the next generation of switching technology based on the so-called crossbar design. By virtue of their intimate knowledge of the French network, the ITT and Ericsson subsidiaries were the best positioned candidates to execute the conversion from rotary to crossbar switches.[15] The ITT subsidiaries proposed a proprietary crossbar design called the Pentaconta, while Ericsson France proposed a model called the CP400. The postwar descendant of Société Industrielle du Téléphone, now called Compagnie Industrielle des Téléphones (CIT), had failed to develop its own crossbar model. Rather than risking dependence on a sole foreign-based supplier, the DGT again contracted for both the ITT and the Ericsson designs. The Pentaconta exchange was selected for Paris and the large cities where the ITT companies already possessed intimate familiarity with the old rotary switches. The first Pentaconta was added to the network in 1964. The Ericsson technology was judged best suited for medium sized cities. Its first switch was installed in 1963, on the condition that the company license the CP400 design for production by the French firms, CIT and AOIP. The latter two were given predominant control over the residual market for rural exchanges.

During this period the DGT sought to gain further control over the ITT and Ericsson technology through the modality of the "mixed enterprise," a research cooperative between the suppliers and the state, which held a minority share. Cooperative research had been tried shortly after the First World War, when three French firms formed a research enterprise (Société d'Etude pour les Liaisons Télégraphiques et Téléphoniques) in important military communications technologies. The first of the fully mixed enterprises in which the French state held a minority share was SOTELEC (Société Mixte pour le Développement de la Technique des Télécommunications sur Câbles), founded in 1947 with majority financial participation from the manufacturers of transmission equipment. The society coordinated research with particular success in the development of coaxial cable. A similar entity, SOCOTEL (Société Mixte pour le Développement de la Technique de la Commutation dans le Domaine des Télécommunications), was founded in 1958 to coordinate research and patents in switching. Although ITT resisted because it had its own extensive research facility in Paris, it eventually joined SOCOTEL in 1961.[16]

The situation was paradoxical because the two ITT subsidiaries were now the leading French producers. Indeed, by manufacturing a switch designed in ITT's Paris research facility, the Laboratoire Central de Télécommunications, ITT and CGCT were responsible for the only large-scale switch of French design. Although it was an ITT subsidiary, LMT in particular had long been one of France's best exporters of telecommunications equipment to other countries. The French manufacturers, CIT and AOIP, were obliged to manufacture the Swedish design under license. By 1965, the market share held jointly by LMT and CGCT had declined from over two-thirds to 47 percent. The Swedish CP400, produced by Ericsson's French subsidiary and the two French firms, accounted for the remaining 53 percent of the public switching market.

The German Context

Although it emerged from very different historical conditions, by the 1960s the organizational context of telecommunications policy in the Federal Republic of Germany reached a remarkably similar configuration to the one in France. In its internal organization as well as its external relations, the German Bundespost (DBP) closely resembled the French PTT. Like the PTT, the Bundespost combined public communications with postal services and consumer banking accounts in a single administration. Like the French PTT, the Bundespost also enjoyed considerable legal autonomy from other state agencies in pursuing its work. Charged by the Basic Law[17] with responsibility for the federal government's sovereign control over telecommunications (*Fernmeldehoheit*), the Postal Ministry (Bundesministerium für das Post und Fernmeldewesen) enjoyed far more freedom from the regional governments (*Länder*) than did most federal agencies in the Federal Republic of Germany. Supervised by a cabinet-level minister and an administrative council (*Verwaltungsrat*) established by federal law, the Bundespost was also governed on a much more centralized basis than any other federal agency except those engaged in foreign policy. Owing to its independence from regional authorities and its mechanism of centralized governance, the Bundespost corresponded more closely to its French counterpart, the PTT, than did perhaps any other German public agency. Like the French PTT, until the 1970s it was constrained most of all by the sluggishness of the telecommunications business.

As in France, the beginnings of long-distance communications were thoroughly embedded in the country's formative political experiences. Soon after the Prussian military recognized the advantages of electrical over optical telegraphy, it constructed a line connecting Berlin with the ill-fated National Assembly in Frankfurt in 1847. Amidst the growing enthusiasm for economic liberalism, the new technology was quickly extended beyond military applications. Lines were soon extended to Hamburg, Stettin, and Breslau; management control was transferred from the military to the new Board of Trade; and in August 1849 the system was opened for ordinary commercial traffic. Under the Imperial Constitution of 1871, control of the telegraph service belonged to the imperial postal authorities (*Reichspost*). The postmaster general, Heinrich von Stephan, initially viewed the telephone as a natural means of extending the imperial telegraph system to small villages which could not afford a full-time clerk.[18] The new device was quickly applied by industrial firms to economic uses beyond the official telegraph system. In 1884, the telegraph authorities linked local exchanges in nearby communities to form a so-called territorial telephone system (*Bezirks-Fernsprecheinrichtungen*) in the Upper Silesian coal district, and several other districts followed suit by 1890.[19] The authorities also allowed private users to establish their own telephone connections to the public telegraph system (according to the administrative order of 22 November 1882), and nothing prevented private persons from constructing telephone connections within the boundaries of private properties. By 1891 there were 2,301 private lines connected to the public service and 2,871 wholly private telephone connections.[20]

With the appearance of new electrical inventions, conflicts arose over the use of public thoroughfares for electrical cables and transmission lines. These technical problems generated jurisdictional conflicts between the imperial telegraph authorities in Berlin and local municipalities, who increasingly needed to provide electric lighting and local transportation systems in order to promote the local economy. The issue was resolved by the law of 1892 which granted priority to whichever lines—either (weak) communication lines or (strong) power circuits—were in place first. The more general issue of imperial versus local control of the telephone network was resolved in favor of the central authorities. The imperial monopoly on telegraph and telephone networks was explicitly recognized with only limited qualifications.[21]

In the post–World War II period, the telephone administration in the Federal Republic may have gained even more centralized control than the French PTT. Except for the administrative council (*Verwaltungsrat*), which was often co-opted by the post minister, the Bundespost had a degree of independence from social and party influence which was remarkable in the Federal Republic.[22] Since the Basic Law included the post and telephone systems among those activities to be governed from Bonn, the Bundespost was exempted from concurrent legislative oversight by the Länder representatives in the Bundesrat. The Bundespost was also unusually free from dependence on Länder civil servants in implementing its policies. While other federal ministries had to rely on the Länder bureaucracies to perform their missions (the military, the diplomatic corps, and the railway administration are among the only other exceptions), the Postal Ministry had the Bundespost's entire staff to implement its decisions.[23] The popularly elected Bundestag also had very little influence over the direction or the magnitude of investment in the telecommunications system because it lacked a role in drawing up the Bundespost's budget.

The Bundespost was, like the French PTT, subject to its national Finance Ministry for most of the years examined here. The Finance Ministry approved the Bundespost's budget, regulated its access to capital markets, and collected 10 percent of its revenues in lieu of VAT. Since this latter provision represented a major contribution to federal revenues (DM 4.6 billion or approximately 2 percent of the entire federal budget in 1985),[24] the Finance Ministry officially refrained from substantive comment on the Bundespost's investment plans or technology policies.

A number of agencies and organizations represented economic interests in telecommunications policy, but their influence was was limited. Most important of these was the Economics Ministry, which had to approve all rate changes in telephone services. Through this power of approval, the Economics Ministry pressed the Bundespost to allow greater competition in new telecommunications services, but the ministry had little power over the Post's long-term investment or procurement plans. The Federal Research and Technology Ministry (BMFT), established in 1972, regularly differed with the Postal Ministry over the agenda of research in communications, but the BMFT had no statutory and very little practical control over the Post's research policies. Although business associations usually enjoyed highly extensive access to policy discussions in Germany, user groups typically had as little influence over telecommunications policies as their French counterparts. Large business users were hampered by a split between the *Zentralverband der Elektrotechnischen Industrie* (Central Association of the Electrotechnical Industry) and the *Verband Deutscher Maschinen- und Anlagenbau* (Association of German Machine and Factory Construction). Smaller business users who were represented by the DIHT (*Deutsche Industrie- und Handelstag*) frequently complained of the Bundespost's monopoly and lack of responsiveness to their needs. The most important economic actors in the politics of telecommunications policy were therefore those in the equipment manufacturing industry."

As in France, the authorities' relations with the telecommunications equipment industry in Germany have long been limited to a small circle of firms—colloquially known as the court suppliers (*Hoflieferanten*). The most important of the court suppliers was Siemens, which obtained licenses to automatic exchanges designed by the American inventor

Strowger in the early 1900s. By the 1920s Siemens equipment had become a virtual standard for the Reichspost. The public authorities quickly recognized the risk of becoming dependent on a technology which they did not control and formed a mixed enterprise for transmission equipment, the Deutsche Fernkabelgesellschaft, jointly owned by the Reichspost, Siemens & Halske, and the two other main German cable manufacturers, AEG and Felten & Guillaume.[25] In the all-important realm of switching exchanges, similar though less stable arrangements emerged. In 1920 and 1922, the Reichspost encouraged its smaller suppliers to form two consortia for manual and automatic exchanges.[26] In 1924, the two consortia merged in an arrangement by which the industry leader, Siemens, made its patents available to the smaller suppliers in return for having its technology accepted as the Reichspost standard.[27] Shortly thereafter, the American-based ITT acquired several of Siemens's former competitors—including Mix & Genest, Telephonfabrik Berlin, and the Berliner Fernsprech-und Telegraphenwerk—which it grouped under the Standard Elektrizitäts Gesellschaft. In 1930 the parent firm bought the well-known firm C. Lorenz of Berlin. The other main competitor to Siemens was the Deutsche Telephonwerke, which had at one point offered designs from the Swedish engineer Ericsson to the Reichspost.[28]

The same basic configuration of suppliers reappeared in the Federal Republic after the Second World War. Even before the American occupation authorities decided whether or not to support reindustrialization in postwar Germany, the need for communications obliged the American military to enter into talks with Siemens. In July 1945, military authorities commissioned the firm to manufacture telephone handsets and within a few months they were helping Siemens obtain the necessary capital equipment for the job.[29] Siemens technology was no longer at the cutting edge, but it was reliable and the firm had extensive knowledge of the German network.[30] Siemens thus continued to supply the bulk of the postwar order for modernized rotary exchanges in the 1950s and 1960s. By retaining other suppliers in order to lessen its dependence on Siemens, the Bundespost was doing precisely what the Reichspost had done before. By the 1970s, the configuration of market participants was remarkably similar to that in France. The domestic leader, Siemens, held 46 percent of the market for public switching exchanges. A smaller German participant, was Telefon und Normalzeit (T&N), a subsidiary of AEG, held 10 percent of the market. ITT, which had regrouped its subsidiaries in Stuttgart under the name Standard Elektrik Lorenz (SEL), held 30 percent. Finally, the Deutsche Telephonwerke, now known as DeTeWe and financially connected to Siemens, commanded 14 percent of the Bundespost's orders.[31] As in France, the telecommunications authorities supported at least two independent domestic equipment suppliers, while foreign-based firms were able to penetrate the market only if they had made longstanding investments in domestic research and fabrication facilities—which in Germany meant only ITT.

The Challenge of New Markets and New Technology

By the 1960s, both the French and the German authorities had settled upon similar organizational mechanisms for maintaining a balance of vertical linkages and competitive bidding among their traditional equipment suppliers. These mechanisms included awarding public orders on a quota basis, using mixed enterprises for coordinating research and patents, and expanding the technical bureaus. Both the French PTT and the German Bundespost had long maintained technical staffs. Initially, these staffs were skeletal units responsible primarily for seeing that equipment met the necessary specifications and performance standards. In the postwar period, the technical bureaus assumed more responsibility for technical and economic planning and, in some cases, took on full-blown research projects in a variety of areas including solid state physics, data processing, space sciences, and materials science.

Through the mid 1960s, these institutional mechanisms enabled the telecommunications authorities in France and Germany to promote orderly growth in their networks. They promoted sufficient cooperative work among the suppliers to minimize the risk that any single supplier might be "innovated out" of the industry. Yet the authorities maintained enough uncertainty in awarding otherwise predictable market shares that the individual firms were pressured to devote some of their own scarce R&D resources to technical improvement. In the 1970s, however, three major changes in the world telecommunications industry disrupted the comfortable and stable relationships between the telecommunications authorities and their equipment suppliers.

The first of these changes was brought on by basic innovations in electronics. The advent of large-scale integration in microelectronics meant that semiconductor devices could carry and process vastly increased quantities of information. The microprocessor, in particular, allowed engineers to think in terms of developing a fully computerized telephone network. Telephone equipment is customarily divided into three classes: switching equipment, transmission equipment, and peripheral (or customer-premises) equipment. Public telephone networks are built around the switching exchange, which serves to identify callers, maintain the connection during a call, terminate the connection when the subscribers hang up, and monitor all control functions such as billing.

Microelectronics promised to transform switching equipment by computerizing all of its functions. Owing to the complexities of the task, however, this transformation was in practice accomplished in two steps, the first involving the *control* function of identifying and connecting callers, the second involving the *contact* function of maintaining the link between callers.[32] Originally, the control function had been performed by operators who sat at long switchboards and plugged jacks into sockets in the old manual exchanges. In the 1920s, automatic exchanges allowed for direct dialing based on mechanical means, of which the Strowger "step-by-step" and the rotary designs were the main versions. In the 1950s, the electro-mechanical crossbar design used both mechanical connections and electrical circuits.

The next type of electronic switching, known as semi-electronic, used computers for the control functions of identifying and billing callers. The link between callers was, however, maintained by a physical contact which transmitted voice signals in analog form. Because a physical space had to be reserved for each connection, the generic design for such switches was called "space-division switching." In fully electronic designs, a computer is used for both the control and the contact functions. In this case, the voice signals are converted from analog signals to digital signals. Conversations are converted into digitized bit-streams, exchanged like computer files and reconverted back to analog form. Because this technique did not involve a dedicated physical link for each connection, it was generically known as "time-division" rather than "space-division."

These developments necessitated a whole range of new technical competencies, including but not limited to computer design. The business of building telephone equipment now required experts in signal processing, large-scale systems design, and, perhaps most important, software writing. These tasks meant that the R&D costs of designing and perfecting a new switch jumped dramatically. By the early 1980s, several firms had already invested over one billion dollars on their first fully electronic switches, and experts suggested that those costs might double before the end of the decade.[33] At the same time, the wave of changes in switching technology shortened the product cycle. Whereas older generations of switches had often lasted thirty or forty years, the first generations of semi-electronic and fully electronic exchanges were superseded so quickly that suppliers had to develop entirely new models within as little as ten or fifteen years.

The second major change was a consequence of increased R&D costs coupled with the shortened product life cycle. Together these factors meant that European equipment suppliers could no longer survive by supplying their national markets alone. In order to amortize the huge development costs for public switches over a shorter time period, suppliers had to aim at selling their products in third markets. Telecommunications equipment had long been a global business in the sense that many major suppliers had always looked to international markets. In the late 1970s, the process of globalization was intensified as international operations became imperative for any firm that wanted to remain in the sector. The process was further intensified in the 1980s by the divestiture of AT&T. Suddenly the largest equipment supplier in the world, formerly restricted to the U.S. market, was allowed to enter international competition.

If the first two changes made life more difficult for equipment suppliers, the third change made the potential rewards higher. As fully electronic switching was combined with digital transmission, a whole new range of telecommunications services became possible. If countries could agree on standards for expanded transmission capacities, it would be possible to combine traditional voice signals with data transmission and video signals. The new technology, known as broadband transmission, held out the possibility of an integrated services digital network, or ISDN. Although ISDN was not expected to be a reality before the year 2000, the prospect promised vast markets for entirely new classes of equipment. From the point of view of national telecommunications authorities, ISDN entailed the reconstruction of the entire worldwide telecommunications system. Such a project raised basic questions of national sovereignty and control over territorial systems, as well as how to help national equipment suppliers remain competitive in the new environment.

These changes meant that public authorities in France and Germany had to accomplish two tasks. First, they needed to promote the development of electronic switching technologies. Second, they needed to increase the export performance of their indigenous producers to help them amortize R&D costs. An economic analysis implies that public policymakers could respond to this challenge in one of two basic ways, either by strengthening vertical links or by resorting to market competition. The first option meant providing state-funded research results, guaranteeing a domestic market share, and subsidizing export distribution or otherwise assuming some of the risk involved in supplying telephone exchanges. The second option meant enhancing competition by reducing barriers to new entrants, whether domestic or foreign. In fact, however, the policy options were not limited to a simple choice between hierarchy and market.[34] A third possible option involved state-led restructuring of the domestic industry. A fourth was doing nothing and allowing events to dictate the response of domestic firms to changing conditions of competition.

This chapter argues that the pattern of policy options chosen by French and German authorities cannot be explained by organizational dynamics alone. Significant constraints and opportunities resulted from the professional relations among the administrative and technical elites involved in policymaking in each country. Policymakers in France and Germany settled upon very different strategies for coping with changes in the world telecommunications environment. After experimenting with enhanced domestic competition in the mid 1970s, French policymakers opted for deepening vertical links with their main national supplier, CIT-Alcatel. German policymakers, after trying to strengthen vertical links with their main supplier in the 1970s, opted for a clear opening to competitive bidding. These very different patterns cannot be explained by organizational structure—which was extremely similar in the two countries. Rather, these choices were shaped more by the occupational worldviews of the different knowledge-bearing elites than by rational calculations that could be inferred from economic incentives alone.

THE DISTRIBUTION OF EXPERTISE IN TELECOMMUNICATIONS

Although the main organizations responsible for telecommunications policy in France and Germany looked very similar by the 1960s, they had emerged from quite different historical experiences. These historical legacies matter precisely because they affect the symbolic context of policy in a way that cannot be understood from the technical characteristics of the organizations themselves.

France

Telecommunications policy in postwar France has been decisively shaped by the increasing influence of the public servants known as the *corps des ingénieurs des télécommunications*. The goals of the ingénieurs

55

des télécommunications were sector-specific, but the themes of their movement resonated deeply with the more general movement toward technical competence that played such a large role in the formation of French elites in the Fourth and Fifth Republics. The ingénieurs des télécommunications sought to maintain national technological prowess in their field, to exert vigilant supervision over the prices paid by French citizens for public goods, and to promote mass democracy through the provision of communication services on an equitable basis. Such goals were readily understandable within an "order of state-created elites," in which technical competence was already accepted as the highest criterion for public service.

The corps des ingénieurs des télécommunications emerged gradually. The optical-semaphore telegraph introduced by Claude Chappe required disciplined personnel to operate the signal towers. With the advent of electrical telegraphy in the mid nineteenth century, technical competence and mastery of a certain body of scientific knowledge became necessary. The telegraph experts were recruited from the famous Ecole Polytechnique, after which they received on-the-job training in telegraphy. A *corps des ingénieurs-télégraphe* began to coalesce in the late 1860s and gained a more tangible identity with the creation of the Ecole Supèrieure de Télégraphie in 1878.[35] Under the Ministry of Posts and Telegraph, formed in 1879, however, the regional administrators who ran the commercial services (*services d'exploitation*) gained control. The telegraph experts were placed under the regional supervisors, who restricted the number of positions to forty. The role of the ingénieurs-télégraphes suffered further when, in 1886, the Ecole Supérieure de Télégraphie was made part of the new Ecole Professionelle Supérieure des PTTs. The new institution was to have two tracks—one for superior officials, from which engineers were excluded, the second for engineers alone. The engineers were relegated within the organization to narrow specialized tasks.[36]

In the first half of the twentieth century, research emerged as the lever that the ingénieurs-télégraphes used to advance their view of the role that telecommunications should play in French society. In 1902, they were recognized as a *corps spécial d'ingénieurs des postes et télégraphes*. The war confirmed a more pressing need to promote communications research, and in 1916 a new Service d'Etudes et de Recherches Techniques was established under the supervision of a Technical Committee founded during the same year.[37] In industry as well as public administration, the small testing departments of the nineteenth century steadily gave way to larger, more formally organized laboratories. The largest

French firm, the Société Industrielle des Téléphones, had a series of "test laboratories" attached to workshops in each of its separate businesses—high-tension cables, telegraph cables, and telephone equipment.[38]

The major event in industrial research was the establishment of ITT's Laboratoire Central de Télécommunication in 1927. Having agreed to create an international laboratory in Paris if the PTT contracted to buy its rotary switch, ITT soon assembled several hundred employees.[39] Although much of the facility's early work concerned short-wave radio, this concentration of expertise thoroughly outstripped all other actors in the industry.

A similar trajectory was apparent in public-sector research. In the nineteenth century, the state's research capacity resided in the testing workshops (*ateliers de vérification*), where performance specifications for telegraph equipment were verified. The establishment of the Service d'Etudes et de Recherches Techniques (SERT) in 1916 gave the PTT its own capacity to publish research results and to set technical specifications for switching equipment—a resource expected to be crucial in the upcoming bidding to supply automatic telephone exchanges. Through the 1930s, the SERT was limited to roughly a dozen engineers, several mechanics, and a single designer.[40] A more ambitious conception of state-directed research was stimulated by the expanding role of radio communications in the affairs of many state agencies. In 1926, the Laboratoire National de Télégraphie sans Fil was established. Although it had interministerial responsibilities, this new facility, renamed the Laboratoire National de Radioélectricité (LCR) in 1931, was placed under the Ministry of War.[41]

The event which later gave the French state the preponderance of technical expertise in telecommunications was the founding of the Centre National d'Etudes des Télécommunications (CNET) in 1944. The CNET was organized as a federation of laboratories, with a general administration and a series of specialized facilities. The old LCR became one of the CNET's specialized facilities, but the new entity's activities extended to other fields including telephony, telegraphy, radio, acoustics, signal processing, sea communications, and security work. Although it was given an interministerial status, the CNET was placed under the general supervision of the Minister of the PTT.[42]

The presence of the CNET changed relations between the PTT and its equipment suppliers qualitatively. With a substantial concentration of expertise under its direct administrative guidance, the PTT could anticipate changes in telephone technologies and direct its suppliers to pursue certain directions. The Vichy government's earlier reorganization of 1941 had split the old Ecole Professionelle Supérieure des PTTs into an Ecole Nationale Supérieure des PTTs (ENSPTT) and an Ecole Nationale Supérieure des Télécommunications (ENST, or "Sup Télécom"). With its own pool of recruits and with responsibility for testing and verifying the equipment developed by suppliers, the CNET emerged as the country's central repository for the study of new technologies in telecommunications.

Of course no institution could attain such a leadership position overnight. The CNET's first endeavor in switching technology was far from successful. In anticipation of competition for the first postwar generation of switches to replace the rotary exchanges, the French Compagnie Industrielle des Téléphones (CIT) developed a modified rotary design with active cooperation from the CNET. The proposed exchange, called the L43, prompted a characteristic tension between the CNET engineers who wanted the to purchase the technology and the commercial operators in the Direction Générale des Télécommunications (DGT) who hesitated to bring new designs into the network and thereby complicate their jobs. The CNET required three years to bring the first prototype into operation in Nancy, and the machinery short-circuited and burned shortly after it was connected.[43]

Although the abortive experiment with the L43 left the DGT largely dependent on ITT and Ericsson for the new crossbar switching exchanges, the CNET engineers continued to play an increasing role in the DGT's evolution. The research effort found a welcome political environment in the late 1950s and 1960s—the period when General de Gaulle prompted the establishment of several national research centers. By 1970, the CNET employed 3,000 persons of whom 2,000 were primarily engaged in R&D. By 1974, the CNET laboratories employed 3,500, persons, including many graduates of the ENST, some graduates of other schools, and over 1,000 short-term contractual employees who helped maintain the CNET's links to university and international research.[44] A research facility of this magnitude could develop new prototypes on its own, conduct joint research with equipment suppliers, or sponsor research undertaken by private enterprises on the basis of public funds.[45]

After consolidating their position in the French research community, the ingénieurs des télécommunications sought to secure their place within the administrative structure of the French state. This effort was led by the official corps des ingénieurs des télécommunications—the select group of *polytechniciens* who chose to begin their public service in the DGT after receiving further training in the ENST. The corps numbered only about 40 members in 1913, when the Association des Ingénieurs des télécommunications (AIT) was officially recognized. By the 1970s, the AIT numbered approximately 650, and by 1985, 850.[46] This growth reflected the changing balance of influence between the engineers and the administrators within the PTT.

In 1951, the *corps spécial d'ingénieurs des postes et télégraphes* was raised to interministerial status as the *corps interministériel des ingénieurs des télécommunications*. The administrative cadres vigorously contested the notion that engineers were well qualified to supervise the nontechnical aspects of the DGT's work. According to the director of personnel at the time, the operation of the phone network required an excellent "general culture" which was not accessible to technically trained polytechniciens.[47] The engineers used precisely the opposite argument. They insisted that the components of a good scientific education—clarity, precision, and rigor—were as important to running an enterprise as the aptitudes provided by legal or literary training. According to a 1963 AIT brochure, "the engineers have demonstrated yet again that a high scientific culture—which inculcates the qualities of clarity, precision, and rigor in those who possess it—is as appropriate for training commercial leaders as legal or literary training."[48] The arguments were couched within the familiar framework of polyvalence, that sign of culture and competence which had become a virtually uncontested requirement in the politics of postwar French elite recruitment.[49]

The ingénieurs des télécommunications did not, however, limit their cause to scientific excellence. They also attacked the administrative cadres for poor financial control and investment planning. These issues surfaced in the early 1960s when a senior member of the corps des télécommunications publicly denounced the ministry for paying inflated prices to its suppliers and investing too little to make the phone system profitable.[50] Public discussion of France's backward phone service soon gave rise to a general sense of crisis in the French telephone system. This sense was reinforced in 1970, when a younger group of engineers delivered another blistering critique of the PTT, written under the pseudonym Jean-François Rugès.[51]

The Rugès critique blamed the "crise du téléphone" above all on inadequate investment. The authors noted that well into the 1960s the telephone remained a luxury in France. There were only 6.6 principal phone connections per 100 inhabitants in France—less than one-fourth the number in Sweden (37), the United States (30.5), and Canada (27.2) and only about half the number in such countries as Norway

(15.6), Finland (13), and the United Kingdom (11.6). Citizens in the provinces complained of having to wait three or four years to get a phone installed, while callers in Paris were given a 50 percent chance that a phone call to the provinces would be completed within the same day. The Rugès authors bemoaned the absence of a separate budget for telecommunications within the PTT's procedures and claimed that financial autonomy was imperative for the system's proper development. From 1951 to 1955, the network's condition worried NATO officials enough that they granted credits of 1.5 billion francs for its improvement—over half as much as the 2.17 billion provided by the Ministry of Finance during the same years.[52]

The Rugès authors argued that the rivalry between the corps des ingénieurs and the corps des administrateurs had weighed especially heavily on the administrative efficiency of the DGT. The rivalry stemmed from the "great difference in training and therefore in the attitude of mind between the members of these two corps."[53] Much of the opposition boiled down to the opposition between the two leading recruitment channels, the Ecole Polytechnique and the Ecole Nationale d'Administration (ENA).[54] The engineers were almost all graduates of the former, while the administrators were graduates of the Ecole Nationale Supérieure des PTTs (ENSPTT), whose courses were run jointly with the ENA. This rivalry expressed itself through the ministry's administrative structure which left control over personnel, construction, investments, accounting, and construction in the hands of the administrators. The Rugès authors chafed under this structure, which they claimed rendered rational planning of network modernization impossible.[55]

If investment funds and better management could be combined, one result would be a great improvement in the DGT's customary procurement methods. According to the Rugès authors, the practice of awarding fixed quotas of the domestic market to a closed group of suppliers made relations between the DGT and its suppliers too comfortable. Interestingly, the authors did not blame industry lobbying for the quota system, but instead they blamed the PTT for seeking convenient and predictable procedures that militated against a more competitive method of awarding contracts. First, absence of genuine competition led to prices which were said to be as much as 20 percent above what other countries paid for analogous equipment. Second, it encouraged large suppliers such as the Compagnie Générale de l'Électricité (CGE), the holding company that owned CIT-Alcatel, to milk their telecommunications subsidiaries for public funds without reinvesting sufficient resources in their own telecommunications capabilities. This tendency was

further encouraged by the CNET's practice of developing new prototypes, which were then adapted by the suppliers for serial production.
Finally, the quota system led to a fragmented domestic industry which
made little or no effort to develop export markets.[56]

In advancing the cause of their own autonomy, the young Turks *(jeunes
loups)* among the ingénieurs des télécommunications also advanced a
vision of France as a modern industrial society where technology was
deployed in accordance with rational and democratic planning. Far from
prescribing technological solutions, they conceived of a public telephone
administration as a commercial and an industrial enterprise, which
required modern techniques of management and planning. Part of the
problem was that the telephone industry was not exposed to competition.
Part of it, however, was the need to "break out of the bureaucratic yoke
that burdens the management and the financing of the telephone."[57]
Far from advocating the free play of the market, the young ingénieurs
des télécommunications asserted that good management and expanded
investment could triumph over economic necessity. The telephone had
assumed "a symbolic value for the France of the 1970s." The Rugès
authors insisted that "proper management of the enterprise will demon-
strate that a dynamic state of mind can replace a purely fatalistic conception of public affairs."[58] It was this attitude of public activism that
informed the French policy initiatives of the next fifteen years.

Germany

The range of policy options considered by telecommunications authorities in postwar Germany was largely determined by the distribution
of expertise in the private sector. The concentration of technical expertise in private enterprises reinforced the preference in the Federal
Republic of Germany for a high degree of market discretion as opposed
to the state dirigisme that often characterized French policy. In the
case of telecommunications, however, market control enabled a single
firm to accumulate the preponderance of scientific knowledge, research
capability, and practical know-how. Almost continually for 140 years,
the center of activity in this industry resided in the workshops and
laboratories of the Siemens company. This degree of concentration
had both advantages and disadvantages in practical terms. It did not,
however, make the telecommunications industry an ideal partner for
the kind of diffusion-oriented policies at which the federal ministries
in postwar Germany excelled.

From the outset Siemens played a key role in the development of Germany's telegraph network. The young Werner von Siemens had founded his first undertaking in 1847 with the Berlin mechanic, Johann Georg Halske, to supply the Prussian telegraph authorities. An officer in the Prussian army, Siemens became a leading official for telegraphy at the same time that the military commissioned his firm to construct the line from Berlin to Frankfurt. There were a number of competitors in the early cable business, particularly Felten & Guillaume of Mulheim and Berlin, but Siemens & Halske established a steady position in the industry. In the 1870s, Werner von Siemens quickly consolidated relations with the Imperial Postmaster General, von Stephan.[59]

In the telephone business, however, the firm had to contend with much more competition. Shortly after the Bell telephone was exhibited in Germany, several firms adapted foreign technologies to supply the Reichpost's needs for telephone handsets and the early, hand-operated switchboard exchanges. For the 1880s and 1890s, most telephone equipment was produced on a nonstandard basis in workshops of various sizes. One Berlin machinist, R. Stock, achieved considerable success offering designs to the Reichspost inspired in part by the Swedish engineer Ericsson. Subsequently the firm was incorporated as Deutsche Telephonwerke R. Stock & Co., which came to be known in the twentieth century as DeTeWe.[60] Additional competition came from the Berlin entrepreneur F. Welles, who obtained Western Electric's early patents and found a German-American engineer from Milwaukee who was particularly gifted at adapting American technologies to European circumstances. In 1897, after Siemens tried for six months to adapt its system to the Viennese network, the Austrian authorities gave the order to Welles. Finally, Mix & Genest, a Berlin trading house that had supplied private telephone equipment to hospitals, banks, and other private users, also entered the bidding for the Reichspost's telephone exchanges. For at least two decades, these smaller firms prevented Siemens from implanting its technology in the German telephone network.[61]

The formative experience in Siemens's relations with the telephone authorities came after 1905, when the Reichspost decided to install Europe's first automatic exchange in Hildesheim. The work was commissioned to the Loewe group, which possessed a license on the American Strowger patents. The firm's weapons factories in Karlsruhe (the Deutsche Waffen-und Munitionsfabriken) were considered well-suited for the series production of precision-engineered parts. During the course of installing the Hildeshiem exchange, however, it became clear that practical knowledge of electrical installations was at least as important as precision engineering. Georg von Siemens disapprovingly described the Loewe employees as a group of newcomers over whom the Reichspost officials ruled like school masters. The Loewe group—overextended by the special electrical engineering tasks required to adapt the American technology to the Hildesheim network—concluded by declaring its disinterest in further switching contracts.[62] In 1907, the Reichspost asked Siemens to enter a joint research consortium (*Studiengesellschaft*) to strengthen the German industry's capability. Siemens agreed on the condition that it be given technical leadership of the new enterprise, which would be called the Gesellschaft für automatische Telephonie. Siemens assumed the Loewe group's licenses for the Strowger technology and also hired the technical personnel who had worked on the Hildesheim project from the Deutsche Waffen- und Munitionsfabriken in Karlsruhe. The firm was now positioned to become the major supplier in the automation of Germany's telephone network. In 1909 the Bavarian postal authorities commissioned Siemens to install Europe's first automatic exchange powered by central batteries in Munich-Schwabing.[63] In 1911 and 1912 Siemens & Halske constructed large urban exchanges in Amsterdam and Dresden.

Rather than scientific research per se, it was the practical know-how and familiarity of Siemens with German communications networks that gave its engineers the leading role in setting development strategies for the German telephone system. This relationship, by which large firms put their accumulated know-how at the service of the state, was not a mere commercial convenience. On the contrary, it was deeply rooted in the respective roles which civil servants, industrialists, and engineers had assumed through the rapid industrialization which Germany experienced in the second half of the nineteenth century.

The concept of "the official" (*Beamter*) was—as Jürgen Kocka has shown in his study of bureaucracy and capitalism at Siemens—crucial to the emergence of new mechanisms of social control in the nineteenth century. As absolutist-mercantilist forms of authority gave way to parliamentary-capitalist ones, newly emerging social groups defined themselves in terms that harkened back to previous grounds of authority. The problem was complicated because the term *Beamter* had been used for employees in royal enterprises. There was a great deal of admiration among employees for the status of the officials. Yet, through the mid-nineteenth century, employees working for private-sector firms of any kind came to be seen as engaged in narrow private endeavors and not serving the larger public interest. As the term *Beamter* became increasingly restricted to public officials, the concept of the *Privatbeamter*—or "private official"—was applied to salaried employees in large firms.[64]

The civil engineers—who played a growing role in German industrialization—had a particularly complex relationship vis-à-vis the civil service. On the one hand, German engineers identified more with the pioneer spirit of the early industrial entrepreneurs than with governmental civil servants. The engineers' social position rested on their individual competence rather than on a role conferred by the state. They were largely blocked from access to senior positions in public service by university-trained lawyers. In their professional association, the VDI, the engineers developed a critique of bureaucracy, which was directed especially against the legal professions. Yet, far from rejecting the principle of the state's authority in technical matters, the VDI generally lobbied to have the state's authority devolved to its own committees for the resolution of technical disputes.[65] As the professional group developed, the engineers were increasingly accorded public responsibilities for resolving technical disputes, even though their livelihood was tied to private industry much more than was the case with their French counterparts.

For communications in general, the public authorities had to develop test and verification facilities, but for telephony in particular, it was Siemens that accumulated the expertise necessary to conduct original research and development. As early as 1888, the Reichspost had a small technical engineering department (Telegrapheningenieurbüro der Reichspost) staffed by a few scientists. At the turn of the century, the rapidly expanding department was renamed the Experimental Telegraph Office (Telegraphenversuchsamt), and in 1920 it became the National Technical Telegraph Office (Telegraphentechnisches Reichsamt).[66]

In its telephone business, Siemens developed a more concentrated staff of technical experts, in part by hiring the best of the Reichspost scientists. In 1896, the company hired Dr. Adolf Franke, a physicist who had worked in the Telegraph Engineering Bureau and who proved crucial to the firm's first successes in the switching business.[67] Numerous personal ties linked Siemens to the Telegraph Engineering Bureau and fostered collaboration between the two. In response to Reichspost plans to expand the long-distance network in 1920, the firm formed the Central Laboratory for Long-Distance Communication (Zentrallaboratorium für Fernmeldetechnik). Technical personnel in telephony had previously been scattered through a number of specialized staffs. Fritz Lüschen, another former employee of the Reichspost, managed to bring them all together in a single facility in the firm's Berlin headquarters, which now contained over one hundred engineers and physicists with hundreds of assistants.[68]

Within a few years, Siemens had a near monopoly on the design of both switching and transmission equipment. To avoid excessive dependence on its main supplier, the Reichspost had little choice but to require that Siemens share its knowledge through mixed enterprises.[69]

After World War II, the elite relations among elites in many fields exhibited great continuity with prewar patterns.[70] In telecommunications, the institutional arrangements that governed relations between the engineers and the public authorities endured particularly well.

Siemens emerged as the dominant supplier of telephone equipment even before the West German authorities had reassumed sovereignty from the Allied Occupation. At this point, the firm's pedigree gave it high status. It was older than the Nazi regime, older than the Weimar experiment which had failed, indeed older than the Reich which had preceded Weimar.

The Bundespost had limited competence to match Siemens. It main source of expertise was the descendant of the National Technical Telegraph Office (Telegraphentechnisches Reichsamt), which was was renamed the Central Office for Long-Distance Technology (Fernmeldetechnisches Zentralamt, or FTZ), and moved, after some political controversy, from Berlin to Darmstadt. The FTZ employed approximately 2,000 people, but its research activities were quite limited.[71] Like its predecessors, the FTZ did neither basic research nor applied research on a self-determined agenda. Most of the FTZ's work was concerned with supervising the development projects undertaken by industrial firms and evaluating competing equipment for government purchase, and its applied research agenda was derived from these tasks. Separate from the FTZ, the Deutsche Bundes Post had a small research institute, also located in Darmstadt, which employed some three hundred persons. They pursued from forty to sixty projects at any given time, with an annual budget of about 50 million German marks, in most years. Total R&D funding by the Bundespost was estimated at about 200 million marks per year.[72]

In the 1980s, the Bundespost's position as a center for learning in frontier areas was also limited by its difficulty in recruiting new communications engineers. The Association of German Postal Engineers (*Verband Deutscher Postingenieure* (VDPI) was a large interest association, whose roughly fourteen thousand members included many of the engineers working in any aspect of the Bundespost's postal or communication

65

services. This organization had nothing like the technological leadership role played by the ingénieurs des télécommunications in France. It concerned itself primarily with the pay and working conditions of the engineers in the Bundespost's employ. In 1986, the VDPI openly complained that salary discrepancies were driving young engineers to industry rather than to public service. As the association noted, the Bundespost had two thousand fewer engineers in 1986 than it needed in the communications divisions alone.[73]

Without an independent research capability like the CNET, the Bundespost relied extensively on industry for technical advice. The FTZ dealt directly with Siemens and the six or seven other firms who made up the modern-day "court suppliers" (*Hoflieferanten*).[74] The FTZ also worked closely with the electrotechnical industry association (ZVEI)—particularly the technical Subassociation for Information and Communications Technology (Fachverband Informations- und Kommunikationstechnik). Although membership in the industry association (ZVEI) was open to all firms operating in the industry, members of the technical subassociations could regulate composition of their affiliated panels (*Gremien*).[75] In the case of telecommunications, these details were significant because membership on the ZVEI panel for norms and standards was a virtual requirement for participating in discussions with the FTZ. The change in name from the traditional German term for Subassociation for Telecommunications (Fachverband für Fernmeldetechnik) to Subassociation for Information and Communication Technology (Fachverband Informations- und Kommunikationstechnik) was the first sign that the computer firms might be excluded from consultations with the FTZ by the "court suppliers."[76] At different points in time, Nixdorf, Ericsson, and IBM all became dissatisfied with the ZVEI for perpetuating these exclusionary channels between manufacturers and the FTZ. As a result these firms worked through the machine building industry association (VDMA) to exert pressure on the FTZ to open its consultations on norms and standards.[77]

Although Siemens was not alone among the firms that enjoyed privileged relations with the Bundespost, it had the dominant voice. The firm's role was signaled by the now-customary inclusion of its telecommunications chief on the Bundespost's administrative council. Observers agreed, however, that the firm's influence was exerted primarily through its discussions on technical matters with the FTZ.[78] Its privileged position in these discussions was based partly on its reputation for superior knowhow. Perhaps even more important, however, was the ongoing imprint of Siemens technology on the entire telephone network, which became institutionalized through *Einheitstechnik*—the Bundespost's policy of maintaining "uniform technology" among all its suppliers.

Einheitstechnik perpetuated the same industry relationships that had existed since the 1920s in the form of the mixed enterprise (*Automatische-Fernsprechanlagen-Baugesellschaft*) in which Siemens and its competitors shared patents and design information. Under Einheitstechnik, Siemens and its competitors enjoyed reliable shares of the public orders for telephone exchanges. Competition was limited to efficient production of a design that was approved by the procuring agency. In this respect, the policy was similar to the quota system employed in France. The balance of influence over technical matters remained, however, completely different in Germany. If Siemens did not possess juridical authority over design choices, its engineers were regarded as the "authoritative" experts. In France, the DGT allocated fixed quotas but also frequently intervened through the CNET in design and development. In Germany, the design was proposed by Siemens and approved by the FTZ, which then required other suppliers to fall into line.

This practice allowed Siemens to build upon its position as the central repository of knowledge about the German telephone network. It also strengthened the company's ability to recommend technical standards and to define the goals of technological advance in a form which supported its larger business strategy. This unusual latitude became an important factor in the evolution of policy through the 1970s.

POLICY

Public officials in France and Germany responded to changes in the telecommunications industry by attempting to mold the quasi–vertical links that tied them to their domestic suppliers in a way that served the public's interest. There was no single or optimal recipe for putting state resources at the disposal of these firms. Indeed, given the very different institutional legacies which governed the distribution of expertise in the two countries, it was not surprising that the French officials made use of different instruments than their German counterparts. This section traces the evolution of telecommunications policy, showing how the collective identities of the technical elites in the two countries shaped policy options and outcomes.

France

Given the dominant position of its own laboratories in the CNET, the DGT tended to use publicly financed research results as one of its favored ways of inducing its suppliers to explore those technologies that it considered most promising. The provision of research results, obtained at the expense of the state, deepened the quasi-vertical links between the DGT as buyer and the equipment manufacturer as seller.

A fully computerized method of effecting telephone connections had been envisioned by telecommunications engineers as early as the 1930s. Preliminary research was begun at Bell Labs in New Jersey and at England's General Post Office facility in Highgate Woods in the 1940s.[79] French engineers first explored digital coding in the domain of transmission technologies, but had developed enough interest in digital techniques that a research department within the CNET was created to explore electronic switching equipment. The first prototypes were conceived as early as 1960—well before integrated circuits were available. Named by the CNET engineers after Greek philosophers, the first two prototypes were called the ARISTOTE and the SOCRATE. The ARISTOTE, based on a large universal computer connected to secondary "explorer" computers at the periphery, was developed by CNET engineers outside Paris (at Issy-les-Moulineaux) and transferred to the CNET's installation in Lannion, Brittany, for internal use in 1964. The SOCRATE was a smaller electronic exchange designed to fit into a configuration of analog contacts based on the earlier CP400 crossbar which had been introduced by Ericsson.[80]

After these two experimental models were built, the decision was made to pursue two different paths of development toward industrial production, one emphasizing semi-electronic space-division designs, the other striving toward fully digital time-division designs.[81] The SOCRATE project was elaborated in the PERICLES model, which employed space-division switching. The contact function, patterned after the crossbar design, used an electro-mechanical system of reed relays (*relais à tiges*) to maintain physical connection between subscribers during a call. The control functions—identifying callers, initiating and terminating contacts, and billing—were all handled by a large general-purpose computer. The PERICLES switch was first installed in Clamart near Paris in 1970. It was later modified and produced in one variant under the name, E-11, by the ITT subsidiary, LMT.[82]

Simultaneously with its entry into semi-electronic switching technology, the CNET also pushed forward in developing a fully electronic, digital switch. The switching specialists code-named their most ambitious effort PLATON (Prototype Lannionnais d'Autocommutateur Téléphonique à Organisation Numérique). It was a visionary project which looked toward an entirely new world of digitized telecommunications.

The project quickly became identified with the CNET's more creative switching specialists, who now began to concentrate at the laboratory in Lannion. Their work was highly experimental and allowed a great deal of potential design latitude since basic algorithms and hardware for digital switching were yet undiscovered. Their self-image was defined partly in contrast to the transmission engineers—whose work was focused on creating cost-efficient and reliable applications of well-known circuit principles rather than on the elegant design of entirely new algorithms.[83]

The projet PLATON shows how the group identity of the CNET's technical specialists enabled the DGT to utilize its quasi-vertical links to the suppliers to promote its own technological aims. The CNET's researchers at Lannion worked in tandem with technicians from a joint supplier firm, the Société Lannionnaise d'Electronique, controlled by CIT (70 percent) and Ericsson (30 percent). By providing much of the design work directly through the work of the CNET's engineers, and by funding the R&D that the firms might not be willing to finance from their own revenues, the DGT encouraged firms to develop technologies long before they might prove profitable. Indeed, the PLATON technology— commercialized under the name E-10—was the world's first commercial, fully electronic time-division switching exchange. It was installed for local switching at Perros-Guirec in January 1970 and for long-distance switching in Lannion in June 1970. When another E-10 was installed in Poitiers in 1972, the Minister of the PTT, Robert Galley, proclaimed it a revolutionary event. Still, the revolution was technological rather than commercial. Even in 1973, the E-10 would account for no more than 2 percent of the DGT's orders for switching equipment.[84]

The E-10 technology was destined to become the predominant product in the DGT's purchasing plans for the next decade, but it did not attain that status easily. As the first fully digitized switch developed for commercial production, the E-10 was clearly the most sophisticated and state-of-the-art technology available. Before the new technology received the full backing of the ministry's procurement credits, however, it had to withstand the tumultuous currents of high industrial politics. Telecommunications procurement became a hotly contested political issue, with product lines compared in the front pages of the daily newspapers and market shares eventually allocated in cabinet meetings. Nevertheless, after the shifting alliances among personalities, philosophies, firms, and politicians, the technology developed by French engineers in Lannion was given the state's backing. Three episodes dominate the contours of these complex interactions: the DGT's call for bids in 1975, which brought Thomson-Brandt into the switching market for the first time;

the revision of DGT purchasing strategies in 1978; and the acquisition of Thomson's telecommunications operations by CIT in 1983.

Events were set in motion in 1973 and 1974 during preparations for the Seventh Plan which designated telecommunications as a priority for economic development. The DGT had already surpassed Electricité de France to become the country's largest public investor by the time an interministerial committee allocated over 10 billion francs for its equipment purchases in 1974. The heightened level of funding was continued when the Commissariat Général du Plan envisioned allocating over 120 billion francs to the DGT over five years (1976–1980). This recommendation vindicated the long-standing calls from the ingénieurs de télécommunications for more funds, but it did nothing to suggest specific technology choices.[85]

The elaboration of an overall strategy for telecommunications was left to the new government to be named by Giscard d'Estaing, elected in April 1974. Giscard's election prompted a repositioning of the various schools of thought within the corps des télécommunications, ranging from the traditional proponents of technology designed by the CNET to younger, more entrepreneurial engineers who questioned the CNET's established relations with its industrial partners. Giscard appointed Gerard Théry, one of the young Turks (*jeunes loups*) to replace Joseph Libois as chief of the DGT. Since Libois had previously directed the CNET, where he steadfastly supported work on electronic switching designs, his replacement signalled a change away from industrial policy directed by the CNET. This shift was confirmed when Théry appointed an outsider from the corps des mines, Jean-Pierre Souviron, to head the division of industrial policy, which was renamed the Direction des Affaires Industrielles et Internationales (DAII).

Théry and Souviron tempered the CNET's customary influence over procurement by adopting the Giscardian notion of enhancing domestic competition. Previously the DGT's goals had focussed on the expansion of the public network and the development of the best possible technology, preferably from French sources. Théry and Souviron emphasized in addition the need for domestic competition among French producers and the desirability of exporting.[86]

The new team was trying to break the hold of the "arsenal" system of procurement that had characterized the DGT's relations with its main suppliers, especially CGE. The arsenal system—named by analogy to the Defense Ministry's procurement practices—exemplified precisely those tensions predicted by theories of nonstandard contracting for asset-specific transactions. That is, both purchaser (DGT) and seller (CGE) wanted the other party to assume a greater share of R&D costs, the asset-specific investments that were part of any contract for a new order of telephone switches. The DGT complained that the holding company, CGE, milked CIT, its telecommunications subsidiary, for cash flow without devoting its own resources for R&D. CGE meanwhile complained that it was asked to undertake major development projects with insufficient public credits. According to one observer, this was an eternal debate. CGE had reinforced its position in 1969 when it signed an explicit accord with its main competitor, Thomson, which agreed not to challenge CGE in the telecommunications market. Some officials in the DGT had long argued that the practice of allocating market shares by fixed quotas encouraged manufacturers to overcharge and underinvest. Under Théry and Souviron, the DGT reopened competitive bidding for switching exchanges. Having relied for many years on CGE as its main domestic supplier, the French state was clearly making recourse to a new degree of market competition.[87]

This new competitive environment in switching equipment was inaugurated in June 1975, when the PTT solicited bids for a major program in semi-electronic switching.[88] The fully electronic E-10, developed at the CNET's work in Lannion, was still only suitable for relatively small, pilot applications (15,000 subscribers or less). A larger version, the E-12 was being planned, but until it was ready, the semi-electronic, space-division switches were still preferred for large, urban exchanges. Bids were submitted by six entrants, in each case a French manufacturer in association with a non-French technology source. CIT, with no semi-electronic model of its own, offered the D10 product of the Nippon Electric Company. SLE, the Lannion champion of the fully electronic E-10, joined with Ericsson of Sweden, its minority shareholder, to offer Ericsson's new space-division switch, the AXE. The ITT subsidiaries, LMT and CGCT, offered ITT's latest switch, the semi-electronic Metaconta, in two variants: the E-11, which used the contact system derived from the CNET's projet PLATON, and the 11A, which used a miniselector developed in-house by CGCT. The smaller French firm SAT (Société Anonyme de Télécommunications) combined with Siemens to offer the German EWS switch. The Dutch giant Philips offered its PRX switch through its French subsidiary, TRT. And the newcomer Thomson proposed a consortium with the Canadian telecommunications giant Northern Bell to offer the SP1.

By December 1975 the PTT eliminated three bids on the basis of price and performance: the Philips product (PRX) because it was too small, the Northern Bell product (SP1) because its technology was outdated, and the Siemens switch (EWS) because it was considerably more expensive than the others. In considering the remaining bids, the DGT clearly used its procurement credits to guarantee French control of production as well as know-how. In early 1976, the DGT began negotiations to bring the subsidiaries of Ericsson and ITT under the control of the Thomson group. A protocol of February 1976 stipulated that Ericsson would sell its majority share of Société Française de Téléphone–Ericsson if Ericsson's switch, the AXE, were selected by the DGT. Similarly, in April, ITT agreed to sell 68 percent of its subsidiary LMT to Thomson, with an understanding that some version of ITT's Metaconta switch would be purchased by the French state. The Swedish firm was to retain a 16 percent interest in its former subsidiary, while ITT retained a share of LMT as well as complete ownership of its other subsidiary, CGCT. In addition, both parent firms were to receive royalties on any exports of their products which resulted from French production.[89]

With French control of the main competitors assured, the final choice of switches was made at a cabinet meeting led by President Giscard d'Estaing in May 1976. The government selected two switches—Ericsson's AXE and a version of ITT's Metaconta—for production under Thomson's management control. Suddenly Thomson had become France's "national champion" in space-division switches. CGE was asked to concentrate its efforts on further development of the fully electronic E-10, which, according to a communiqué of 13 May, would be systematically purchased for new exchanges starting in 1978.[90]

The government's decision clearly signified the DGT's desire to reduce its dependence on CGE by establishing a major new supplier for public switching equipment. The effort to stimulate domestic competition was, however, far from an appeal to unrestrained competition. The highest levels of the French state had endorsed the DGT's view that management control of the new suppliers should stay in French hands. In addition, even as they sought to weaken the arsenal mechanism of procurement, Théry and Souviron maintained the CNET in a major role by having it adapt foreign technologies instead of accepting them outright. Rather than accepting either of ITT's variants, the DGT contracted to purchase a switch designated as the 11F. This switch, based on a computer developed in ITT's Paris research facility, was combined with a French-developed contact system from CGCT's laboratory and software developed by the CNET.[91] These details were more than purely symbolic; they gave the DGT leverage in bargaining with ITT and they helped insure that the French network employed a variety of technologies which no single supplier understood as well as the engineers at the CNET.

The DGT's decision to bring Thomson into the public switching business can be parsimoniously explained by straightforward bargaining dynamics, but the idiosyncratic knowledge and the collective identity of the ingénieurs des télécommunications continued to play a role in subsequent developments. As events were to show, the promotion of robust French manufacturers proved to involve more than just buying off foreign investors and specifying technologies to be produced in the newly "Frenchified" factories. The rapidity of technological change in the industry, more than anything else, undermined the strategy of relying primarily on competition among domestic suppliers to move technology development forward. Up through 1976 many experts believed that time-division (fully electronic) switching technologies could not become cost competitive. Yet in October 1977, consensus first emerged—at a conference of telecommunications experts in Atlanta, Georgia—that component costs had declined to the point where fully electronic time-division exchanges appeared to offer cost and performance advantages over all other options.[92]

The announcement created huge difficulties for Thomson, the DGT's new supplier. Although Thomson's semi-electronic 11F switch was not to be ready for installation until September 1979, the firm had to finalize the product in order to fulfill contracts already signed with the DGT. Thomson's other semielectronic switch, the Ericsson AXE, was also rendered archaic at the Atlanta conference. Ericsson announced that it would no longer sell the semi-electronic AXE in third markets, leaving Thomson in the position of trying to export a licensed product which had been abandoned by its own original manufacturer. Thus, while continuing work on these two transitional switches, Thomson was faced with the daunting task of developing a fully electronic successor product if it wished to remain in the business. Quite surprisingly, the firm found a file on LMT's premises containing its plans for participating in ITT's digital switching program. Thomson's directors decided to use the LMT plans to develop their own switch by 1980 to be called the MT20.[93]

In retrospect, the discovery of LMT's electronic switch blueprints turned out to be a major pitfall. The plans were only preliminary designs from one of ITT's subsidiaries. Virtually all major switch manufacturers substantially underestimated the time it would take to bring their fully electronic exchanges to market. In an effort to produce its planned MT series as quickly as possible, Thomson's managers combined LMT and the old Ericsson subsidiary, but had difficulty integrating the former competitors' development teams with their own specialists. By late 1982, morale in Thomson's development teams was reportedly flagging. Although the MT20/25 switches had a larger capacity than CGE's E-10, the DGT brusquely cut its orders for the Thomson model in late 1982. Not until March 1983 did Thomson receive the DGT's final technical approval that the MT20 was ready for installation.[94]

By 1981, the E-10 had become the DGT's favored product. This development represented a delayed vindication for the CNET members whose work on the PLATON project had been deemphasized by the Giscardian strategy of promoting technological advance through domestic competition. Although Thomson's accumulated orders through 1981 gave it a slightly larger share of France's public switching market than CIT-Alcatel (46 percent compared to 39 percent), the latter produced all of the 1.65 million lines of digital switching connections that had been installed through June of that year. During the course of 1982, the DGT reduced Thomson's share of new orders for electronic exchanges to 35 percent while CIT-Alcatel received 50 percent. By September 1981, CIT-Alcatel's product had also been ordered by over twenty countries, while Thomson's export orders remained modest. Perhaps most important, CIT-Alcatel had developed a larger capacity version of its E-10, installed in Brest in 1981, before any of Thomson's fully electronic exchanges had actually been emplaced.[95]

Thomson definitively ended its stake in public telecommunications when its executives arranged a thoroughgoing reorganization of its activities in conjunction with CGE in 1983. This move immediately became known as the "second Yalta" of French electronics, because of its similarity to a merger which Thomson's executives had negotiated with CSF in 1969. According to the agreement worked out between the firms, CGE took over Thomson's activities in civil telecommunications, while Thomson assumed management control of CGE's operations in defense electronics, consumer electronics, and other components.[96] CGE returned to its pre-Giscard role as the country's national champion in telecommunications, while Thomson was effectively confirmed as France's premier entrant in defense electronics.

The reorganization was ironic as well as controversial because of its great secrecy and the fact that such a momentous reorganization had taken place without the knowledge of the socialist government. Members of the government were not pleased to read in the press about the restructuring of the country's two largest nationalized firms in a sector which they had themselves designated as a showcase for socialist industrial policy. This type of restructuring had certainly been mentioned in government circles, but many observers had thought that managers working under nationalized ownership would discuss such major changes with the public authorities before acting.[97]

Though not consulted on this major reorganization, the Socialist government had already effected extensive changes in the telecommunications sector. Most important, ITT had been obliged to sell its second subsidiary, CGCT, in 1982.[98] Jacques Dondoux, the Socialists' successor to Gérard Théry in the DGT, had opposed the nationalization on economic grounds but was over-ruled by others who found ITT a politically repugnant partner for any Socialist government.[99] It quickly became clear that CGCT, whose 16 percent share of the public switching market had been set by the government in 1976, was barely viable without ITT's technology or capital. Suddenly, the DGT had one weak equipment supplier for 16 percent of its orders and the remaining 84 percent concentrated in the hands of CGE.

In the end, the government accepted the restructuring initiated by Thomson and CGE.[100] The notion of "recentering" the country's public communications resources under CGE's control fit well with the idea, elaborated by the one of the government's economic theorists, Alain Boublil, of coordinating policy toward an entire industrial sector as an integrated whole *(filière)*. One aim of this approach was to rebuild national champions to make them large enough to compete in world markets. At a less theoretical level, many in the DGT had been exasperated by Thomson's performance on the MT series. In addition, those who succeeded Théry in the DGT had to recognize the argument for consolidation in the world switching industry.[101]

The "second Yalta" was motivated by a variety of factors, but its main consequence for public efforts to promote innovation was a thoroughgoing rationalization of R&D resources in telecommunications. Financial details of the agreement stipulated that Thomson would retain minority interest in a new entity which would be called Thomson Telecommunications, placed under CGE's management control, and merged by 1987 into Alcatel. This arrangement meant that Thomson's various development teams could be kept intact in order to service outstanding contracts for Thomson's semi-electronic (11F) and fully electronic (MT20/25) exchanges.[102] For future projects, however, the French state would henceforth be able to rely on unified design teams. Although the assimilation of formerly competing engineers was not a trivial matter, informed observers agreed that CGE had more successfully integrated the various firms it acquired from Thomson than Thomson itself had ever managed to do.[103]

In the all-important field of switching technologies, the merger allowed CGE and Thomson to announce plans for a joint research enterprise, effectively reuniting remnants of the teams which had atrophied after Gérard Thèry made competition the leitmotif of DGT policy in 1974. The new research enterprise was to be located where CNET had its first successes in electronic switching, Lannion. The communist Left saw the merged research facility in Lannion as part of a larger policy meant to disguise layoffs by forcing employees to transfer job sites. Others saw the joint research effort as one way of meeting the huge expenditures necessary to develop the next generation of switching exchanges. During discussions of the fusion between Alcatel and Thomson Telecommunications, the idea of a joint research center was the one point that the PTT had never contested. Within two years, the merged research group had indeed dropped further development of Thomson's MT product line and concentrated its efforts on the E-10.[104]

By 1985, the contours of policy in the telecommunications sector had shown numerous twists and turns. Nonetheless, through the entrances, exits, nationalizations, and mergers, the position of the ingénieurs des télécommunications remained central. At the level of technology, it often barely mattered who worked in which laboratory or which firm because the engineers had important suprafirm sources of identity. This identity rested on the prestige of public service in France and the ability of the corps des télécommunications to advance their vision for the telephone system as an infrastructure of symbolic value. The identity of the ingénieurs des télécommunications also extended to more tangible issues of research agenda and technical specifications, in which the DGT, advised by the CNET, remained the central actor. By the mid 1980s, the corps des télécommunications had gained a central position in the larger discussion of technology and its role in French society. An increasing number of the top graduates of the Ecole Polytechnique were opting to work in telecommunications.[105] The DGT was given overall financial responsibility for the largely nationalized electronics sector, which had come to be known in policy circles as the *filière electronique,* in 1983. And the labs of the CNET were among the leaders in research on satellites, components, and data processing in addition to its traditional focus on communications.[106]

In the latter half of the 1980s, developments outside France began to transform the organizational arrangements within which the ingénieurs des télécommunications exercised their broad influence. First, the Commission of the European Community seized upon telecommunications as one area where it could strengthen European industry by opening national markets to greater competition. Beginning with its Green Paper of 1987, the commission issued a series of directives that called for steady liberalization of telecommunications services, culminating in plans to open basic voice networks to competition in 1998. In addition, the example of British Telecom, privatized in the early 1980s, suggested that independent enterprises rather than state administrations might be better able to compete in the new and more open environment for telecommunications.[107]

Equipment suppliers responded to these changes with a series of acquisitions that moved the industry toward greater concentration. Most important, Alcatel's parent company, CGE, dramatically strengthened its presence by acquiring ITT's European subsidiaries for telecommunications in early 1987. The new European holding company, Alcatel N.V., thereby gained control of Germany's second supplier for public switching equipment, SEL, which had played a lead role in developing ITT's System 12 switch. Soon thereafter, France's new right-of-center government under Jacques Chirac announced its intention to privatize CGE. Privatization was pushed further the same year when the government sold control over one of the DGT's traditional suppliers, CGCT, to a consortium of the Swedish Ericsson and the French firm Matra. Although French officials effectively denied German producers any foothold in France's public switching market, the Bosch group acquired the communications interests of the French Jeumont Schneider later in 1987. The main German producer, Siemens, had to content itself with expansion in the British market by taking an interest in Plessey telecommunications in 1988.[108]

In the public sector, the impetus for change came from the DGT itself. Well before the center-right coalition gained power in 1986, the ingénieurs des télécommunications took up the cause of reform. The select group of roughly 800 polytechniciens who had joined the public service as engineers in the corps des télécommunications advocated in 1985 that the DGT be changed from an administration to a nationalized enterprise. Though quickly opposed by the unions, the idea of greater autonomy for the telecommunications authority appealed to the higher officials in the DGT. After Jacques Chirac became prime minister, the new minister of the post and telecommunications, Gérard Longuet, pressed for further reforms. Eschewing the industrial policy aims of the Socialists, Longuet handed financial control of the nationalized electronics sector *(filière électronique)* from the DGT back to the Ministry of Industry and opened the phone network to competition in value-added network services (VANS).[109]

When the Socialist Party regained power in 1988, it continued reform measures and began paving the way for legal changes in the DGT's status. Under the new minister, Paul Quilès, the Socialists renamed the agency, henceforth known as France Telecom, and created a new regulatory bureau, the Direction de la Réglementation Générale (DRG), to approve all additional equipment for the public network. While giving France Telecom a more entrepreneurial image, Quilès also proclaimed the rebirth of "the concept of the public service" and recruited Hubert Prévot, a former union member, to build a consensus before attempting any legal reform. Through a process of extensive consultation, Prévot was able to win support from all of France Telecom's major unions except the communist-led Conféderation Générale du Travail (CGT). In June 1990, the national Assembly adopted a law that established France Telecom and the Postal Service as two independent public enterprises *(exploitants publics)*. A second law, passed in December 1990, gave France Telecom the exclusive right to own the public network and provide basic voice service, while opening most other services to competition.[110]

Between 1990 and 1994, the government led a continuing discussion of the alternative regulatory frameworks to govern France Telecom's activities in a more open competitive environment. Much of the organization's top management favored privatization, which was viewed as a prerequisite to the cross-border alliances that France Telecom wanted to conclude with other service providers. By 1993, however, many of France Telecom's employees had come to oppose privatization, and in October 1993 roughly 75 percent of the employees went on strike to protest further changes in the organization's status. The majority union, the Conféderation Française Démocratique du Travail (CFDT), which had cooperated in the reform legislation of 1990, began to resist further steps toward privatization. A dissident grouping known as SUD, which had split from the CFDT in 1990, emerged as a substantial force and joined with the Force Ouvrière (FO) and the CGT to solidify the resistance. By the middle of 1995, the new government under Jacques Chirac's presidency decided to postpone privatization until 1997.[111]

These legal and organizational changes introduced great uncertainties into France Telecom's relations with its suppliers. In the sphere of technology development, the new arrangements were tantamount to the end of France's arsenal system. Since the new Alcatel holding company received most of its revenue from outside France, the company attempted to align its new R&D capabilities with non-French market needs. At the same time, France Telecom became more cautious in sharing the

CNET's new technologies with Alcatel for fear that they might be transferred through Alcatel's non-French subsidiaries, such as SEL, to other public operators with which France Telecom was beginning to compete in third countries. This question grew increasingly pressing in the 1990s because France Telecom and Alcatel both relied on work done earlier in the CNET in the 1980s for the new switching technology, known as ATM (asynchronous transfer mode), that was to be deployed for high-speed multimedia communications.[112]

The shift in France Telecom's supplier relations was also illuminated when Alcatel executives suggested that the firm should take an equity position in the public operator if it were privatized—an idea dismissed as preposterous by France Telecom officials, who were still accustomed to thinking of Alcatel as a manufacturing dependency. Further tensions were evident in a series of billing controversies in which Alcatel was accused of overcharging France Telecom for public switching equipment. Several executives were removed for fraud in a set of court proceedings that fully displayed the extent of the renegotiation that the new arrangements entailed.[113]

Despite these changes in the structure of the supplier industry, however, France Telecom retained a continuous source of engineering talent from the special schools under its supervision. In addition to its other students, the ENST continued to train approximately forty graduates of Polytechnique who were preparing for public service in the corps des télécommunications. As the field of telecommunications grew, the DGT had established another school in Bretagne (ENST-Bretagne) in 1977 as well as the Institute National des Télécommunications in Paris in 1979. By the late 1980s, all three establishments were broadening their curriculum to include international internships, more work on foreign languages, and greater emphasis on organizational skills and teamwork.

These changes were intended to help the ingénieurs des télécommunications adapt to the environment of more open competition. After the privatization of France Telecom in 1997, the schools were expected to lose their privileged links to France Telecom's research teams in the CNET. France Telecom's director of education made it clear that the ties between the schools and the CNET were likely to remain strong. Since France Telecom would have no "vested interest" *(droits acquis)* in these links, however, the schools would have to sustain them by producing the best students.[114] As at earlier stages, the public interest in telecommunications technology would hinge on the expertise of the ingénieurs des télécommunications and the way they defined their professional loyalties.

Germany

Lacking a research capacity similar to that of the CNET, the Bundespost was far more dependent on its industrial suppliers to set the R&D agenda and far less able than the Direction Générale des Télécommunications to use its equipment procurement budget as a lever for technological modernization.

Through the 1960s, the West German network was dominated by Siemens technology, which had regained its prewar reputation. At the end of the Second World War, the network was based on the step-by-step Strowger design which Siemens had modified earlier in the century. The Federal Republic was one of the only industrialized countries that did not move to a crossbar switch in the 1950s and 1960s. Instead, the Bundespost opted for the modernized Siemens design, known as the EMD (Edelmetall-Motor-Drehwähler)—essentially a Strowger design with improved parts and a motorized preselector. The technology was considered extremely reliable for its vintage and was described in the English language trade press as "the Mercedes of public switching."[115] The Bundespost's policy of *Einheitstechnik* made this technology available to the three other main suppliers who built switching equipment: ITT's subsidiary, Standard Elektrik Lorenz (SEL); DeTeWe, the Berlin firm originally formed in the 1880s by R. Stock; and AEG's subsidiary, Telefonbau und Normalzeit (T&N).

Despite the general satisfaction with the EMD exchange, the telecommunications industry clearly faced momentous changes. Since the Bundespost was running deficits in the early 1960s, declining procurement prospects threatened to idle much of the industry's capacity. In 1965, an expert commission (Sachverständigen Kommission) was convened to consider strategies for making the Bundespost more efficient.[116] The second source of change was the emergence of computer technology. As the world industry moved toward computer-controlled semi-electronic switching designs, the inexperience of Siemens and the Bundespost's smaller suppliers in data processing became more worrisome. In the 1960s, the Bundespost solicited bids for a new generation of semi-electronic exchanges. Siemens proposed the EWS (Elektronisches Wählsystem), a switch in which miniature electro-mechanical connections were governed by a central minicomputer. Standard Elektrik Lorenz proposed a semi-electronic design based on ITT technology. The Bundespost quickly opted for the Siemens design, reaffirmed its policy of uniform technical specifications, and called for joint development by Siemens, SEL, DeTeWe, and T&N in 1967.[117]

With the election of the Social-Liberal coalition in 1972, a new conception of the state's role in promoting technology came to the fore. This conception—associated with the notion of rational coordination of policy and planning—was advanced by a group of younger officials and politicians linked to the SPD. One of the first achievements of this impulse was the formation of the Ministry for Research and Technology (Bundesministerium für Forschung und Technologie, or BMFT) to coordinate research programs that had previously been administered through the Ministry for Science and Education. This impulse was championed by Horst Ehmke, the director of the chancellor's office, who took several of his younger colleagues from that office to the BMFT in 1972. The importance of telecommunications to the new advocates of policy coordination was symbolized by the nomination of Ehmke as a double cabinet member who simultaneously held portfolios for the BMFT and the Postal Ministry.[118]

The new view of technology policy was central to the Social Democrats' broader efforts at economic modernization. The link was enunciated by Horst Ehmke's parliamentary secretary, Volker Hauff, and co-author, Fritz Scharpf. These men sought to elaborate a state-led structural policy (*aktive staatliche Strukturpolitik*) which would be well adapted to the West German economy. The circumstances that called for such a policy conception included secular increases in raw material prices, particularly oil; growing competition from the developing world, and an impending saturation of the worldwide market for existing products. The coincidence of product-cycle changes with more fundamental technological stagnation suggested to the new policy chiefs that a long-term structural transformation was under way.[119]

In telecommunications, the advocates of technology policy sought to implement an ambitious broadband fiber optics network which would carry computer data and cable television as well as telephone signals. The main instrument of this effort was a special Commission for the Expansion of the Technical Communication System (*Kommission für den Ausbau des technischen Kommunikationssystems,* or KtK). The KtK was charged by Minster Horst Ehmke with an explicit industrial policy agenda, which would make the Bundespost the driving force for technological modernization in microelectronics, data-processing, and fiber optics.[120]

In the end, the KtK decided not to convert to a broadband network. The commission met over the course of two years and submitted its report in January 1976. The proponents of structural change through innovation were unable to gain approval for their policies. The commission itself included representatives of social interests whose counterparts in France had little access to the policy process. In particular, it included five academic specialists, delegates from the political parties, and representatives from the *Länder,* the municipalities, industry, and labor, as well as radio broadcasters, publishers and journalists, and officials from the Bundespost and the BMFT. There were several explanations for the KtK's refusal to recommend broadband technologies. The proposals for cable television apparently ran into numerous institutional obstacles. The Bundespost and several members of the commission opposed the involvement of private parties in developing the new medium. Broadcasters, who had been regulated on a regional level since the Nazi period, feared that cable television could provide the national government with an entirely new and possibly dangerous means of building public opinion. Finally, the adoption of broadband technologies would have meant the obsolescence of the new semi-electronic switch on which Siemens and the other firms had already invested a great deal of R&D. A broadband (or any fiber-optic) network would necessitate transmission by digital signals, thereby requiring fully electronic switching methods.[121] In this case, the telecommunication industry's own agenda for R&D was perceived as slowing down the adoption of the SPD's new anticipatory technology policy.

Within a few years, however, Siemens and the other equipment suppliers did move into fully electronic technologies in line with international market trends which indicated that the world industry was rapidly turning away from semi-electronic designs. When world telecommunications experts met in October 1977, it became clear that large-scale integration was making microelectronic components powerful and cheap enough that fully computerized switches could be commercialized. First, high performance hybrid integrated circuits would be able to translate analog voice patterns into digital signals, so that fully electronic switches could be installed before the networks were completely digitized. Second, microprocessors made possible entirely new and smaller ("distributed," or "modular") designs in which the control function was exercised through decentralized microcomputers instead of a single larger machine. In view of the changes, Siemens initiated new design efforts on a completely digital exchange, to be called the EWSD (Elektronisches Wählsystem Digital), in 1977.[122]

Meanwhile, the prototypes for the Bundespost-commissioned EWS switch required ongoing revision. According to *Der Spiegel,* hundreds of highly qualified engineers at Siemens and the three other suppliers were deployed on the project.[123] The trade press reported that the entire

project had become "caught up in the spiral of advancing technology
. . . [and that] the development engineers, in an attempt to keep abreast
with technology, went through an almost continual process of rede-
veloping the system, which saw development costs soar to alarming
levels."[124] Particularly difficult were the daunting software requirements
of the new switches, which had to be met without the help of the programming tools developed later in the decade.[125]

If this degree of technological change caused problems with the Siemens engineers, it wreaked havoc with the Bundespost's policy of uniform standards. The problem became the subject of a lengthy in-house
memorandum circulated by a senior official of the Bundespost. This
official asserted that the uniform standards had great operational advantages, but disadvantages in keeping pace with technological change.
The description of the development process was illuminating: ". . . in
very close consultation with a very small group of supplier firms or within
the ZVEI, the Bundespost (FTZ) develops very detailed specification
volumes for technical systems. The FTZ also intrudes in the development
process itself down to the 'last screw' and expects custom-tailored technical systems from the firms."[126] The cumbersome process by which uniform specifications were hammered out among the suppliers seems to
have made it virtually impossible to change the specifications mid-stream.
Even after Siemens had shifted much of its attention to fully electronic
designs, the firm remained tied through the FTZ's requirements to the
EWS project.

After numerous delays, Siemens and the Bundespost decided to abandon the semi-electronic switch.[127] Siemens could only have less and less
interest in a product which it would have trouble selling on the world
market.[128] And the Bundespost also saw advantages in purchasing technology whose cost basis could be spread over international sales. The
costs of the write-off were contested. Siemens and Bundespost officials
said that most of the investment was applied to subsequent products
and was therefore not lost at all.[129] Others insisted that the project had
been extremely costly. Officials at the BMFT, which had long wanted
the Bundespost to push Siemens to fully digital designs, called it the
"Waterloo of the German telecommunications industry."[130] The controversy showed that much of the German public expected the country's
industrial firms to supply competitive technology and subjected them
to intense scrutiny when they seemed unable to do so.

The twelve-year episode precipitated a basic change in the Bundespost's procurement practice. The policy of Einheitstechnik was dropped
and the ministry announced its intention to call for competitive bids

on a fully electronic digital design. For the first time in sixty years the postal authorities announced that they expected to install non-Siemens switching designs in the public network. In August, the Bundespost invited bids for a fully electronic system from all four of its customary suppliers as well as the Phillips communications subsidiary TaKaDe. The Bundespost was to install prototypes for a test period beginning in 1981 and would begin deliveries in 1984.[131]

Although the episode represented an undeniable setback for Siemens, it was resolved in a way that suited the company's changing business strategy well. As Siemens spokesmen pointed out, the end of Einheitstechnik held real advantages for the firm. It could now control its proprietary designs, orient them more quickly toward changes in the world market, and still compete for the domestic market and the Bundespost's label of quality.[132] Siemens had been developing its fully electronic switch, the EWSD, since 1977, and it now submitted the system for the Bundespost's new competition. The firm also demonstrated its "surge" capability by putting 1,500 of its own engineers on the project.[133] Even before the Bundespost made its final choices, Siemens had received orders for the electronic switch from a dozen countries.[134]

For Standard Elektrik Lorenz, the new competition represented a unique opportunity to implant its own proprietary designs in the West German network. Although owned by ITT, SEL was considered a German firm because of its independent research and manufacturing capability. Indeed, SEL had played a major role in developing ITT's modular electronic switch, the System 12. The firm entered its version of the System 12 for the Bundespost's consideration and launched a concerted effort to develop a prototype in conjunction with ITT's subsidiaries in Belgium, Spain, Italy, and France. This international effort was needed in order to meet the Bundespost's deadline of May 1983 for working prototypes.[135]

It turned out that SEL, with its own considerable research staff, was the only supplier which gave the Bundespost any competitive choice. The Phillips subsidiary TaKaDe dropped out of the competition because it had little hope of meeting the deadline. Though no longer obliged by Einheitstechnik to do so, the other two suppliers, DeTeWe and the AEG subsidiary T&N, accorded Siemens its old leadership position on a private basis.[136] In October 1983 the Bundespost announced that SEL's System 12 would be accepted for some 26 percent of the switches ordered over the next several years, while Siemens would receive the remainder, of which a small number would be produced by T&N and DeTeWe.

Given its relatively modest technical expertise, the resort to the market was the only solution open to the Bundespost. Without the capacity to initiate a state-led agenda on technical matters, even one of Germany's few mission-oriented agencies such as the Bundespost was highly dependent on the industrial firms with a preponderant concentration of know-how and expertise. In the case of telecommunications, the Bundespost's project for a semi-electronic switch became mired in outdated development goals, while Siemens took its cues increasingly from the international market. Siemens and the Bundespost were both struggling to discover the possibilities inherent in the new technology. The professional authority enjoyed by the Siemens engineers meant that they largely determined the technologies to be considered and adopted. The net result was that the public's interest in exploring different technology options was increasingly entrusted to the R&D managers of the country's main equipment supplier.

In the late 1980s, the processes of internationalization and market liberalization began to affect Germany as much as France, but with very different implications for the tasks of developing and managing new technologies for telecommunications. Like the DGT in France, the Bundespost took an important role in efforts to open the German market. Yet the process in Germany was characterized by more formal reliance on outside actors and sources of expertise.

Liberalization necessitated much less adjustment by the equipment industry in Germany than in France. Siemens and SEL remained the Bundespost's major suppliers, even after SEL was acquired by Alcatel. Other equipment producers—especially IBM and Nixdorf—pressed anew for liberalization of the Bundespost's procurement policies. Firms in other sectors contributed to the reform impetus by calling for lower prices and more flexibility from the Bundespost.

When the Christian-Liberal coalition took power in 1982, it soon established an independent commission to study the sector. Chaired by an economist, Professor Eberhard Witte, the commission included twelve members from the various political parties, industrial sectors, unions, regional governments, and the media. The commission's report, issued in 1987 after lengthy discussions, recognized the Bundespost's monopoly on basic voice services, but called for competition in other services and in peripheral equipment.[137]

Although the Witte Commission did not reach unanimity on its recommendations, the government used them as the basis for reform legislation. As in France, the postal workers, represented in Germany by the Deutsche Postgewerkschaft (DPG), opposed changes that they feared would weaken their role on the governing boards or split the more profitable telephone division from the postal service. After extensive parliamentary debate in 1988, Chancellor Helmut Kohl eventually met with union representatives in early 1989, paving the way for passage of the bill. The new law divided the Bundespost into three entities that were organized as nationalized enterprises. The new telephone authority—to be known as Deutsche Telekom—became separate from the postal service (Postdienst) and the postal savings bank (Postbank).[138]

This initial legislation left important regulatory questions unresolved. The reform coalition, citing changes at the European level, pressed for competition in basic network services and for the privatization of Deutsche Telekom. Given the constitutional status of the state's monopoly in telephone services, these steps required a constitutional amendment. The opposition Social Democratic Party (SPD) made its agreement contingent on several provisions safeguarding the welfare and job security of Telekom's employees. In the summer of 1994, the necessary two-thirds majority in both legislative chambers approved a packet of ten reform laws that turned Telekom into a joint-stock company and prepared the way for partial privatization in 1996.[139]

Reorganization of the telecommunications market accentuated certain changes already under way in Deutsche Telekom's relations with its suppliers, but caused nothing like the turmoil that disrupted France Telecom's relations with Alcatel. Since the policy of Einheitstechnik was dropped in the early 1980, the public operator had purchased distinct switching technologies from its main suppliers, Siemens and SEL. This practice continued with little change in the 1990s. The procurement process was decentralized to allow for shorter decision making and better cost control. It was no longer self-evident that Telekom would buy equipment only from the old "court suppliers," but the unification of East and West Germany in 1990 obliged Telekom to rely heavily on its customary suppliers to provide new network equipment in the eastern Länder. When Telekom announced a five-year investment program to replace the antiquated eastern network of 1.5 phone lines and to add 6 million new lines, the work was largely done by Siemens, SEL, and the German subsidiary of Phillips, with a few smaller contracts assigned to smaller firms.[140]

While the reorganization of the Bundespost did not overturn existing procurement practices, it did raise the issue of Deutsche Telekom's in-house technology capabilities. By 1987 France and Germany displayed almost diametrically opposed patterns in funding telecommunications R&D. In France, the DGT funded 60 percent of the country's R&D

budget for civil telecommunications, of which roughly two-fifths was performed by the DGT itself. In Germany, where a great deal of development work was performed through procurement contracts, the Bundespost directly financed only 10 percent of the country's R&D in telecommunications, of which it performed approximately half. While aggregate expenditures for telecommunications R&D in the two countries were similar ($2.1 billion in France, $2.5 billion in Germany), the in-house R&D capacity possessed by the Bundespost was dwarfed by that of the DGT.[141]

This asymmetry illuminated an important weakness in Deutsche Telekom's ability to develop new products and move into new geographic markets. Public operators were increasingly following the pattern established by their equipment suppliers in concluding cross-border alliances and mergers. Deutsche Telekom formed a number of joint ventures and alliances. In 1993 Deutsche Telkom joined forces with France Telecom in a high-profile service venture known as Atlas, and in 1994 the two European carriers invited the U.S. carrier Sprint to join in a venture called Phoenix. While such relationships provided access to a range of research resources, Deutsche Telekom needed its own sources of technical information in order to avoid unwanted dependence on its new partners.

These initiatives showed how both public operators and equipment suppliers were trying to expand their international activities. In order to play effectively in the new game of mergers and alliances, however, Deutsche Telekom needed to bolster its internal development capability dramatically. It also needed to restructure the FTZ in Darmstadt, whose previous role of supervising technology development by supplier firms had been rendered almost superfluous by the new international reach of commercial development efforts. In early 1993, Telekom reorganized roughly 500 of the FTZ employees into a new software development center. In December 1995, the FTZ was entirely restructured as an internal project-oriented research facility. The new FTZ (which now stood for Forschungs- und Technologiezentrum) was to focus on application-related research. It would not perform basic research, which Telekom might finance at universities, but it would provide support for new services and product development at Deutsche Telekom's branch offices throughout Germany.[142]

Organizational structure did not alone dictate the different strategies adopted by the French PTT and the Deutsche Bundespost. The different professional orders that informed technical negotiations in the two countries were equally important. They explained why certain organizational solutions were open to French authorities while others were open to the Germans. Despite the similarity of the organizational structures in the two cases, the professional relations that linked technical experts in the private and public sectors in the two cases were virtually reversed. These professional relations decisively constrained and, at certain junctures, promoted policy initiatives.

In France, the existence of a dominant in-house research facility gave public authorities the technical competence necessary to push technology in the direction they wished. The ability of the ingénieurs des télécommunications to articulate a technological vision for French society in politically persuasive terms reinforced their influence within the French state. Even when the corps des télécommunications framed their message in terms of Giscardian liberalism, the state dictated the technical agenda to a degree that was both impossible and unthinkable in Germany. The DGT decided not only how many competitors would bid on contracts for the public network, but also what technologies, components, and materials they would use. Indeed, the record suggests that the Giscardian experiment in domestic competition in telecommunications procurement was not well adapted to the resources available to the firms. Thomson, the newer entrant, experienced great difficulty mounting its own R&D efforts. Once the Socialist government came to power, it was not surprising that the company took the first opportunity to exit the sector by initiating a restructuring agreement with its foremost competitor, CGE.

The lack of an extensive public research capability in the Federal Republic of Germany left the telecommunications authorities far more beholden to their major supplier, Siemens. When that supplier was unable to innovate, their only option was to open procurement to a wider market. Even when the younger Social Democratic proponents of structural change came into the administration, they found it quite impossible to wrest the agenda in telecommunications policy from Siemens, the traditional industry leader. In part, they confronted political influence of the conventional variety, which Siemens, the Bundespost bureaucracy, and the regional broadcasters exerted through the KtK commission. Yet, it was not simply the influence wielded by Siemens in organizational terms that prevented the young reformers from attaining their aims. It was also the considerable influence that Siemens had won through its longstanding authority in technical questions which enabled the firm to shape the agenda for technological change. Although the Bundespost approved every detail in public switching equipment through the policy of Einheitstechnik, the suppliers, and especially Siemens, determined which technologies would be submitted for approval.

In addition to opening different options to public policymakers, these institutional legacies also exerted different effects on the organizational capacities of the suppliers. French firms—accustomed to a world where technical specifications and research agendas emerged from the CNET—expected to cooperate intimately with the DGT on matters ranging from research and development to investment and marketing. German firms—accustomed to a modus vivendi in which leading suppliers submitted research plans and technical proposals to the FTZ for approval—expected to make their own decisions on matters integral to their own strategies. These firm-level expectations existed in more than a metaphorical sense. They were evident in organizational capacities which emerged from historical experience. They can be traced to the level at which firms deployed engineers in different roles. CGE had, for example, long been designated an arsenal firm. It did little if any basic research and, until the early 1980s, had no marketing division.[143] From the very outset, by contrast, Siemens developed the organizational capacities necessary to design and market telephone equipment independently of state tutelage. Siemens lacked the research support that the French state gave to its suppliers during the early development of an all-electronic switch. Once it perfected its product, however, Siemens was equally well positioned to sell it on world markets.

As the movement toward more open telecommunications markets gained strength in the 1980, relations between the PTTs and their traditional equipment suppliers began to shift. Alcatel, deprived of its nearly automatic access to research done in France's public laboratories, sought new R&D capabilities through its acquisitions abroad. Siemens, which had never relied on the kind of research support traditionally granted to French equipment suppliers, had less trouble adapting to the new policies of the Bundespost's successor, Deutsche Telekom. Increasingly, public authorities shaped the development of the telecommunications infrastructure through regulation rather than direct technology promotion.

Even as public attention shifted from technology issues to regulatory questions, however, the inherited distribution of technical expertise remained central to the strategies pursued by the public operators. With its reservoir of knowledge in the CNET, France Telecom confronted the new competitive landscape from a position of real technological strength. With unusual expertise in ATM switching, France Telecom could afford to emphasize exclusive knowledge of advanced digital services, particularly in its growing commitments outside of France. Deutsche Telekom, by contrast, needed to bolster its in-house R&D capability in order to monitor its external relationships. The organization was more likely to move into advanced digital services through alliances with other technology leaders.

In both cases, the ownership changes entailed by privatization left the future role of the public operators undetermined in important ways. It was clear that both France Telecom and Deutsche Telekom would be obliged to compete in their home markets by the end of the 1990s. In each country control over technologies for the public infrastructure could evolve in different ways. Some of these changes would hinge on the regulatory regimes adopted in the two countries. As in earlier decades, however, many of the changes would hinge on the professional identity of the technical elites involved in the industry.

In France, a relatively small group of elite civil servants had long decided which technologies should be developed for the public telephone system. The choices (and the mistakes) were reached in the central ministries by brilliant officials who were expected to determine the optimal way to promote innovation. In the 1990s, it appeared likely that public experts would exercise their influence as much through a regulatory function as through the planning function of earlier decades. It appeared far from likely, however, that the French elites would cede control to a process of market competition, whether it favored France Telecom or its newer competitors. In the Federal Republic, it was politically impossible for any group of officials, no matter how well trained, to make such binding decisions. Here the choices emerged from a broader process in which many actors jointly determined the preferred way to promote innovation. Even as Germany's market for telecommunications opened in the 1990s, it appeared unlikely that German officials would abandon the norms of consultation among public and private experts as they prepared to allow market mechanisms greater scope in shaping the public infrastructure. Both the French and German approaches showed collectivities seeking rational solutions. The different paths they chose show how deeply the concept of rationality in matters of technology was affected by institutional legacies and traditional sources of authority.

CHAPTER FOUR

Retooling the Industrial Plant: Machine Tools

This chapter compares policy efforts in France and Germany to promote the use of microelectronics in the machine tool industry. The tool making industry—certainly among the least glamorous of industries—turns out to provide unexpected insights into the way societies organize economic production. Machine tools are defined as power-driven equipment for cutting and forming metal. They produce all other production equipment used in industry and can also reproduce themselves. As such, they are the core technology for manufacturing firms in industrial economies.[1]

The comparison of French and German policies to promote this industry reveals a striking contrast in the way policymakers defined the task of technology promotion. If the telecommunications sector showed that French officials were better equipped to implement mission-oriented policy strategies, the machine tool sector illuminates the advantages of Germany's way of linking administrative and technical occupations. French policymakers persisted in top-down, centrally coordinated efforts to push machine tool builders into using microelectronics. As a result, virtually all participants agreed that the policies had failed. Employment, production, and French shares of world trade fell. Numerous firms went bankrupt. And other firms survived only through acquisition by foreign buyers. By contrast, German policymakers devised instruments that gave firms more discretion over the timing and purposes for which the new technologies were brought into their product lines. The result was an unusually successful response to competitive challenge from East Asia. After substantial declines in employment, production, and German share of world export trade, German firms began to recoup their position in 1983 and 1984. By the late 1980s, the German industry had largely regained its position within the new conditions of competition. This chapter explores three questions: How did these different policy strategies emerge? How were they implemented? And why did they have such different consequences for the industrial autonomy and vitality in the two countries?

The two different approaches to industrial renewal are rooted in relationships that link administrative and technical occupations. The French state—with a highly trained technocratic elite which operates from deductive principles—is likely to define policy in terms of mission-oriented strategies. The German state—composed of a more loosely connected group of generalist civil servants—is more likely to define policy in terms of diffusion-oriented strategies. Even in cases where a sector's structure calls for measures of a particular kind, the inherited predispositions of policymakers are still likely to influence the shape of policy in persistent and sometimes decisive ways.

The challenge posed by the machine tool sector in the 1970s was how to encourage an industry of mostly small, specialized, and geographically dispersed producers to adapt the new technologies of computer control to their products. For the firms, this process often meant incremental improvement rather than radical innovation. For policymakers, the challenge was not so much to develop technology as to diffuse it. This task led policymakers in both countries to formulate a number of similar goals. They tried to cultivate sector-specific research capabilities often with the help of non-state agencies. They worked with the industry to provide funds for the use of microelectronics in these products. They tried to bolster demand from other sectors for these new products. And they promoted educational efforts to train and retrain workers with the new combination of mechanical and software skills that were needed by the industry.

Despite the similarity of their objectives, however, French and German policymakers settled on very different strategies. In dealing with the machine tool sector, French policymakers devised a succession of centrally coordinated plans that closely resembled their standard recipe for mission-oriented policies. Through these plans, the French state allocated large sums to specific firms for retooling their plants and updating their product lines. The state also engaged in substantial restructuring, by making financial bailouts conditional on mergers and acquisitions recommended by elite administrators in Paris. Other measures included the establishment of sectoral research centers, allocation of credits through the Ministry of Education to purchase French-made tools, and encouragement of state-owned firms to purchase machine tools at home instead of abroad.

In the years between 1975 and 1985 by contrast, German policymakers learned how to design a collection of policies that exemplified a diffusion-oriented strategy. Instead of centrally coordinated plans, German policy strategies rested on something awkwardly known as "indirect-specific measures" (*indirekt-spezifische Maßnahmen*). These were programs which made modest subsidies available to firms to adopt certain new technologies. These programs were not aimed at specific industrial sectors, but they were limited to certain key technologies (*Schlüsseltechnologien*) such as microelectronic controllers or electronic sensors. They were typically administered by industrial research centers or regional development bureaus. Through these programs, policymakers in Bonn encouraged technological retooling without disrupting the industry's own capacities for self-regulation. It is difficult to say whether the successful adjustment of the German industry should be attributed mainly to federal policy or the industry's own intrinsic strengths. It is, however, indisputable that German policy did not produce the kind of dramatic decline that followed upon French efforts to support the French machine tool industry.

This comparison, like the others in this book, shows that policymaking does not depend only on formal procedures and material resources. The accord between the outlook of administrative elites and the self-images of professional groups in a particular sector is equally important. For the machine tool sector, two professional groups are crucial: mechanical engineers and skilled machinists. In France, both of these occupational groups were separated from the central administrative elite by well-nigh insuperable barriers. Mechanical engineers were trained in practical skills that have traditionally conferred much less status in France than the polyvalence attributed to the elite civil servants. Yet, because so many of the civil servants were themselves nominally trained as engineers, the mechanical engineers in France have generally been deprived of an independent basis for asserting their sphere of competence.

In the Federal Republic of Germany, the corresponding groups enjoyed deliberate relations among themselves and a greater voice in the evolution of public policy efforts. Mechanical engineers have been one of the prominent and respected groups in German professional life since the mid nineteenth century. From their nineteenth-century membership in the Dampfkessel-Überwachungs-Verein (DÜV), mechanical engineers have established themselves in today's TÜV (Technische-Über-wachungs-Verein), which not only inspects all German automobiles but also monitors compliance with industrial standards for a whole range of production installations.[2] Skilled machinists work in the top echelons within the large and well-organized union, IG Metall, through which their interests are articulated. To be sure, these groups are separated by hierarchical distinctions in Germany as much as in France. Yet, the hierarchies are different in quality. Rather than having impermeable divisions, as in France, they have more organic links. The different groups tend to recognize their respective areas of competence. Coordination occurs through consultation and deliberate negotiation rather than top-down instructions, which often encounter resistance. The norms of competence and consultation that informed the permeable hierarchy of professional groups in Germany were crucial to the public programs for modernizing the machine tool sector. In sum, the contours of policy in this sector were determined as much by the self-images of these different professional groups as by the structure of the agencies and firms in which they worked.

THE ORGANIZATIONAL CHALLENGE

In their efforts to promote technological advance in machine tools, policymakers in France and Germany had to deal with very different industrial resources. Although both countries were counted among the world's six major exporters through the 1960s, France's industry was always overshadowed by its counterpart across the Rhine.

Germany led the world in machine tool exports for most of this century. Its machine tool builders supplied manufacturers of all kinds and made Germany's own metalworking sector the largest source of industrial employment in the country. France's machine tool industry has been much less celebrated. Although its exports surpassed Japanese exports in 1971, the French industry was consistently outperformed by the United Kingdom and Italy and was surpassed in exports by Czechoslovakia and East Germany in the 1980s. French machine tool builders increasingly turned for export markets to less sophisticated users in developing countries or the Eastern Bloc, and they rarely supplied more than half of French industry's own needs for capital equipment. In 1970, West Germany's machine tool builders outproduced their French counterparts by a factor of four and outsold them abroad by a factor of seven. (See Table 1.)

Table 1. Market value of metal-shaping tools produced by selected countries, 1970–1985 (millions of U.S. dollars)

Country	1970			1975			1980			1985		
	Value	%	Rank	Value	%	Rank	Value	%	Rank	Value	%	Rank
FRG	$1,479.0	18.95%	1	$2,399.5	17.59%	1	$4,707.0	17.76%	2	$3,168.4	14.75%	2
USA	1,433.1	18.36	2	2,364.9	17.34	2	4,812.3	18.16	1	2,717.8	12.65	4
USSR	1,073.1	13.75	4	1,984.4	14.55	3	3,065.0	11.57	4	3,035.8	14.13	3
Japan	1,109.4	14.22	3	1,059.9	7.77	4	3,630.3	13.70	3	5,316.6	24.75	1
UK	476.9	6.11	5	728.3	5.34	6	1,204.7	4.55	6	417.8	1.95	9
Italy	433.0	5.55	6	889.0	6.52	5	1,726.0	6.51	5	1,115.5	5.19	5
France	316.5	4.06	7	678.3	4.97	7	954.0	3.60	8	444.7	2.07	8
Switzerland	242.0	3.10	9	626.8	4.60	8	994.0	3.75	7	822.1	3.83	6
E. Germany	252.3	3.23	8	585.2	4.29	9	891.5	3.36	9	730.4	3.40	7
Sweden	66.0	0.85		147.4	1.08		232.9	0.88		161.4	0.75	
PR China	52.0	0.67		300.0a	2.20a		420.0b	1.58b		341.2a	1.59a	
Yugoslavia	26.0	0.33		69.0a	0.51a		231.8	0.87		239.2	1.11	
Brazil	33.8	0.43		137.0	1.00		314.8	1.19		265.0a	1.23a	
Romania	17.0	0.22		106.0a	0.78a		590.0	2.23		324.1	1.51	
Taiwan	14.2	0.18		21.0	0.15		245.1	0.92		276.2	1.29	
Total	$7,024.3	90.01%		$12,096.7	88.69%		$24,019.4	90.63%		$19,376.2	90.21%	
Other	779.4	9.99		1,543.3	11.31%		2,481.9	9.37		2,103.9	9.79	
All countries	$7,803.7	100.00%		$13,640.0	100.00%		$26,501.3	100.00%		$21,480.1	100.0%	

aEstimated from fragmentary data.
bUnrevised figure.
SOURCES: National Machine Tool Builders Association, *Economic Handbook*, various years.

These differences were accentuated in the policy process by the tremendous organizational complexity of the sector. The machine tool industry is constituted by a multitude of small and medium-sized firms, with few enterprises employing more than one thousand people. Machine tool builders maintain close links with their customers in the huge and even more variegated metalworking industry. Since reliable production tools are the core of their customers' manufacturing operations, a major segment of the machine tool sector competes on quality, service, and attention to customer specifications as well as price. Because of the multifarious relationships in such an industrial landscape, the industry's own internal capacities for self-regulation and adjustment are at least as important as the state's capacity for directing the process of industrial change.

The complexity of the sector also gives intermediary organizations a pivotal role in public innovation strategies. Since public officials cannot hope to understand or shape all the variegated supplier-user links in the industry, they must rely on organizations staffed by experts who possess a close understanding of the sector and ongoing communications with the firms. Since many of the firms are too small to finance high-risk innovations on their own, they often turn to regional development bureaus, trade associations, or other outside bodies for assistance. The availability of such intermediary organizations—or the ability of public officials to create them—often becomes a key determinant of policy effectiveness.

In the absence of such intermediary organizations, public officials relate more directly to the industrial users of machine tools than to the machine tool builders themselves. As direct suppliers, for instance, aircraft producers are of immediate concern to defense bureaucracies. As major employers, automobile makers receive ongoing attention from labor ministries. When state agencies do address the problems of the machine tool industry itself, they do so from a general concern for the national economy's overall vitality, not as part of their particular missions.

From an organizational perspective, then, one would expect the machine tool case to illuminate the significance of industry size and strength for the shape of policy. The argument made here is very different. The organizational characteristics of the industry defined the challenge that confronted policymakers but in no way dictated their response. Indeed, close examination shows that policy response followed from the inherited beliefs of policymakers more than from any organizational imperatives inherent in the industries themselves.

The Distribution of Expertise

The machine tool industry depends more than perhaps any other on industry tacit forms of knowledge. The way different machines work with different materials is a question of such idiosyncratic variation that it is extremely difficult to codify. Since the skills needed to build machines and operate them are part and parcel of industrial development, their distribution is something like a living map of a society's economic history.[3] Unlike the specialized engineers who staffed the telephone systems in the two countries, the mechanical engineers and skilled workers in the machine tool sector typified broad reaches of each country's industrial skill-base.

France

In the case of France the emergence of mechanical skills shows that the deductive style was ascendant, but far from universal. The Ecole Polytechnique itself included practical instruction in mechanical arts during the Revolution. Only after it became a preparatory school for the prestigious *écoles d'applications* in the first years of the nineteenth century did the Polytechnique's curriculum come to rest primarily on math and physics.[4]

Until the 1850s, France's machine building industry was almost entirely an artisanal industry. It was characterized by shop culture and dominated by the *mécaniciens,* mostly self-made men who learned their trade from British visitors and then from the incipient network of French machine shops. The hierarchy grew more complex with the advent of more theoretically oriented industrial training at the Ecole Centrale des Arts et Manufactures in 1829. The *centraliens* moved into more senior positions in railways, metallurgy, and brickworks. They were instrumental in founding the Société d'Ingénieurs Civils, which, however, never managed to overcome the corporatism of the schools. Certification of engineers in France began on a piecemeal basis and included the name of each school, thereby encouraging fine distinctions and leaving the younger mechanical engineers subordinate in status to the older state engineers from Ponts et Chaussées or Ecole des Mines. All of these elite schools were separated by sharp status distinctions from the *gadzarts,* the technical graduates of the smaller *écoles des arts et métiers* that were established in the nineteenth century.[5]

Similarly sharp status distinctions persisted through the twentieth century. By 1980, less than half (approximately 100,000 of 230,000)

97

of the engineering diploma holders in France actually worked in jobs classified as engineering positions.[6] The remaining 192,000 employees who fulfilled engineering roles without higher diplomas were *ingénieurs non-diplomés*—mainly skilled workers and technicians known as house engineers (*ingénieurs maison*), so called because they got promoted on the basis of plant-specific experience within the firm. The remaining 130,000 holders of engineering diplomas who did not hold engineering positions worked in public administration, in private-sector managerial or executive positions, or in other capacities altogether.

While certification at the level of school-trained engineers was finely graded, certification of shop-floor skills was never well developed in France. In the nineteenth century, industrial apprenticeships were poorly regulated, and by the twentieth century they were offered overwhelmingly by the smaller firms. The basic *certificat d'aptitude professionelle* was plagued by attrition rates as high as 60 percent and was not regarded as responsive to the changing needs of larger firms. In sum, a high proportion of skilled workers and technicians in France in the 1970s and 1980s were still trained through on-the-job programs which emphasized plant-specific skills that limited the mobility of employees as well as their ability to assimilate new skills and techniques.[7]

The educational distinctions between ingénieurs diplomés, house engineers, technicians and skilled workers were typically reproduced in the hierarchical form of organization found in most French firms.[8] The status distinction between the graduates of the elite schools like Polytechnique and the house engineers was especially important. Because the elite engineers usually lacked the specific knowledge necessary to run a factory, French firms relied on in-house training for the technical personnel who maintained and upgraded production equipment. The result was usually disastrous. The elite engineers strongly resisted consulting their junior colleagues about technical problems while at the same time the junior colleagues monopolized the needed knowledge. In the early twentieth century, one critic remarked of an ingénieur diplomé that "this *polytechnicien,* who by definition knows everything, would have considered it a dishonor to have had to ask for the help of outsiders to solve a technical question."[9] The same insularity engendered a strained relationship between the polytechnicians and their nominal subordinates, the technical directors, in large industrial organizations. As Michel Crozier's classic work has shown, the in-house technical directors used their superior knowledge of plant technology to reinforce their status. The younger polytechnicians meanwhile sought to avoid face-to-face encounters where the technical directors had the advantage.[10] Through educational distinctions as well as enterprise hierarchies, the occupations most tied to the machine tool sector—mechanical engineers as well as technicians and skilled workers—were precisely those that were subordinated and marginalized by France's order of state-created elites.

Germany

In Germany, the occupations most important to the machine tool sector enjoyed a better supported and more prominent place in the order of state-certified occupations. The mechanical engineers were not subordinated to previous cadres of civil and mining engineers. In addition, they were central to the relatively rapid industrialization experienced in Germany. The mechanical engineers were therefore a central constituency in the Verein Deutscher Ingenieure (VDI), which did not discriminate on the basis of educational background and therefore became a better integrating force for the profession as a whole.[11]

During the second half of the nineteenth century, these professions became central examples for Germany's permeable, or organic, hierarchy of state-certified professions. The engineers won the right to have the *technische Hochschulen* award the *Diplom-Ing.* in 1899.[12] Meanwhile, the *Ingenieurschulen* were established where skilled workers and technicians could upgrade their certification. And in 1897, the *dual System* was legally established, making requirements for apprenticeship uniform throughout Germany and thereby giving all firms a greater stake in a system of collective education.[13]

Following from these nineteenth-century origins, university-trained engineers came to be supported in the workplace by a large number of graduate engineers (*graduierte Ingenieure*), who attained engineering status by virtue of continuing education courses undertaken during their careers.[14] These were the graduates of the *Ingenieurschulen,* known more recently as *Fachhochschulen,* or in Baden-Württemberg as *Berufsakademien.* There was no close equivalent to this group in the French vocational hierarchy. In 1980, the number of German employees (469,000) whose primary job responsibilities involved engineering accounted for approximately 1.75 percent of the active labor force, whereas the corresponding group (292,000) in France constituted only 1.25 percent of the active labor force.[15] Thus, in more advanced technical training as in general education, the German educational system provided more manpower through vocational training at intermediate levels of technological sophistication than the French system.

Because Germany's order of state-certified professions confers a well-defined sphere of competence on each profession, the division of labor among technical elites is based on a high degree of mutual recognition. The university-trained engineers (*Diplom-Ingenieure*) enjoy a considerably easier relationship with nonuniversity engineers (*graduierte Ingenieure*) than do the elite French engineers (*ingénieurs diplomés*) with their professional subordinates (*ingénieurs non-diplomés*). To be sure, the distinction between the two types of engineers in Germany has at times been contentious, but their strong identification with the goals of industrial production has given them a common language and a large area of shared interests.[16] On the one hand, Diplom-Ingenieure do not need to defend their claim to nearly transcendent status in the way in the way that the elite engineers in France must do. On the other hand, the nonuniversity engineers have their own training and a certified realm of practical competence, which, while different from the more theoretically trained Diplom-Ingenieure, still affords them a larger sphere of autonomy than the ingénieur maison in France.

A similar stable and deliberate articulation of tasks characterizes the different production-related occupations in the machine tool industry. Certification of different skill levels means that employers can hire from the labor market for quite specific competences. Since individual workers have good access to further training, they can also raise their qualifications and advance through different levels in the occupational hierarchy. As a result, the skilled worker *(Facharbeiter)* became a valued and pivotal figure who gained much of the recognition long accorded to craftsmen in Germany. In machine tool plants, the *Facharbeiter* played a particularly important role in surveying and coordinating the activities of other shop-floor personnel.[17] In addition, in the 1960s and 1970, the majority of graduate engineers, technicians, and foremen had all qualified initially as skilled workers.[18] This pattern of sectoral expertise accorded well with the expectations of German policymakers, who were also socialized into an order of state-certified professions where a high value was placed on recognized competence.

POLICY HISTORY IN FRANCE

French and German policymakers took very different approaches in their efforts to promote technological change in their machine tool industries. In this sector, as in others, industrial policy consisted of numerous related decisions which were themselves driven by a multitude of factors. Through this complex tapestry, the thread that emerges most clearly is the persistence of policies which, whether suited to the organizational challenge or not, were intellectually familiar to the elites who dominated the policy process.

The machine tool sector differs from other industrial activities in several ways. As the sector that provides production equipment for other sectors, it occupies a central position in the logical structure of industrial economies. Yet, characterized by tremendous specialization, the sector is comprised of a broad range of small and medium-size producers. Finally, rooted in historically evolved supplier-customer relationships, the sector is embedded in a series of local, national, and international markets.

The organizational complexity of the machine tool sector left policymakers heavily dependent on others for information about the industry, its needs, and its internal dynamics. As argued throughout this study, policymakers in different contexts make use of different institutional resources. These resources include organizational structures, but are not limited to them. They also include the visions and self-images of the professional groups that inhabit those structures. As policymakers confronted the organizational structures of the sector they were trying to change, one of their main tasks was to understand and mobilize the different occupational groups that worked in the sector.

France's stratified hierarchy of professional networks gave the top policymakers a great deal of freedom in formulating policy, but also made it difficult for them to gather information about the dynamics of a highly dispersed industry like machine tools. In the absence of ongoing communication with the sectoral elites, central administrators in Paris resorted to their standard methods of policy formulation without much ability to imagine the consequences for the industry. The results dramatically illustrated how their mission-oriented policy could, in the wrong circumstances, fail. The vaunted expertise of the administrative elite provided little help to a sector dominated by traditionally organized firms. Nowhere was the incapacity of the French state's instruments for planning and financial restructuring more starkly revealed than in this industry.

The crucial years for the technological challenge in machine tools were 1975 to 1985. During this period, there were two policy initiatives, one inaugurated by Giscard d'Estaing's Minister of Industry, Michel d'Ornano, the other one inaugurated by Mitterrand's Minister of Industry, Pierre Dreyfus. In both cases, administrators strongly emphasized the most sophisticated technologies of the day. Both times, when policy goals appeared to be in jeopardy, administrators expanded the original impulse from machine tools proper to a much broader and more advanced class of automated production technologies such as robotics and flexible manufacturing centers. Both times, the consequences for the machine tools firms were devastating.

The War and Reconstruction

Policy efforts on behalf of this industry were dominated by the general predispositions and analytic methods that grew out of the planning movement of the early postwar years. Between 1941 and 1946, there was a clear shift from the corporatist business-state relations of the Vichy period to the dirigiste methods associated with postwar planning. State officials steadily assumed the initiative for sector-wide planning from the industrial committees (*comités d'organisation*) created by the Vichy regime. One of the earliest explicit planning documents—the Five Year Program for Machine Tools developed by Paul-Marie Pons of the Direction des Industries Mécaniques et Électriques (DIME) in the Ministry of Industrial Production in April 1945—plotted production goals and discussed forms for establishing a national machine tools enterprise. In 1947, when Jean Monnet adopted projections close to those of the Pons Plan, it seemed clear that state officials would take primary responsibility for devising public measures to promote the retooling of French industry.[19]

Over the next thirty years, the policy debate regarding capital goods ranged between the promotion of nonspecific investment and specifically targeted efforts to expand production. Shortly after the war, industrial retooling was subsidized through the Caisse de Crédit pour l'Achat de Machines-Outils (CREDIMO). In the mid-1950s, discussion returned to the prospects for a nationalized machine tool company. During the resurgence of indicative planning in the 1960s however, the planners preferred the *grands projets* to smaller, dispersed sectors; as a result, the machine tools business was again supported mainly through investment tax credits and preferential depreciation allowances.[20]

None of these efforts produced much success, but they continued to describe the boundaries of administrative imagination in France. To be sure, there was a discernible decline in the influence of the Commissariat Générale du Plan from the mid 1960s, but this decline involved the scope rather than the quality of state action. During Giscard's presidency, state assistance was viewed as more appropriate to declining sectors than to dynamic growth sectors.[21] But when the Giscardians addressed themselves to machine tools, their repertoire of strategies and instruments was much the same as those of earlier planning efforts.

Under Giscard's first Minister of Industry, Michel d'Ornano, the main themes of industrial policy were familiar: investment, concentration, and export promotion. Even under a center-liberal government, Paris officials saw industrial concentration as an imperative for effective competition. The dispersed structure of sectors like textiles and capital goods made them especially troublesome. According to Andrew Shonfield's classic account, the planners believed that nothing would help these sectors more than "the demise of a lot of small businesses and the emergence of a few dominant large ones." By 1970, the desirability of concentration was widely accepted and textbook wisdom held that larger firms were invariably more profitable than small ones. Export promotion was a subsidiary principle, but sectoral trade deficits frequently merited official attention. Indeed, within six months of Giscard d'Estaing's election, officials in the Ministry of Industry spotted the import penetration in machine tools and made the sector a priority for state assistance.[22]

These themes were transferred from the Commissariat Général du Plan to the Ministry of Industry with little alteration. The only exception was that the Ministry typically involved industrial representatives more extensively in its discussions. In the case of machine tools, formulation of the d'Ornano Plan was led by the ministry's top staff, but industry was given a strong voice in six advisory committees that debated various aspects of the sector's situation. True to previous planning practice, large firms were given primary weight in the discussion. Five of the six advisory groups were chaired by managers from the largest firms. Smaller firms were heard only through the trade association (the Syndicat des Constructeurs Français de la Machine-Outil, or SCFMO), which provided information and reactions to the work of the advisory groups.[23] Notably absent from the deliberations were labor unions, particularly the CGT and the CFDT, which were heavily represented in this sector.

The d'Ornano Plan

When the d'Ornano Plan was unveiled in early 1976, it showed that policymakers had thought of a broad range of instruments. The plan had four major elements.[24] First, the state sought to stimulate demand for more advanced machine tools. The rationale was to break the French producer industry's dependence on traditional technologies and push it toward those market segments which policymakers expected to grow fastest. Public demand was to be reinforced by urging the Ministry of

National Education and the military arsenals toward a "buy-French" policy. In order to stimulate private demand for advanced tools, a 1972 procedure known as MECA (Materiéls et Equipements de Conception Avancée) was updated in two ways. First, the financial solvency of purchasing firms could be guaranteed through the banks. Second, firms could lease high-tech computer-numerical-controller (CNC) tools on a trial basis for two years after which the state would subsidize their purchase or help offset any losses incurred by the original producer upon their return.

Second, incentives for firms moving into more advanced product lines would be supported by promoting and coordinating research. A special research center for machine tools, CERMO (Centre d'Etudes et de Recherches de la Machine-Outil), and another for mechanical engineering, CETIM (Centre Technique des Industries Mécaniques), were to spearhead the research efforts. Training in advanced technologies was to be strengthened by directing the Ministry of National Education to purchase top-of-the-line equipment.

Third, the state was to encourage machine tool exports by underwriting any associated risks. Financing was to be made available for firms that wished to establish production or sales facilities abroad. The ministry also announced its interest in financing market research and trade exhibitions for foreign markets.

Fourth, the ministry was to create *pôles*, or axes of orientation, for smaller producers by encouraging industrial concentration around the larger firms in the industry. This industrial restructuring was considered inevitable in the long term. In order to insure that it occurred on terms that served the public interest, however, officials sought to coordinate investment among the larger industrial groups and sometimes to effect restructuring directly through publicly provided capital loans. For both purposes, officials relied primarily on the state's industrial finance agency, the Institut de Développement Industriel (IDI). This entity had been created in 1970 as a joint public-private investment bank.

Of these four elements, all but the last proved exceedingly difficult to implement. Unlike the first three objectives, the last did not require much cooperation among different types of organizations. When a firm fell into financial trouble, an unambiguous opening for state leverage appeared. In exchange for needed capital infusions, the state gained substantial influence over the firm's policies and often over its management structure as well.[25] These interventions were one of the few policy instruments that did not require the top civil servants to venture far outside their own customary networks. The larger firms that did much of their business with the state were frequently managed by graduates of the same elite schools. In the machine tool sector, many firms were managed as family operations; when they fell into trouble, the price of state assistance was often the installation of new overseers whose background and education more closely resembled those of the Parisian policymakers than the traditional owners.

The use of capital grants to influence firm-level behavior initiated a pattern which was seen repeatedly in many different sectors in French industrial policy. Individual firms engaged in intricate maneuvers to capture capital distributed by the Institut de Développement Industriel under the banner of industrial concentration and technological modernization. The bilateral negotiations between state and individual firms created a zero-sum dynamic. Whatever the top civil servants said they wanted, inevitably the top managers of a number of firms were willing to oblige. Other firms found it difficult to renounce participation, for if any particular firm ignored such an important source of capital, it risked giving its competitors in the sector a substantial advantage. In short, this method of allocating capital grants through bilateral firm-state relations made efforts at adjustment through interfirm cooperation efforts all but impossible.

Since those firms with the best connections to the state bureaucracy held significant advantages, the game reinforced the influence of the Parisian elite that controlled state-allocated capital. Through the trade association, some limited progress was made in interfirm efforts to promote exports.[26] For the planners' other two goals—pushing new product lines and promoting cooperative research—there is little evidence of any progress in the first three years. Policymakers in Paris had neither the organizational levers at hand nor the taste for dealing directly with the mechanical engineers or the family owners on such topics. For the first iteration of policy, the dominant leverage provided by instruments of financial restructuring was the most apparent result.

The maneuvering began as the third largest firm in the sector—Forest, S.A.—recorded increasing losses through 1977. When Forest filed for bankruptcy in 1979, the Institut de Développement Industriel had already taken the main equity position (34.6 percent) in the holding company, Ratier-Forest, which itself filed for bankruptcy a month later.[27] As a result, Ratier-Forest's assets not only went on auction at a cut-rate price, but with a virtual guarantee that the IDI would protect its stake. Of these assets, the production facilities supported by national aerospace programs were quickly reorganized. Ratier-Figeac, the subsidiary whose equipment made specialized aerospace fasteners, was nourished by Airbus and sold to Générale de Forgeage in 1978. The Forest unit at Capdenac also supplied specialized tools to the aerospace industry and was rescued through an IDI subsidiary known as Equipements Mécaniques Spécialisés (EMS). Another Forest unit at Courbevoie (which made milling machines, boring equipment, and machining centers) found no takers; it was put under the management control of another IDI subsidiary known as Technique et Mécanique Industrielles (TMI) in 1979 and bought outright at the end of 1980. The last Forest unit, at Châteaudun (which produced radial drill presses and machining centers), stimulated considerable discussion among private firms. One of the sector leaders, Liné, considered acquiring the Châteaudun unit with the British firm Kearney-Trecker-Marwin, but eventually Muller et Pesant of Mauberge put together an acquisition plan with the assistance of the Comité Interministériel pour l'Aménagement des Structures Industrielles (CIASI), a state agency involved in industrial restructuring.[28]

Policy Evolution: Robotics

The setbacks experienced by Ratier-Forest and several other well-known firms—particularly H. Ernault-Somua and Dufour—provoked a highly characteristic reorientation of policy. Prevailing diagnoses of the industry's problems focused almost entirely on CNC technologies. These concerns came to the fore at the industry's biannual trade show in May 1980. A contemporary study showed that only 13 percent of the small and medium-sized enterprises in mechanical engineering had purchased numerical control machines.[29] At the same time, industry spokesmen announced that Japanese firms offered simple CNC machines as much as 40 percent cheaper than the few French producers who offered them. The Japanese competition therefore stood to garner the entire gain in capital investment which French producers had been awaiting after the lean years of 1978 and 1979.[30] Finally, there was a realization among the Parisian policy elite that almost nobody in France had the joint expertise in electronics and mechanics needed to survive in the technological forefront of the machine tool industry.[31]

In theory, these observations suggested a range of alternative policy responses—each aiming at a different point between incremental improvements and radical jumps in technological levels. Under the incremental approach, the state would have fostered technological advance indirectly by strengthening the market for machine tools that already existed in France. Incremental progress in machine tools would have been governed by the ability of the user industries to assimilate the new technologies. The state's main levers of influence would have been limited to upgrading technological capacities such as skill levels and information resources within the user industries. In contrast to the incremental approach, the radical one aimed at the technological frontier from the outset. Under this approach, the state would assemble the resources to produce sophisticated technologies, which would then be imposed through a combination of incentive and coercion on user groups.

The latter approach—emphasizing radical technological jumps—was congenial to two central assumptions in the Parisian elite's way of thinking. First, promotion of radical technological jumps fit well with the notion that the state could direct high-tech innovation better than small firms. Second, radical innovations emphasized economies of scale which could best be generated by the larger firms with whom French planners were accustomed to dealing. These two beliefs were reflected in the new policy orientation, which submerged the machine tools plan within a much broader effort to promote robotics and automated production equipment throughout French industry.

This policy change took shape through a new agency for strategic industries, the Comité d'Orientation des Industries Stratégiques (CODIS) created in 1979. Initially, the role for CODIS was debated as a bureaucratic choice between the DIMME (Direction des Industries Métallurgiques, Mécaniques et Electriques) and the DIELI (Direction des Industries Electroniques et de l'Informatique)—each of which claimed competence for the state's efforts in production technologies. Soon, however, discussion took a more philosophical turn among two groups, the *mécaniciens* and the *électroniciens*. The mécaniciens advocated a bottom-up approach (*approche ascendante*) to factory automation, according to which each machine would be linked through decentralized networks. The electroniciens favored a top-down approach (*approche descendante*), which conceived robots and machines as peripheral equipment within a centralized computer system.[32]

Although this rarefied debate was conducted among the policymakers, it had very real consequences for the industry. The top-down approach implied a substantial loss of control for the machine tool builders. If senior state functionaries set priorities for the production technologies to be used by the large industrial groups, machine tool suppliers would have to develop new products to suit politically determined priorities. This was particularly threatening in view of the openness to the international economy favored by Giscard's Prime Minister, Raymond Barre. Those machine tool producers that could not deliver what Paris wanted would be completely exposed to powerful foreign competitors. As one official in the Ministry of Industry said in May 1980, "It would be better if the French machine tool industry made money with 10,000 employees than lose money with 20,000."[33]

Later that year, the machine tool association responded to the debate with a formal document asking the Minister of Industry whether France wanted to keep its machine tool industry. If so, the association argued that the state needed to take several steps: large industrial firms should commit capital to the machine tool industry; certain Japanese tools should be blocked from France through tariffs; public procurement should be firmly directed to French products; and finally, "national solidarity" and "common sense" should be encouraged in private purchasing."[34]

Proponents of the top-down view triumphed in early 1981, when Jean-Pierre Souviron was made Directeur Générale de l'Industrie. As one of the central figures in the renovation of the public telecommunications system under the Sixth Plan, Souviron was an expert in large-scale, state-led projects. His entire experience led him to give priority to France's electronics firms rather than to the smaller, more traditional specialists in machine tools. Under Souviron's leadership, the state committed resources to an ambitious effort in robotics and flexible manufacturing centers. Even the venerable Académie des Sciences joined the enthusiasm with a report declaring that the mechanical engineering industry was experiencing a technological revolution. The *electroniciens* and *mécaniciens* were to be joined by the *roboticiens* in a major effort to automate French industry.[35]

Souviron's efforts combined a dirigiste approach to technology development with a policy of openness toward the international economy. The state directly funded several elaborate factory automation systems, but refused to guarantee a protected market for the machine tool firms that built factory automation components. Through CODIS, the state funded elaborate pilot projects in flexible manufacturing centers. The most spectacular examples were assembled by the automobile firms, Renault and Peugeot-Citrôen, while Peugeot bicycles commissioned another system. These futuristic projects confirmed the state's preference for state-of-the-art technology, even when it was too advanced to be assimilated by much of the industry. The factory automation pilot lines provided a showcase where foreign buyers could view French production equipment, but they were exceedingly expensive to operate. Even the chief of Renault Machine-Outil estimated that the market for such systems was modest in the early 1980s.[36]

The industry segment where Souviron's approach worked best, though indirectly, was in CNC technology. Under the d'Ornano plan, a number of French firms had tried to enter this business without much success against the larger foreign competitors, particularly General Electric in the United States and Siemens in the Federal Republic of Germany.[37] In 1977–78, a new entrant called La Société NUM, was organized by Télémécanique (75 percent) and Thomson (25 percent). NUM was given public aid through contracts to develop numerical controls.[38] Since the only market for NUM's products were machine tool builders, the weakness of the French machine tool builders in CNC machines forced the firm to look abroad. In 1979, the firm began selling controllers to machine tool builders in West Germany, Switzerland, Italy, and the Soviet Union. Through its international strategy, NUM turned the weakness of the French machine tool sector to its own advantage. Although the larger French industrial groups often bought their machine tools abroad, they frequently asked their foreign suppliers to use NUM controllers in order to maintain compatible systems. Thus, NUM supplied numerical controllers to the Italian firm, Mandelli, for machining centers that were returned to the French aerospace firm, SNIAS. Similarly NUM supplied controllers to the German firm, Diedesheim, for vertical lathes that were sold to Renault.[39]

Souviron's approach undoubtedly aided French users of advanced machine tools as well as NUM, which supplied the controllers. It did little, however, to support the French producers of machine tools themselves. If anything, Souviron's emphasis on advanced pilot projects encouraged cross-national subcontracting networks that cut French machine tool builders out of the business.

The political stakes were heightened by a bitter confrontation over the bankruptcy case at Dufour, the precision milling specialist in Montreuil, near Paris. When plans for 700 layoffs were announced in July 1980, members of the CGT and the CFDT began a day-and-night plant occupation that continued for three months. The workers opposed a takeover of Dufour by a nearby machine tool firm, Profel, fearing that Profel would terminate Dufour's flagship milling machine, the T-7000. Supported by local residents, union members preferred a direct takeover by the state through the IDI. Later that year, the CIASI negotiated a privately financed plan which was accepted by the CFDT as the least problematic solution, and the firm reopened with 350 employees instead of 680.[40]

The story of Dufour was highly visible, but other, larger firms in the sector continued to suffer financial difficulties. Ernault-Somua, France's third largest machine tool firm, suffered losses in 1979 and 1980. After shedding factories in St.-Etienne and Lisieux, the firm entered into a coproduction agreement with the Japanese firm Toyoda, the machine tool subsidiary of Toyota. The agreement, under which Toyoda took a 35 percent stake in the plant at Montzeron (near Dijon), heralded the first major entry of a Japanese producer into France. Ernault-Somua's other plants in Moulin and Cholet required further capital infusions and the firm's parent company, Empain-Schneider distanced itself increasingly through 1981.[41] Further financial problems loomed at legendary firms like Graffenstaden and Liné, which were soon to require public rescue efforts from the Socialist government that took over after François Mitterrand's election in May 1981.

The Plan Machine-Outil

Mitterrand's election created the possibility for a thoroughgoing reassessment of policy for machine tools. Just before the Socialist party won a legislative majority in the June elections, the new president promised to make the machine tool problem a high priority. Given its central role in economic production, the sector was accorded a symbolic role by the left-of-center government. The Socialists had opposed their predecessors' strategy of adjusting French industrial structures to international conditions and instead announced the need to reconquer the internal market. The Giscardian aim of "redéploiement industriel" gave way to the Socialists' rallying cry, "reconquérir le marché interne." It was expected that the capital goods industries would be featured in industrial policy. In addition, the Socialists were anxious to stem employment losses, which had reduced the machine tools industry from 27,000 employees in 1974 to 20,000 in 1980. Given their links with the labor movement, the new government seemed to have better information about the industry and could be expected to negotiate more constructively on industry restructuring.[42]

In fact, however, the Socialists' policy for the machine tools sector showed remarkable continuity with earlier efforts. Despite important differences in the economic doctrine they espoused, Socialist leaders were dependent on the same administrative elite to formulate particular policy initiatives. The possibilities for industrial policy remained tightly bounded by this administrative elite's collective memory. In particular, the familiar themes of investment promotion, industrial concentration, and state-led innovation persisted. These policy goals had never produced much success for machine tools in the past. Yet, since these goals left the Parisian elite in the central decision-making role, they supported the administrators' view of themselves as arbiters of the nation's interest in specific policy arenas. As before, the administrators refrained from devolving discretion over public resources to the industry association, but they were themselves too removed from the industry to engage any but the larger firms in detailed consultation. The result was continued reliance on bilateral negotiations with the larger firms in the sector.

The Parisian administrators also avoided extensive consultation with organized labor. Elected Socialist leaders certainly viewed labor as a constituency; given the tense relations among the CGT, CFDT, and the Force Ouvrière (FO), however, the new government found itself obliged to listen dutifully to all three without taking any action. The solution was to rely on the technocratic elite for detailed policy formulation.[43] Although the individuals were sometimes different, the policy discussion was only modestly expanded beyond the customary circles of Parisian administrators, experts, and industry representatives. For the machine tool industry, the result was a continuing reluctance to engage labor and a commensurate inability to upgrade the skill-base available to individual firms.

The continuities between the Plan Machine-Outil and previous policies quickly became evident. From August through October, several working groups were formed to prepare recommendations. They included representatives from the trade association and the Ministries of Industry, Finance, and Employment. The working groups were particularly careful to bring industry into the discussion, interviewing over two hundred interlocutors from the sector, user firms, and supplier firms. Trade unions were, however, given no significant role.[44]

Without good links to the trade association or organized labor, policymakers frequently relied on outside consulting firms that drew on the prevailing international consensus without challenging the assumptions of the Paris policy elite. Details of the plan were elaborated by two administrators in the DIMME, which relied heavily on a report commissioned from the high-profile consulting firm, Telesis, a spin-off of the prestigious Boston Consulting Group (BCG).[45] Its report focused on the strengths and weaknesses of the French machine tool industry compared to those of Japan and Italy. Like BCG, Telesis made its name by espousing economies of scale and learning curves, which led to lower production costs over a larger volume.[46] Thus, it was not surprising that the Telesis report again recommended that the state emphasize general-purpose CNC machine tools, where it was commonly thought that larger production runs could generate economies of scale. The report did not minimize the difficulty of the task. According to the Telesis authors, "France must therefore fight in highly competitive markets where the Germans, Italians and Americans seek to regain terrain lost to the Japanese, but with certain assets which France does not possess: specialized sub-contracting in Italy, strength of the component suppliers and distribution networks in Germany, size of the internal market in the United States."[47] In short, the Telesis report told administrators that major public resources would be needed by the machine tool sector, but it did not move them to develop fundamentally new methods or institutions for distributing those resources.

When the plan was approved by the Council of Ministers in December 1981, the proposed measures were very similar to those announced by Michel d'Ornano six years earlier.[48] First, as before, the state sought to organize demand in support of more advanced machine tools. Private demand was stimulated by extending the previous plan's MECA procedure, to be overseen by the Agence pour le Développement de la Productivité et de l'Automatisme (ADEPA) with increased funds. Public procurement was again to be effected through the Ministry of National Education, but in much higher amounts. Starting in 1982, the ministry was slated to spend 400 million francs annually—or almost 10 percent of the industry's total revenues—for three years. Through such measures, the plan aimed at a thoroughgoing industrial "reconversion," which would more than double the nationwide stock of CNC tools from under 10,000 in 1981 to 26,000 in 1985.[49]

Second, the plan projected a training program in the new machines. The Ministry of National Education would train new generations of workers in advanced techniques. Though less emphasized, plans to have the ministry develop a technical degree (*brevet de technicien supérieur,* or BTS) in *informatique industrielle* was also announced.

Third, as before, research efforts were to be strengthened and coordinated. Minister Dreyfus spoke of three national research "pôles" to be organized around CERMO in conjunction with the Ecole Nationale Supérieure des Arts et Métiers in Paris, ADEPA, and CETIM. In addition, the ministry planned to negotiate development contracts with individual firms which would require them to increase their research expenditures to 5 percent of revenues.[50]

Fourth, direct industrial grants would be made available to individual enterprises to "specialize" their product lines in coordination with other firms in the sector. The aim of such specialization was threefold: first, to avoid "ruinous competition"; second, to create firms of sufficient size to finance the R&D needed to move into numerical control; and third, to organize the supply by replacing the multitude of small, family firms with a few sectoral "leaders," which would presumably be better placed to compete in world markets.

A fifth element, which harkened back to Souviron's modification of the d'Ornano plan, was explicit state support for the efforts of Société NUM in automation. As part of the development contracts negotiated with individual firms, they would be asked to privilege computer-control modules from NUM over other suppliers.

In the end, the major difference in the Socialists' approach concerned the magnitude of resources. Over three years, the state expected to devote 2.3 billion francs to the sector and to attract another 1.7 billion francs in investments from user industries. With these means, the planners aimed at a doubling of production by 1985. This goal was predicated on the "reconquest of the internal market" and on the ability of French producers to become competitive in the most sophisticated machine tools. French producers were expected to increase their share of the internal market from 40 percent to 70 percent by 1985. The trend lines did make a doubling of production within four years appear plausible—but only if one assumed 40 percent annual growth in the domestic market for CNC tools without any disruptions in the international economy.[51]

Although the Socialists paid more lip service to the significance of education and human resources, the logic of their plan rested as heavily as ever on the conventional recipe of seeking economies of scale through size. The remarks of the minister were instructive. Upon announcing the policy, Dreyfus told a journalist, "You know, I do not have an obsession with size. . . . [I]t is not strictly the structure of the productive apparatus which needs to be improved. It is also necessary to act in support of research and manpower training." A few minutes later, however, while discussing international competition, Dreyfus flatly voiced the conventional view that "competitiveness vis-à-vis foreign rivals nonetheless imposes a minimum size in each market segment."[52] The officials responsible for implementation also subscribed to the conventional view. As much as they mentioned the importance of human resources, they unfailingly repeated the time-worn wisdom that French industry was disadvantaged by its small size.[53] According to this view, the state's first task was to relieve this handicap by encouraging industrial concentration.

Despite its sway, the argument for economies of scale was not universally accepted. Indeed, Jean-Claude Tarondeau, an economist from the University of Paris at Dauphine had questioned the applicability of this argument to the machine tool sector. According to this author, a comparison of French and German machine tool builders provided no evidence that larger firms were more efficient. His point was bolstered by the observation that average firm size, 180 in Germany and 155 in France, was only 49 in the highly successful Swiss industry. On Tarondeau's view, the problem with the French machine tool firms was not their size; it was rather their inability to meet user specifications without falling into thoroughly customized production methods. The solution was not industrial concentration, but rather what Tarondeau called "modular" production methods by which even small firms could meet the needs of their customers efficiently. Since Tarondeau's work was published in a leading management review and summarized on the front page of *Le Monde*, it was clearly available to policymakers who wanted to consider it.[54]

During the implementation of the plan, the operations of industrial restructuring once again took precedence over the other policy goals. Under the guise of keeping industrial reorganization compatible with the public interest, Parisian administrators again became preoccupied with financial bailouts. The firms, as before, sought either to acquire assets cheaply or to prevent their main competitors from doing so.

Even before the Socialists' plan was finalized, the sector's second largest group, Liné, required attention. The firm's president, Henri Liné, had played the restructuring game to perfection under earlier governments. From 1976 to 1980, Liné had employed aid from Paris and regional authorities to gain control of an impressive group of firms in Eastern France.[55] Through the holding company, Liné/PMO (Participations-Machines-Outils), Henri Liné shrewdly limited his equity stake in the new acquisitions to 10 percent. As long as he could acquire troubled firms, his efforts were appreciatively backed by the state. By early 1981, however, lack of capital brought Liné himself toward insolvency. As one account said, "the miracle man has become the sick man of the machine tool industry."[56]

Obliged to deal quickly with Liné, the Socialists relied on the IDI. The result was ironic. While the new government was discussing grand plans for a national investment bureau, the managers of the IDI patterned themselves after the private investment bankers and strategic consultants. As they described their role, they were "simultaneously the Lazard Frères and the Boston Consulting Group of the public authorities." They held a special meeting with Liné in July 1981. In their role as investment bankers, the IDI managers financed half of a capital infusion of 360 million francs. In their role as strategic consultants, they installed their own man to chair the executive board alongside Henri Liné, the firm's traditional patron.[57]

The result was a poignant embarrassment. Liné's employees promptly decided that the new director wanted to "chloroform" the firm or turn it into an "assembly hall" for other IDI-backed firms. Within three months, 94 percent of the shop-floor workers voted for the resignation of the IDI director, Louis Tardy. By way of a parallel to the bitter Dufour standoff, the workers were backed by the communist-led local government. By early 1982, the affair required one of Mitterrand's economic theoreticians, Alain Boublil, to write the company's workers to assure them that the Machine Tool Plan did not aim at dismantling the firm.[58]

Problems at Liné placed particular pressure on the government to conclude a series of rescue plans for the industry. The idea was to create several major pôles to specialize in complementary product lines. The first pôle, to regroup French production in heavy-duty customized machines, was called Machine Française Lourde (MFL). Announced in July 1982, MFL combined Liné's milling operations with the heavy lathe operations of Berthiez (a subsidiary of SNECMA). Capital was split on a thirty-five/sixty-five basis between the IDI and nine large user firms: Dassault, SNECMA, SNIAS, Peugeot, Renault, Alsthom-Atlantique, Creusot-Loire, Sacilor and Usinor.[59] Since several of the user firms were nationalized, as much as 86 percent of MFL's equity was effectively held by the state.[60]

A series of other pôles were envisioned for different market segments. A major effort was made to finance a merger of Huré (subsidiary of the Bank of Suez) and Graffenstaden (subsidiary of CIT-Alcatel), which specialized, respectively, in precision milling machines and lathes. The possibility of bringing Empain-Schneider into the arrangement through its subsidiary, Ernault-Somua, was frequently broached. An additional pôle for grinding machines was expected to join Constructions de Clichy (a subsidiary of Renault) and Gendron (formerly of Liné), while a pôle for large presses would combine the assets of Colly, Promecam, and Sagitta. Policymakers also debated merging the recently combined Dufour-Profel with other firms in the Seine–St.-Denis area (namely, Cazeneuve and RAMO)—or of merging Cazeneuve and RAMO with other lathe producers (Société d'Innovations Mécaniques) while combining the Dufour remnant with its traditional competitor, Vernier, in a pôle for milling machines that would also include Alcera-Gambin.[61]

The proposals and permutations kept the officials at the ministry entirely absorbed in negotiations with the firms. In order to confirm its independence from the industry, the DIMME sent each development contract to an outside consultant. In those cases where mergers were involved, officials had difficult negotiations with firms that were often traditional competitors. Finally, where rationalization was required, the state had to hammer out compromises with labor organizations on compensation offered to those who lost their jobs.[62] Further difficulties resulted from the continuing suspicions held by large user industries regarding the machine tools sector. The large groups increasingly sought to jettison their interests in the sector. Renault steadfastly resisted taking on the burdens of the industry. SNECMA sold most of its interest in Berthiez to MFL. Suez and CIT-Alcatel were each anxious to lower their exposure in their respective subsidiaries, Huré and Graffenstaden.[63]

If these complex financial reorganizations preoccupied the administrators, they also disrupted day-to-day work at the firms. Managers did not know what products they would be producing for more than a few months, while workers did not know how long their jobs would last. But the biggest question was simply whether the newly organized firms would fare any better than their predecessors. Despite the ministry's frenetic activity, firms continued to file for bankruptcy. One industrialist commented skeptically on the government's plan: "I can hardly see how one forms fruitful enterprises by marrying cadavers."[64]

Policy Evolution: The Plan Productique

As the evidence mounted in 1982 and 1983 that financial interventions alone were not likely to improve the technological capabilities of the industry, a push for a reassessment of policy gained momentum. The official reassessment was paralleled by an unofficial critique, which brought different perspectives to the problem. The lines of this discussion were far from clear. All actors sought a new understanding of the links between industrial competitiveness and employment. Meanwhile, French public opinion displayed dramatic changes in the prevailing estimation of business and its role in French society. The traditionally negative views of business, profit, and enterprise gave way to a burst of fascination with entrepreneurship and innovation.[65]

Although none of the actors took a simple position for or against technological change, the basic alternatives were as investment in human resources or rationalization through automated technologies. Organized labor moved away from simple opposition to innovation and tried to develop proposals for protecting labor while also supporting state efforts to promote technological advance. Technocrats in the ministries continued to mention the need for human competence but increasingly equated progress in the machine tool sector with reductions in employment. As in Boris Souviron's efforts a few years before, the reorientation of policy effectively subordinated the goals of education and human-resource development to the mission-oriented strategies of the central ministries in Paris.

The unofficial critique emerged first from organized labor. With much closer links to occupational groups in the sector, labor spokesmen advanced prescriptions that were quite different from those favored by the ministerial elites. The Féderation Générale de la Métallurgie (FGM) of the CFDT argued that French industry in general suffered from the inadequate recognition given to production workers in the capital goods sector. According to one such analysis, the first key to improved competitiveness lay in a general revaluation of manual labor: better training within the plant for unskilled and semiskilled workers; better possibilities for promotion; and greater emphasis given to worker qualifications when defining of new products. The latter point was particularly important in matching technological advances in machine tools to the skills and capabilities of those expected to operate the new equipment. The CFDT analyst recognized this point by asserting that "it is essential to transform the design process for machines so that the operators' jobs conform better to the type of work that the workers (especially the younger ones) expect, to the qualifications they have acquired and can acquire."[66] According to this view, it was important to resist the tendency to design more and more intelligence into the machines at the expense of the qualifications of the manual worker.

The same analyst also proposed novel remedies for the problems of small and medium-sized firms. Instead of sacrificing these firms on the alter of rationalization, the state should promote healthier relations between small and large firms. This goal hinged on reinforcing the autonomy of the smaller firms through a number of steps. First, the large, nationalized groups should change their subcontracting policies to minimize the volatility of demand for particular subcontracting firms. Second, the large groups should diffuse the knowledge intensive aspects of their work to the provinces instead of concentrating brain-power in Paris and treating the provinces as assembly centers for unskilled workers. Finally, the state should promote cooperative associations among the smaller firms so that they could support the research and development activities necessary to preserving a degree of autonomy from their larger customers.[67]

In contrast to the CFDT, the CGT placed less stress on qualified work and more importance on state policy. The CGT argued that the owners of machine tool firms had not fulfilled the production goals of the development contracts they signed with the ministry. Like the CFDT, however, the CGT authors argued that more resources be allocated for regional research centers. Also like the CFDT, they argued that nationalized groups purchased foreign matériel when they could have supported French machine tool builders. In order to promote better supplier-user links within France, the CGT itself assembled a detailed data bank on French components and machines which could be substituted for foreign-bought goods.[68] In fact, the issues of worker qualification and supplier-customer links were connected. There was widespread agreement that French machine tool firms devoted too little effort to cultivating customer relations. Even within the firms, a deductive, top-down understanding of technology prevailed. Unlike machine tool shops in some countries, French producers rarely employed sales engineers. According to an observer with the French industry association, research bureaus in France were occupied strictly with design. As a result, noted the industry observer, "French firms produce material that is poorly adapted to many of their markets."[69] Once again, the tendency to design capital machinery without regard to the needs of the users appeared to compromise supplier-user relations. Of course, there were different ways to interpret user needs. Following the CFDT critique of the design process, the heart of the supplier-user link lay in designing products that suited the machine operator's needs, a conception in marked contrast to the urge to automate production technology and eliminate operators altogether.

In the official reassessment of policy, the Socialists increasingly sought a solution for the problems of the manufacturing industries through a state-led plan to encourage automation of production technologies. The first step in this approach was a reaffirmation of the state's role in a period where user needs were gaining importance in the discussion of technological change. The seemingly esoteric issue of supplier-user links was addressed in a report commissioned by the Prime Minister on the government's overall plan for an integrated policy toward the electronics sector *(programme d'action en filière électronique)*. This report, submitted in January 1983, questioned the assumption that the state could effectively determine the content of new technologies. Instead, the author argued that only users could determine the content and applications of new products.[70] This assertion suggested the novel view that the state should play only a passive or indirect role in promoting technological advance. As the author developed the argument, however, his language betrayed a familiar tendency to put public officials in a central role. The state's duty was to "release" user preferences "by not imposing its views on the content of the products." In order to relieve the problems caused by inadequate support for modern technologies, the report asked for "a profound reorganization of administrative structures and the adoption of new methods of intervention dedicated to a resolutely proactive policy."[71] Keeping well within familiar categories, the author envisioned a "commissariat for information technologies" to be supervised by an interministerial committee. The idea of user preferences was gaining recognition, but was hardly overturning the received assumption of the Paris policymakers that technological change could be planned and administered by central state agencies.

The main proponent of state activism in the cause of factory automation was the Minister of Industry and Research, Jean-Pierre Chevènement. In July 1982, Chevènement highlighted the links among electronics, capital-goods, and manufacturing through his neologism, *la Productique*. The precise meaning of "la Productique" was explored by an advisory group to the CGP on the mechanical engineering sector. This group integrated a broader range of perspectives than previous efforts. Its report advanced a mixed set of recommendations, including some important modifications from the usual recipe for top-down, mission-oriented technology policy.[72] The authors recited the standard list of technologies that were said to be transforming the production process: new materials, microprocessors, robots and CNC machine tools, automated materials-handling, and computer aided design. In contrast to earlier efforts, however, the authors took exception to the conventional views on firm size. Instead, they noted the importance of small, specialized firms that dominated their market niches. They also noted the importance of enhanced training for the introduction of computer-supported technologies. Particularly in the preparation of work, the need for a close link between programmers and machine operators made it very difficult for firms to find employees with the necessary double competence in mechanics and electronics. Rather than hiring technicians who were trained in software skills, firms in this sector often did better by providing in-house training to machine operators or by seeking new graduates in mechanics who had also learned some programming.

The report's recommendations regarding small firm strategies and professional education were, however, quickly submerged within the wider enthusiasm for automation. Public discussion of the report focused on the productivity gains ostensibly attainable through automation—which were said to reach 15 to 25 percent for a robot, 40 to 60 percent for a CNC machine, and 20 to 30 percent for a computer-aided-manufacturing system. The summary in *Le Monde* reinforced the prevailing conception of dirigiste technology policy by citing the report's introductory recommendation that mechanical engineering be placed alongside telecommunications, aerospace and nuclear power as an essential "vector in a proactive industrial strategy [*stratégie industrielle offensive*] for the country." Having almost forgotten their mechanical engineering industry, the reporter noted, the French were "rediscovering it through robotics and more generally 'la productique,' according to the syllogism adopted last year by Mr. Chevènement."[73]

When the Plan Productique was announced in November 1983, it parallelled the shift in priorities prompted by Jean-Pierre Souviron three years earlier. State funding was now to support robotics and flexible manufacturing cells. The Ministry of Industry also pronounced itself receptive to European cooperation, particularly in CNC machine tools and in textile equipment. As before, the main instrument for implementing the new plan would be contracts by which companies agreed to pilot projects. Intentions to improve training procedures were again to be implemented through the Ministry of National Education.[74]

For machine tool firms in particular, the Plan Productique signalled a change in priority rather than a change in the quality of policy. Machine tool shops were not excluded from the new plan, but their problems were now subsumed within the larger effort to automate French industry. The new orientation did little to change the way ministerial officials thought about the sector. Their view was well-reflected in one of the few articles that *Le Monde* devoted to machine tools in June 1983. According to the paper's high-tech analyst, ministerial officials complained about expending vast reserves of diplomacy in order to overcome the "archaic habits" of the firms so that growth contracts could be concluded. The same sources emphasized the Japanese example and the need to specialize in CNC technologies. As had so often been done before, the author explained the weakness of the internal market according to the psychological barrier which led small firms to resist the new machines that the state wanted to promote.[75]

In implementing the Plan Productique, the public agencies held true to past practice. A nearly exclusive preoccupation with financial restructuring meant that the machine tool sector was thrown into continuing disarray while its human-resource base eroded. The first of the three major pôles, MFL, had already been formed. The second, linking Graffenstaden with Huré under the new name Intelautomatisme was thought capable of producing a integrated line of medium-sized CNC machines

(*machines à catalogue*)—based on Graffenstaden's expertise in lathes and Huré's expertise in milling machines. After considerable negotiation, the entity was formed when the IDI agreed to finance a good part of CIT-Alcatel's liability for Graffenstaden.[76] The major unresolved case concerned Ernault Somua. Extensive negotiations revealed that neither Intelautomatisme nor Renault would commit funds to the firm. Finally, the Japanese Toyoda, which had already started coproduction with Ernault Somua in Montzeron, took a 50 percent interest in the firm, while minority shares were retained by Schneider and the Institut de Développement Industriel. According to those responsible for the Machine Tool Plan through 1984, the foreign takeover of "the brightest jewel" in the French industry signified a "very serious reverse in comparison to the initial ambitions of the plan."[77]

A penultimate series of smaller restructuring arrangements also took place in 1983 and 1984. The lathe producer, RAMO, filed for bankruptcy in April 1983. In early 1984, the celebrated Dufour was obliged to close its doors for the last time, while its traditional competitor, Vernier, survived only with a capital infusion from the state. The DIMME had some success in assembling a pôle for grinding machines when it combined Gendron (formerly of Liné) and Constructions de Clichy (formerly of Renault) under the designation Société de Rectification Cylindrique Française (SCRF).[78]

Since financial reorganization had overshadowed other aspects of the Machine Tool Plan, policymakers only belatedly acknowledged the glaring deficits in human resources and research capabilities that afflicted the sector. If only in retrospect, however, it seemed clear that human resources had been one of the major bottlenecks. As one official familiar with the plan said:

> We had certainly underestimated somewhat the gravity of the problems of certain firms. We realized that in fact some firms either entirely or very severely lacked qualified persons. It was often at the level of human competence, which is more difficult to appraise, that we saw how the firms were basically condemned and how they could not simultaneously make investments, train personnel, change product lines, introduce numerical controls in their products, and do all that in the space of three years. . . . There are human limits at this level that were undoubtedly underestimated.[79]

In fact, from the outset, the Ministry of Education had encountered resistance in efforts to upgrade the technological level of the machine tools used in vocational education. Following the Socialists' efforts to promote administrative decentralization, the Education Ministry no longer coordinated purchases on a centralized basis. Once particular schools controlled their own materiél, it became painfully clear that instructors did not want the advanced machines that the policymakers had thought they would. As those in charge of implementing the plan wrote later, "We should recognize that the Education Ministry's handicap will not be easy to overcome, because it is not limited to obsolete equipment but also rests on the poor qualifications of the professors, very few of whom have mastered the new technologies."[80] Other officials in the DIMME also stated flatly that because the professors at the vocational schools were not trained in the new technologies, they continued to order traditional machine tools.[81]

The human resource problem was not limited to curriculum. It extended deeply into the sociology of French professional groups. The policymakers responsible for the Machine Tool Plan soon discovered how strongly French engineers disliked the manufacturing sector. This disaffection for production was surely one reason why the new technologies were so slowly assimilated: "As a group, French engineers preferred in the 1970s to join the ranks of the computer or electronics firms or to make the jump into management positions. This disaffection for production, which touched an entire generation and which has probably not entirely disappeared, explains the current dearth of competent persons in this field."[82] It was also revealing that officials in the Ministry of Industry did not consider the role of apprenticeships or intermediate professional groups. Their assumption that engineers alone were enough to spread the new technologies was itself symptomatic of the stratified professional relations which hindered the emergence of the double competence needed to integrate electronics into the traditional mechanical engineering trades.

Basic apprenticeships remained a problematic proposition in France. Enterprises found them burdensome, apprentices risked being trapped in programs that taught only plant-specific skills, and the approximately two hundred inspectors remained too few to monitor the programs.[83] Given the weakness of industrial training, ministry officials were probably correct when they asserted that a traditional lathe operator could not be retrained to program a CNC machine.[84] At the other end of the spectrum, engineers from the more prestigious of the grandes écoles could get much higher salaries from electronics and aerospace firms than they could from small mechanical engineering shops. The big nationalized firms would "pay any price [cassent les prix] in order to get an engineer from Supélec or Sup Aero."[85] Holders of the baccalauréat de technicien meanwhile fell between the cracks of industrial and academic careers and indeed often sought further certification through the BTS (*brevet de technicien supérieur*).[86] Holders of the BTS degree were the most available to firms in the metalworking trades. The problem was that relatively few of them possessed the double competence in mechanics and electronics that was needed. From the lowest to the highest skill levels, the vocational education system remained one of the greatest unstated obstacles to technological advance in the manufacturing industries.

In addition to training, the Machine Tool Plan had aimed at strengthening institutions for cooperative research, particularly CERMO and CETIM. There was little positive evidence for their contributions, however, and French observers of the sector were skeptical of their success.[87] Given the combination of difficulties facing the sector by the 1980s, direct financial aid from the state overpowered any single firm's interest in contributing to cooperative research efforts.

The only part of the plan that showed much success was, as before, the state's effort to support France's CNC supplier, La Société NUM. Once it obtained the state's backing, NUM was able to establish a near monopoly within the French market.[88] From 1978 to 1987, the firm raised its share of the French market for CNC equipment from 20 percent to 80 percent—raising its revenues from 22 million francs to approximately 247 million francs. Sales were also supported by orders from French user-firms to other European machine tool builders. Exports grew from 12 million francs (8 percent of revenues) in 1981 to over 70 million francs (30 percent in 1987). NUM itself always viewed these orders as a wedge in other European markets. The firm quickly established subsidiaries or affiliates in Switzerland, Italy, and Germany. By 1988, the firm had even attracted some of the Stuttgart machine tool builders that normally bought from German offerings.[89]

It was not surprising that computer controls were the one market niche in which the French state effectively promoted advanced machine tool technologies. The dirigiste instruments of industrial policy were ill suited for cultivating the kinds of sector-wide resources and capabilities that small and medium-sized machine tool builders needed. These same policy instruments did, however, give NUM its initial boost toward a critical threshold of business. By encouraging large French machine tool users to request NUM controls, the state also helped to pull NUM into business relations with many of Europe's most sophisticated machine tool builders outside of France.

These policy measures were supplemented by NUM's efforts to maintain a high level of training in its Nanterre headquarters. The firm invested substantially in continuing education for its employees, spending 2.5 percent of its payroll for non-product-related training.[90] Owing to its small size (about six hundred employees worldwide) and high profile, NUM was able to find the engineers it needed from a few lesser-known engineering schools outside Paris. With a relatively solid skill-base in France, NUM was able to assimilate lessons from its customers abroad as well as at home. This was precisely the kind of self-sustaining practice which so many of France's machine tool builders had not managed to cultivate.

Consequences

In assessing French policy toward the machine tool sector, it is difficult to avoid the view that the state severely weakened those self-regulative capabilities that were crucial for individual firms as they adjusted to new technologies and new conditions of competition. Official efforts at rationalization disrupted the interfirm relations that were so important to developing new products and prevented the industry from generating useful collective institutions for adjusting to shifts in demand. And, finally, the national policy forced thousands of workers out of the sector. Because public policy in this case was so heavily skewed toward top-down restructuring, those firms that attracted official attention suffered while those that did not often succeeded.

Between 1975 and 1985, the sector experienced a drastic decline in size. As measured by membership in the trade association, the number of firms dropped 20 percent from 185 to 148 (see Table 2). Employment dropped more than 50 percent from over 26,000 to 12,050. The employment drop itself constituted a major loss of practical skills. It also reduced average firm size from 145 employees in 1975 to 82 employees in 1985—casting doubt on the administrators' belief that larger firms were likely to be more efficient and robust. Indeed, changes in firm size contradicted the official views quite clearly. During the ten-year period, the number of firms with 500 employees or more declined from fifteen to five. It is unlikely that such a large decline reflects marginal layoffs designed to enhance productivity gains. Moreover, the decline in size did not occur proportionately throughout the industry. There were pockets of dynamism, and they were located in the small-firm segments. The number of firms with 20 or fewer employees dipped from fifty-eight in 1975 to fifty-five in 1980, but then jumped back to sixty-eight.

Table 2. Number of firms producing metal-shaping tools in France and Germany, 1975–1985, by number of employees

Country	1975			1980			1985		
	Employees	Firms	%	Employees	Firms	%	Employees	Firms	%
France	Up to 20	58	31.4%	Up to 20	55	33.7%	Up to 20	68	45.9%
	21–50	46	24.9	21–50	44	27.0	21–50	35	23.6
	51–100	28	15.1	51–100	17	10.4	51–100	19	12.8
	101–200	20	10.8	101–200	18	11.0	101–200	14	9.5
	201–500	18	9.7	201–500	20	12.3	201–500	7	4.7
	501–1,001	11	5.9	501–1,001	9	5.5	501–1,001	5	3.4
	Over 1,001	4	2.2	Over 1,001	0	0.0	Over 1,001	0	0.0
Total		185	100.0%		163	99.9%		148	99.9%
Germany	Up to 50	165	35.9%	Up to 50	155	34.4%	Up to 50	169	39.8%
	51–100	81	17.6	51–100	75	16.7	51–100	81	19.1
	101–200	96	20.9	101–200	100	22.2	101–200	84	19.8
	201–500	60	13.0	201–500	60	13.3	201–500	46	10.8
	501–1,000	44	9.6	501–1,000	45	10.0	501–1,000	34	8.0
	Over 1,000	14	3.0	Over 1,000	15	3.3	Over 1,000	11	2.6
Total		460	100.0%		450	99.9%		425	100.1%

SOURCES: VDMA statistics, cited in Bernhard Nagel and Hildegard Kaluza, *Eigentum und Markt im Maschinenbau* (Baden-Baden: Nomos, 1988), 85–86; SCFMO statistics reported in the *Economic Handbook* of the National Machine Tool Builders Association, various years.

Individual cases reinforce the hypothesis that pockets of dynamism were emerging outside the scope of state activity. Managers at La Société NUM, the official plan's only case of success, reported that their domestic customers shifted noticeably toward the small-firm sector in the 1980s. For example, Realmeca, a family-owned firm established in the early 1980s in Clermont-en-Argonne, quickly became a significant producer for flexible manufacturing cells that used NUM controllers. Another firm, SOMAB, started in Moulins with regional support from Bourgogne, reopened an old facility of Ernault Somua, and emerged as one of France's few successful producers of CNC lathes in the 1980s.

While unofficial efforts were generating several successes, firms that received state aid continued to falter. The pattern was remarkably consistent. The Société de Rectification Cylindrique Française (SRCF), formed by the DIMME in 1984, filed for bankruptcy in 1986 and its assets were acquired by two small producers of tools for the leather industry, Mercier Frères (Annonay) and Promat (Bordeaux).[91] An especially telling case was that of Promecam, a small but well-known specialist in building sheet-metal presses. The firm had about 150 employees and an illustrious list of customers including Boeing Aircraft. After abortive efforts to establish export branches brought the firm into difficulty, the public authorities made loans as well as capital available. When the IDI took a 33 percent equity stake, it also asked that a former manager of Thomson-CSF be hired as general director. Fourteen months later, the firm filed for bankruptcy and was soon acquired by the Japanese leader in sheet-metal presses, Amada.[92]

The fate of the three main pôles in the Machine Tool Plan was even less ambiguous. The fortunes of Ernault-Somua, the "jewel" of the French industry, improved dramatically as soon as management control was shared with the Japanese machine tool specialist, Toyoda. The new entity, Ernault-Toyoda-Automation (ETA) operated the Ernault plant at Cholet and invested heavily in Montzeron, where 93 employees produced flexible machining centers. Work practices at Montzeron were overhauled to the point where white gloves were required for quality-control personnel—a novelty in France.[93] French acceptance of the new venture was confirmed when its president became president of the national machine tool builders trade association. By early 1987, Toyoda had installed entirely new production equipment and was considering further investment. ETA expected to boost its exports from 20 percent to 40 percent of production and to become an ideal base for Toyoda's efforts to compete in European markets as its Japanese rival, Yamazaki, was building a new factory in Worcester, England.[94]

The pôle that was controlled by French institutional investors, Intelautomatisme, fared less well. A new line of medium-sized CNC products achieved little success. In September 1986, the group separated Graffenstaden's operations in traditional cutting machines, filed for bankruptcy, and began searching for new European or Japanese partners. Within a few months, Comau, Fiat's subsidiary for manufacturing systems, purchased the group and began a long effort to return it to profitability.[95]

The final chapter of the Machine Tool Plan was concluded when the major pôle for specialized machines, MFL, was disbanded. MFL had been weighed down by elaborate ambitions to sell the most advanced flexible manufacturing cells in international markets. Products of this magnitude required a major service presence. In 1983, MFL opened a branch in Essex, Connecticut, with seven sales and technical engineers to penetrate the American markets in aerospace, automobile, and railway production. The strategy was simply too expensive and after four years, the group was still recording losses. In 1988, after the group had received roughly a billion francs in public funds, MFL was dissolved into its two original constituent firms, Liné and Berthiez, and sold to new owners.[96]

The legacy of the Machine Tool Plan—frequent ownership changes, investment fluctuations, and declines in employment—made it difficult for managers and policymakers to replenish the pool of skilled personnel needed to rebuild the industry. Indeed, the patterns established in the 1980s persisted as the industry experience renewed turbulence and crisis in the 1990s. A major blow occurred in 1992 when Toyoda announced that it was abandoning its investment in Ernault-Toyoda-Automation. The next year, the remnants of the firm were absorbed by a new holding company known as CATO, which had been built around Cazeneuve, Dufour, and somab. Employment in the sector continued to fall, from 12,050 in 1985 to 8,295 in 1992 (see Table 3). Once again, the firm that performed well was the software provider NUM, which had become one of the to worldwide suppliers of controllers by 1995. As in earlier years, those parts of the industry that relied on experience-based skills fared poorly while the one firm that specialized in software-intensive expertise to sell controllers succeeded.[97]

POLICY HISTORY IN GERMANY

Germany's more permeable hierarchy of professional elites allowed central policymakers much less latitude than their French counterparts in formulating policy but gave them far superior access to the informa-

Table 3. Aggregate employment in machine-tool firms,
France and Germany, 1970–1993

Year	France	Germany[a]
1970	26,125	125,000
1975	26,859	102,000
1980	19,650	99,000
1981	18,984	99,000
1982	17,661	94,500
1983	15,502	83,700
1984	13,433	83,000
1985	12,050	88,000
1986	11,450	93,000
1987	10,025	93,500
1988	9,190	94,000
1989	9,475	99,500
1990	9,810	103,000
1991	9,430	98,000
1992	8,295	89,500
1993	6,885	82,500

[a] Does not include former East Germany.
SOURCE: VDMA and SCFMO statistics reported in the
Economic Handbook of the National Machine Tool Build-
ers Association, various years.

tion and manpower needed to implement those policies in a sector like
machine tools. Officials in Bonn were bound by regulation and custom
to consult producer groups and academic experts. Once these actors
had hammered out their compromise positions, the dense links among
sectoral professional groups became a great asset in implementing policy.
The same networks that obliged public officials to negotiate seriously
with societal actors over the formulation of policy provided the means
by which policymakers allocated funds and tailored programs toward
the achievement of policy goals in a variety of regional and sector-specific
circumstances. The result was a surprisingly effective case of diffusion-
oriented policy.

German policy outcomes differed from the French experience in
three respects. First, the intermediary organizations used by the state to
implement policy became vibrant institutions. Called *Trägerorganisationen*
(literally, carrier organizations), they grew in size, became quickly integrated into the larger institutional landscape, and became important
stakes in the struggles among contending professional groups. Second,
the policy instruments designed by public officials—known as "indirect-
specific measures"—were intended to reach the *Mittelstand,* or small

and medium-sized firms, as well as their larger competitors. Third, the importance given to labor representatives in the policy process made possible a completely different vision of factory automation. The French notion of "la Productique" pointed toward fully automated production without human intervention. The German discussion by contrast included alternative visions, some of which kept the skilled worker at the center of the production process. The human-resource problems that plagued French policy efforts were grasped more quickly and more thoroughly by German authorities. The result was a more halting, but much more effective adjustment to the possibilities and risks inherent in the new technologies for production.

Of course these outcomes did not follow immediately from Germany's distinctive pattern of professional relations. They were the conclusion of a process of bargaining, persuasion, and reassessment that stretched from the early 1970s through the mid 1980s. German policy was not characterized by the clearly demarcated cycles of initiative and assessment found in France. Rather policymakers in the federal ministries worked continuously to devise a bundle of instruments that encouraged firms to adopt so-called key technologies such as microelectronics on a more incremental basis. The following discussion shows how these efforts were guided by the various professional groups that had a stake in the way new production technologies were introduced to German manufacturing industries.

The Terms of Debate

Policy for machine tools emerged within a larger debate between the proponents of *Ordnungspolitik* and *Strukturpolitik* in the 1970s. Ordnungspolitik was a particularly German economic doctrine that prescribed an important but limited role for the state in maintaining proper framework conditions (*Rahmenbedingungen*) for orderly competition and growth. Partly in reaction to the wartime economic policies of the Nazi period, this so-called ordo-liberal approach became nearly uncontested among academic economists in the Federal Republic through the 1960s. Strukturpolitik was the alternative concept advanced by the enthusiasts of economic planning in the Social Democratic Party in the 1970s. Its proponents favored a more anticipatory and activist role for the state, particularly in investment and industrial policy. After a brief fascination with macroeconomic planning in the late 1960s, Strukturpolitik became the main rationale for state involvement in the economy and became the early doctrine for the Ministry of Research and Technology (BMFT), founded in 1972.[98]

Both Ordnungspolitik and Strukturpolitik assigned the state a more integral role in economic processes than the free market versions of liberalism familiar in the United States. Yet, neither doctrine gave state officials the autonomy from social actors that was implicit in French dirigisme. In France, ongoing consultation with social actors was viewed as tainting the policy process with private preferences. In Germany, such consultation was required by regulation and custom.[99] The proponents of Ordnungspolitik assumed that major economic decisions would be made by private actors. The proponents of active Strukturpolitik gave state bureaucrats a larger role, but also insisted on the need to build consensus by bringing expert deliberations into the public, political arena. In the realm of research policy, the Social Democrats explicitly agreed with their Christian Democratic counterparts on the need "to transfer the setting of priorities out of the bureaucratic arena into the field of public debate and resolution."[100] Thus, while liberals and statists could be found in both France and Germany, the range of debate was very different in the two countries. In France, it was assumed that higher civil servants should play the leading, often the exclusive, role in defining the public interest. In the Federal Republic, the public interest was thought to emerge from a process of negotiation which was guided but not dictated by public officials. The precise degree of state guidance was controversial, but the basic formula was not. The proponents of Ordnungspolitik and Strukturpolitik alike assumed that the state could only formulate effective policy in close consultation with various societal actors.

Given the norm of consulting societal actors, it was not surprising that the indirect-specific measures eventually adopted to promote the machine tools sector showed the influence of the main social groups implicated. It would be a mistake, however, to interpret this influence as evidence of the state's weakness. When German officials brought labor, management and academic experts into the policy process, they were not capitulating to private interests. They were doing exactly what administrative and professional norms required them to do: namely, recognizing the competence of groups that resided outside the state.

Moreover, if the initial adoption of indirect-specific measures might be seen as the result of competing social interests, the successful implementation of these measures cannot be explained through interest-based dynamics alone. Rather it was a cognitive factor—the mutual recognition of managers, engineers, technicians, and skilled machinists—that provided the positive context for public-policy initiatives. This mutual recognition did not eliminate conflict or divergent interests from the shop floor. Yet, it did make possible a level of deliberate consultation and communication that was glaringly absent in France and that was crucial to the successful introduction of new technologies in Germany. With time, it also became clear to officials in the federal ministries that the inclusion of organized labor in the policy process was not only politically expedient, it was demonstrably necessary to achieving the technological advances that policymakers in Bonn desired.

Early Initiatives

Concern for the capital goods sectors in Germany appeared in the mid 1970s after the oil crisis and exchange rate fluctuations raised the fear of continuing instabilities in the international economy. These shocks were particularly threatening to industrial sectors that exported heavily. Among these, the machine building industry, which produced 14,000 products and accounted for 14 percent of Germany's manufacturing employment, depended on export markets for almost 50 percent of its revenues in 1973. Within machine building, the machine tools sector had seen its export sales rise from 47 percent of total production in 1965 to 71 percent in 1974.[101]

The impulse to identify the machine tool sector as an object of national policy came from several different sources. The first signs of trouble were macroeconomic disturbances in Germany's traditional export markets, but the issue of technology was closely related. The analogy of the watch industry was prominent in the public discussion. If they did not adopt the new electronic technologies, it was feared, German machine builders might be dislodged from their markets as dramatically as German and Swiss watchmakers had been from theirs in the previous decade.

In contrast to the French case, virtually all observers in Germany emphasized the importance of small and medium-sized production runs. There was no assumption that only large firms could survive in the sector. Technological advance was seen as a means of enhancing the flexibility of the smaller firms rather than as a condition which required further concentration. These views were advanced by academic specialists in a major Commission on Economic and Social Change, appointed in 1974. In its discussion of technological change in the machine tools sector, the Commission emphasized both high-speed machining techniques and numerical control. Far from being tied to concentration, however, the new techniques were presented as means of keeping German firms competitive in business lines where fully customized and small-batch production ("*Einzel- und Kleinserien*") were the rule. The metal workers union, IG Metall, also gave great attention to the introduction of NC machine tools in their review of structural changes in the mid 1970s. Once again, the need to develop flexible operating systems (*flexible Handhabungssysteme*) was stressed as essential in small-batch and medium-batch production ("*Klein- und Mittelserienfertigung*").[102]

The formulation of German policy did not proceed by the clear pattern of repeated initiatives that characterized the French case. As soon as the Commission on Economic and Social Change had begun its work, the BMFT simply began pilot projects on new technologies for automation in machine tools. These early grants typified the brief period where policy was quite consistent with the idea of anticipatory Strukturpolitik. Grants were carefully designated for specific projects, generally accompanied by funding for research institutes on the same problem. In 1974, a number of the larger machine tool users received substantial grants for flexible handling systems (*Handhabungssysteme*). Recipients included the Bosch Group (Stuttgart), IBP Pietzsch (Ettlingen), Industrie-Werke (Augsburg), MAN (Munich), and Pfaff Industriemaschinen (Kaiserslautern). The research was paralleled by a similar project at the Fraunhofer Institute for Production Technology and Automation in Stuttgart.[103] In 1975, one of the country's largest lathe producers, Gildemeister, received DM1 million to develop a flexible, integrated operating system for numerically controlled lathes in conjunction with the Institute for Machine Tools at the Technical University of Berlin.[104] Within the next five years, direct grants for work on CNC technologies went to at least a dozen additional machine tool builders.[105]

Representatives of labor were directly involved in these efforts at Strukturpolitik through a program for the Humanization of Work (*Humanisierung des Arbeitslebens*). For labor organizations, this program was the heart of state-administered technology policy. It was inaugurated after the leader of the SPD's technocratic wing, Horst Ehmke, was succeeded in the BMFT by the pragmatic unionist, Hans Matthöfer.[106] Through a series of advisory bodies and expert committees, organized labor had a substantial voice in policy elaboration. The advisory committee appointed in July 1975 to guide the program included twenty-four members, with eight from industry, eight from the unions, and eight from other research institutes. The program included grants to enhance work safety, reduce noise and reduce physically stressful work requirements, but it also included many of the BMFT's efforts to promote new production technologies in capital goods industries.

Within organized labor, the SPD's efforts at Strukturpolitik remained controversial. Some unionists saw the Humanization of Work as a fig leaf to cover state subsidies for automation and industrial rationalization. Others saw it as a mixed blessing that could, with careful oversight, be turned to labor's advantage. Parallel to this program, organized labor stimulated a broad training campaign *(Qualifizierungsoffensiv)* to provide the skills required by the new workplace technologies. By comparison to the French case, these efforts clearly evidenced a greater concern for the role of labor.[107]

More concerted opposition to Strukturpolitik emerged from the small-firm sector, known in German as the *Mittelstandswirtschaft.* Because so much of BMFT's early funding went to nuclear power and data processing, small firms could argue that they were severely disadvantaged by massive subsidies granted to the large firms involved in these capital-intensive fields. Germany's business associations—the guardians of Ordnungspolitik—were especially opposed to state interventions that resembled sectoral planning or substantive investment guidance. The Bundesverband der Deutschen Industrie called for recentering public research policy around general framework policies such as R&D tax credits and nontargeted subsidies for R&D personnel. The Association of Young Entrepreneurs called for dismantling the Technology Ministry altogether and argued that direct research grants were a drug that started independent firms toward an addictive dependence on state aid. The president of the German Chamber of Commerce and Industry asserted similarly that firms should themselves remain responsible for the normal business of innovation. By 1980, criticism of the BMFT had become a constant feature in parliamentary debate.[108]

The basic tension between anticipatory technology policy and framework-setting policy had already prompted a vigorous debate within the government on the role of small and medium-sized firms. Within the governing coalition, the Free Democrats championed the Mittelstandswirtschaft through their control of the Economics Ministry. FDP Ministers for Economics and the Interior were especially concerned that 80 percent of BMFT's research funds went to fifteen large companies.[109] In 1978, a general statement for promoting research and innovation among smaller firms was issued by the SPD's Minister of Technology, Volker Hauff, and the FDP Minister of Economics, Otto von Lambsdorff.[110] Rather than resolving the opposition between the two images of the state's role in promoting industrial R&D, however, the joint statement served as the starting point for further competition between the Economics Ministry and the BMFT.

The Economics Ministry had long financed cooperative research among small firms through a nonstate umbrella association, known as the Arbeitsgemeinschaft industrieller Forschungsvereinigungen (AIF). The AIF was founded in 1954 to coordinate joint research activities in small-firm sectors. By 1980, it counted eighty-seven member organizations and had monitored DM572 million in research funds from the Economics Ministry. The AIF provided an ideal mechanism for those who favored indirect research support over the SPD's anticipatory policy. In 1979, the Economics Ministry initiated a program of subsidies for R&D personnel in small and medium-sized firms. The program was limited to firms under 1000 employees or less than DM150 million in annual sales. (The limits were lowered to 500 employees and DM50 millions in 1982.) Grants were limited to a scaled percentage of R&D personnel costs—(25 percent to 40 percent), with a ceiling of DM400,000 (DM120,000 after 1982).[111] The program was an effort to promote R&D activities, while leaving substantive choices of technologies and strategies at the level of the firm. It provided the support that small and medium-sized firms said they needed in order to match the research capabilities of their larger competitors, who were increasingly supported through the BMFT. Since applications were evaluated and grants monitored through the AIF however, the program had no hint of state-led, anticipatory policy.[112]

Proponents of anticipatory structural policy in the BMFT also developed programs for small and medium-sized firms. They sought, however, to channel public resources toward those areas considered likely to become bottlenecks in social and economic development. This position was outlined in the BMFT's official report of 1979. According to this report, small and medium-sized firms had superior flexibility in matching products and services to market opportunities. Yet, the report also reflected the view, often found at BMFT, that German entrepreneurs were too slow to adopt new technologies: "The relatively short-term orientation of research and development toward changing market imperatives often blinds small and medium-sized enterprises to the danger that they are not applying fundamentally new technological solutions quickly enough."[113] On this view, the Economics Ministry's subsidies for R&D personnel were not discriminating enough to promote adjustment to technological change. According to some critics in the trade unions, such subsidies demonstrated only the "watering can principle" *(Gießkannprinzip)* by which public authorities returned resources to industry without channeling them toward long-term goals.[114]

As an alternative, BMFT officials sought to advance the concept of "indirect-specific promotion." The first example was the Special Program for the Application of Microelectronics, developed in 1978 and implemented on a trial basis in 1979. The program was indirect because it was to be administered through a nonstate intermediary organization without the BMFT's direct supervision. Yet the program was informed by a specific technological vision inasmuch as it was only available for developing new products and components in which microelectronics defined the technical functions. Although the program would not exclude larger firms, it included a cap of DM800,000, which made it more suitable for smaller enterprises. Equally important, funding was limited to 40 percent of the total costs (personnel, consulting and hardware) to ensure that firms did not contrive projects solely to capture public subsidies. Even after the first pilot program, the proposal was resisted by the opponents of Strukturpolitik. Indeed, the Economics Ministry insisted that the proposal be registered with the European Community bureau for monitoring subsidies. Only after it was bounded within strict time limits was the program acceptable to the defenders of Ordnungspolitik. After several years of preliminary work, the program received funding of DM450 million from 1982 through 1984.[115]

Implementation

The indirect-specific measures represented a compromise formula through which followers of Ordnungspolitik and Strukturpolitik found uneasy agreement. On the practicalities of implementation in the metalworking industries, however, differences in doctrine continued to surface. Only the links among occupational groups and the norms of mutual recognition permitted policy in this sector to proceed.

Organized labor quickly concluded that it needed its own organizational entity to help guide the practical implementation of new technologies in the workplace. For the metalworkers union, IG Metall, a continual role in the introduction of new technology became an essential condition for maintaining control over job content and the organization of work. If the union was to maintain a protechnology position, it needed to insure that its members were prepared to assimilate innovations at the workplace. As early as 1976, the union staff began to press the federal government to establish a series of consulting bureaus to assist firms and labor in the assimilation of new technologies (*Innovationsberatungsstellen,* IBS).[116] In 1979, the federal government helped finance union-operated innovation consulting bureaus in Hamburg and Berlin. The Hamburg bureau, staffed by three engineers and a psychologist, was concerned with practical education for union officials in shipping related sectors. The Berlin bureau, initially staffed by an economist, was heavily involved in establishing links to engineering research institutes on the subject of CNC machine tools.[117]

The Association of German Machine and Factory Construction (VDMA) already dealt with a densely populated landscape of research institutes affiliated with its sectoral membership associations. It had established its own research coordinating agency, the Forschungskuratorium Maschinenbau (FKM), in 1968. The FKM was funded mainly through the AIF and member contributions, with some support from BMFT. Its primary mission was promotion of joint research projects to compensate small and medium-sized firms for their competitive or structural disadvantage relative to large firms. These projects either involved more than one firm in a single subsector (*Fachgruppe*) or cross-cutting projects (*Querschnittsforschungsvorhaben*) of interest to several sub-sectors within the machine building industry. The FKM was particularly skeptical of the Technology Ministry's early policies, which offered little that fit the needs of the small firms in the machine building branch. In contrast to the BMFT, the FKM was not only concerned with the front runners, but also with firms that took more time to integrate new technologies more slowly—and perhaps more carefully.[118]

In an unusually sharp dispute which revealed the stakes involved in industrial innovation, the VDMA reacted strongly against the BMFT's support for the metalworkers' innovation consultation bureaus. The president of the VDMA attacked Minister Hauff's policies of taking responsibility for R&D away from private enterprise: "Our credo, now as before, is the social market economy with its competitive order and the self-responsibility of the firm. R&D in industry is the concern of the private sector and should stay that way."[119] For the VDMA's research arm, public support for the union's consulting bureaus threatened to dilute an important prerogative. The Forschungskuratorium raised the debate to a higher pitch by arguing that "IG Metall has no say in this area, because it has no expertise [*Sachverstand*]. The union itself knows as much and therefore resorts only to the politics of naysaying."[120] Given the close association between technical competence and political competence in Germany, this denial of the metalworkers' expertise represented a serious attempt to deny IG Metall's political voice in the introduction of new technologies.

Although this denial of labor's competence was in the VDMA's institutional interest, the view was not widely shared in the industry. The practical know-how of skilled workers was a basic element in the business strategies of many machine builders— particularly those in the specialized machine tool branch. This view was expressed as early as 1977 by the vice president of the machine tool builders association, VDW (Verein Deutscher Werkzeugmaschinenfabriken), Hans-Jürgen Marczinski. Marczinski pointed out that changes in the industry were pushing German machine tool builders to deliver complete production solutions, rather than stand-alone machines. The restructuring of the industry involved "shifting the crucial know-how from pure machine tool construction to the related [production] process."[121] As the industry moved toward customized products, however, design capabilities still rested on practical experience which also required familiarity with serial production. The industry needed a foundation on which to "build and accumulate know-how." This necessitated stable markets in order to support stable employment. As Marczinski put it: "We have to keep our people employed because we can't work with stark fluctuations in personnel. In our core personnel, there is hidden know-how."[122] Individual firms also favored more cooperative labor relations in the matter of technological innovation. Even as the VDMA staff attacked IG Metall's role in innovation, for example, a machine tool firm near Hamburg met with the union's new innovation consulting bureau regarding organizational changes to accompany plant renovations. Firm managers said the union's consultant was "very expert" and had come to "the same recommendations" as had management.[123]

At the level of national policy, SPD officials continued to consider labor's participation in the indirect-specific programs technically advisable as well as politically expedient. One SPD official in the Technology Ministry spoke of labor's "immense expertise" and said it was "very sensible as well as necessary" to include labor in programs for new production technologies.[124]

Internal discussions had, however, convinced BMFT officials that many small firms would deal more readily with a separate organization than with the ministry directly.[125] For this purpose, the Association of German Engineers (VDI) provided an excellent solution. As the largest engineering association in Western Europe, the VDI possessed the organizational independence as well as the technical expertise that the BMFT needed.[126] Owing to its size and historical pedigree, the VDI had cultivated longstanding relationships with public and private research institutions.[127] Under the umbrella of the VDI, the ministry established the VDI-Technologiezentrum in Berlin in 1978 and assigned it responsibility for administering grants and consulting firms in the Special Program for the Application of Microelectronics.

Pressure from the Economics Ministry insured that the microelectronics program was not defined in sector-specific terms. Nonetheless, two-thirds of the supported firms came from the electro-technical or mechanical engineering sectors. The Technologiezentrum became particularly important as a forum for the interest groups implicated in automated production technologies. Through the Technologiezentrum, the BMFT financed a study of microelectronics in the machine building industry, with an advisory committee that rejoined representatives of labor, firms, trade associations, and academic institutions. The same individuals who had publicly clashed over the IG Metall consulting bureaus sat together at the Technologiezentrum.[128] Of the DM450 million allocated to the program from 1982 through 1985, roughly 20 percent went to machine builders. The majority of products promoted in all sectors involved measuring, regulating, or controlling technologies; machine controllers and guidance mechanisms were frequently mentioned among the program's emphases.[129]

The proponents of long-term structural policy were not forced to channel all of their support for advanced machine tools strictly through the new indirect-specific measures. In January 1980, the federal cabinet approved a program aimed at the entire field of advanced manufacturing technologies (Programm Fertigungstechnik). Over four years (1980–1983), the BMFT distributed DM165 million for approximately four hundred projects that involved 270 different recipients. As before, many of the grants went to firms in conjunction with research institutes.[130] The technologies to be supported included computerized efforts to design products for machining (CAD or computer-aided design), computerized methods to govern work flow and machining (CAM or computer-aided manufacturing), automated handling systems, and robotics.

These programs evidenced an emerging consensus among technology policymakers in Bonn that a mixture of direct and indirect measures was needed. Already in 1979, the ministry's official reports deplored the "blanket value judgments" that the anodyne terms, direct and indirect, had acquired in the public debate. Direct and indirect measures were not mutually exclusive options, but reciprocal, complementary instruments of policy. As formulated in the report, the state's role was neither to intervene in the firm's internal technology decisions nor to provide funds to firms that had already determined their technology strategy.[131] Rather, as it emerged over the next few years, the ministry's strategy aimed at accumulating know-how that would be publicly available to all societal actors for their chosen ends.

This policy trajectory continued when the Christian Democratic party replaced the Social Democrats as coalition leaders in 1982. The Christian Democrats' Minister for Research and Technology, Heinz Riesenhuber, announced a major new policy orientation which stressed freedom in research, a restrained role (*Zurückhaltung*) for the state in industrial research, pursuit of competitiveness through technical progress, and acknowledgement of excellence in research.[132] In terms of policy instruments, Riesenhuber wanted to reduce the Ministry's dedication to large projects and increase funds for indirect technology promotion. Like previous ministers, however, Riesenhuber found it difficult to effect more than marginal changes.[133] The combination of policy instruments that had evolved through discussion and reassessment could not be quickly overhauled without disrupting the professional networks on which technology policy depended.

In the area of production technologies, the first program to be extended was the one which most clearly showed the traces of earlier impulses toward anticipatory Strukturpolitik. In 1983, the federal cabinet formalized and extended the Programm Fertigungstechnik for a four-year period (see Figure 1). Lengthy discussions between the BMFT and industry associations led to the view that computer aided design and computer aided manufacturing should be considered key technologies.[134] The first part of the program involved a series of indirect-specific projects to be administered by a new *Trägerorganisation* staffed by a nonministerial staff located in Karlsruhe. Indirect-specific measures were seen as the best way to streamline application procedures for small and medium-sized firms. In addition, the Karlsruhe staff would judge the merit of each proposal and work with firms in a new CAD/CAM laboratory built for the program. Explicitly mentioning the Special Program for Microelectronics, the ministry once again renounced a direct role in setting the substantive agenda for technological development projects and instead created a new Trägerorganisation which became a nodal point for small and medium-sized firms.[135]

The second part of the program for Fertigungstechnik involved the linking of firms with research institutes at universities or Fraunhofer Institutes. This practice had already produced good results and was formalized under the name, *Verbundprojekte* (joint projects). By obliging firms to work with other firms and with research institutes, the joint projects insured that they would not be using public funds for their own proprietary R&D. Instead, the joint projects aimed at "overarching, future-oriented issues in production technologies [which] were to be cooperatively solved."[136] The explicit aim was the cultivation of know-how in the public domain. As BMFT's literature acknowledged, there were already good links between industry and the applied research institutes for production technology. Nonetheless, owing to the substantial know-how and human capital available in these institutes, it was felt that such links were well worth intensifying. The entire program was funded at DM530 million for four years, of which DM350 million was reserved for the indirect-specific programs administered through the staff at Karlsruhe. This combination of direct and indirect measures in practice was paralleled in language as well. According to the ministry's official report, the Programm Fertigungstechnik aimed at promoting "positive structural adjustment" for the capital-goods industry. Yet, it did so by helping enterprises to help themselves: "Through strengthening their internal resources, enterprises are to be supported in accomplishing the high-risk and know-how intensive step of integrating modern information technologies in their products and processes."[137] The juxtaposition of positive structural adjustment and entrepreneurial self-help on the same page of an official report would have provoked vehement argument a few years before. A common emphasis on deepening the reservoir of knowledge in the public domain was replacing the earlier confrontation between advocates of Ordnungspolitik and StrukturThe second initiative to be extended under Christian Democratic leadership was the Special Program for the Application of Microelectronics (see Figure 1). This program was considered highly successful by participating firms and external referees.[138] The Economics Ministry had required that all indirect-specific programs run for a strictly limited time period, but the government extended the work of the VDI Technologiezentrum through a modified follow-on program. This program for so-called microperipherals focused on microelectronic sensors and other integrated circuits for industrial applications. In keeping with the emerging emphasis on public know-how, the program was implemented through a mixture of indirect-specific measures and joint projects. Indirect-specific grants were administered through the VDI Technologiezentrum to assure that there was "no state influence over the conception of the product to be developed or the development process." At the same time, the ministry argued, joint projects between industrial firms and research institutes were the best way to build a "foundation of internationally competitive know-how in the most important technologies for the future." The program allowed for DM400 million over

Figure 1. Amounts budgeted for selected BMFT programs for production technologies, 1980–1992 (millions of deutsche marks)

1980	1981	1982	1983	1984	1985	1986	1987	1988	1989	1990	1991	1992

Direct grants in Fertigungstechnik
Total = 158

1980	1981	1982	1983
39	40	40	39

Programm Fertigungstechnik
Total = 530
(Amount devoted to indirect-specific measures = 350)

1984	1985	1986	1987	1988
70	125	130	135	70

Programm Fertigungstechnik II
Total = 502
(Amount devoted to indirect-specific measures = 300)

1988	1989	1990	1991	1992
32	125	125	130	90

Sonderprogramm Anwendung der Mikroelektronik
Total = 450

Mikroperipherik
Total = 400
(Amount devoted to indirect-specific measures = 200)

1986	1987	1988	1989	1990
45	76	95	94	90

NOTE: All figures as budgeted. Actual amounts disbursed were sometimes higher.
Fertigungstechnik, 1980–1992: 163 + 530 + 502 = 1,195.
Mikroelektronik and Mikroperipherik, 1982–1989: 450 + 400 = 850.
SOURCES: BMFT brochures: *Fertigungstechnik*; *Fertigungstechnik, 1988–1992*; *Förderungsschwerpunkt*, no. 23, "Mikroperipherik"; *Forschungsbericht*, 1984, 124ff.

4 years, half of which was designated for indirect-specific measures (see Figure 1).[139]

By the mid-1980s, the mixture of indirect-specific measures and joint projects was well established as a fruitful way to cultivate know-how in the public domain. This mixed strategy was also combined with assistance from the institutes for mechanical engineering at the main technical universities, such as Aachen, Stuttgart, and Berlin. The point of the indirect-specific programs was not to work with a particular firm, but to create a "bandwagon effect."[140] Since the program administrators in Karlsruhe or Berlin were in close touch with the major institutes, they were well positioned to help small and medium-sized firms adapt the latest knowledge to their often less exalted needs. The need for cultivating firm-level know-how was explicit in the guidelines for the Programm Fertigungstechnik. All proposals required a minimum of six man-months of work during the preliminary phase in order assure a base of human know-how in the plant (*personengebundenes Mindest-know-how im Unternehmen*) during the proposed project. For CAD/CAM projects, the designated personnel could be university engineers, physicists, technicians, graduate engineers, master craftsmen, or persons of similar job classifications. For robotics and automated handling systems (*Handhabungssysteme*), designated personnel could also come from the ranks of skilled machinists or laboratory assistants. In no way were links between the firms and research groups limited to highly abstract or theoretically codified knowledge. The inclusion of shop-floor personnel showed that practical experience was also valued as an essential resource in technological change.

Policy Evolution

Once these policy instruments were in place, they reinforced certain institutional arrangements more than others. Policymakers consciously tried to strengthen those resources most important to the smaller firms: public know-how and qualified personnel. In so doing, their efforts fed into the subsequent evolution of the sector and thereby influenced the terms of debate for future policy. In particular, German policy actively supported a plurality of visions for factory automation that contrasted starkly with the largely uncontested French view of fully automated production. These effects can be traced through changes in industry structure at the sectoral level and industrial organization at the firm level.

In terms of industry structure, German policy efforts differed from those in France by supporting a variety of electronics suppliers for

machine tools. The introduction of CNC meant that an increasing proportion of the sector's gross product lay in the electronic steering mechanisms or so-called controllers. This change created a tendency toward
vertical disintegration, inasmuch as only the larger machine tool firms
could develop their own CNC devices in-house, leaving other firms to
purchase their controllers externally.[141] It also created the risk that
smaller machine tool producers would become dependent on large
electronics concerns, and that the large firms' control of the CNC units
would limit the design and specifications of automated machine tools.

In the early 1980s, the market for computer numerical controls was
dominated by a few large firms. Working with the Japanese firm, Fanuc,
Siemens held the largest share. Except for Gildemeister, the other early
suppliers were electronics firms such as Bosch, Phillips, Olivetti, General
Electric, or Allen Bradley. Yet the ability to design CNC units was quickly
generated by other, large machine tool firms including Traub, Deckel,
and Maho. These firms were able to buy out small software houses or
hire engineers who had gained software expertise. Expertise in writing
software for industrial applications was also cultivated in the machine
tool divisions of the major technical institutes. A specialized research
association for programming languages in production technologies
(Forschungsvereinigung Programmiersprachen für Fertigungseinrich-
tungen) had been founded as early as 1968 and had collaborated with
the machine tool institutes at Aachen, Stuttgart, and Berlin. By 1980,
university institutes for data processing in Karlsruhe, Darmstadt, and
Stuttgart were also involved in programming for CAD/CAM systems
and other industrial applications. There were also a few independent
software houses that BMFT could bring into its early program for production technologies at this time.[142] Finally, the ministry was able to support
software development efforts through direct grants to machine tool firms
including Boehringer, Gebruder Heller, Heidenreich and Harbeck, and
Liebherr-Verzahntechnik.[143]

Such developments in industry structure cannot be attributed simply
to national technology policy. In contrast to the French, however, officials
in Bonn seized on these activities and promoted them. Whereas French
policymakers encouraged all machine builders to buy controller technology from Société NUM, German policymakers helped finance controller
hardware and software across a broad range of firms. At the very least,
German policy was consistent with a broader range of technological
options than was French policy. By 1984, different controller models
were available from more than twenty domestic electronics firms, while
over twenty CNC machine tool builders developed their own control

mechanisms. Compared to the single domestic French supplier, over forty German firms had started producing CNC technologies since the early experiments of the 1970s. Counting foreign suppliers, more than sixty firms in the German market were disseminating CNC devices, either in their own products or for sale as subsystems to the machine tool producers.[144]

This range of technological options turned out to be crucial for the further assimilation of automated production technologies. As information processing grew more sophisticated, computer technology offered programmable automation for much more than stand-alone machining equipment. Programmable machine tools became one element in a thoroughgoing restructuring of industrial processing. The new view, summed up under the label, "Factory of the Future," held that all of the computer-aided technologies would be connected together in a single, integrated network. Simulation and computer-aided design of products would be linked to CNC machine tools. Computer inventory and orders-booking functions would be linked to computer-aided planning and automated material transport, which would in turn be linked to CNC machine tools and then grouped into flexible manufacturing systems. Ultimately, fully automated production, known as CIM (computer integrated manufacturing), seemed possible.

The goal of CIM—explicit in the French Plan Productique—gave rise to a major debate in the Federal Republic. The case for fully automated production corresponded to the "classical engineering ideal" of an automatic, self-regulating factory that required human supervision only from a distance. The other view saw programmable automation as a means of achieving more autonomous and "complete" forms of work.[145]

These two positions were personified by two leading figures, the "two popes" of the mechanical engineering establishment. Professor Spur, director of the Fraunhofer Institute for Production Installations in Berlin, advocated centralized information processing to link all parts of the production design in a single, centrally controlled network. Professor Warnecke, director of the Fraunhofer Institute in Stuttgart, moved increasingly toward advocacy of decentralized information-processing and autonomous "islands of production."[146]

For the smaller firms that constituted the bulk of Germany's metalworking industry, the decentralized concept of factory automation proved extremely helpful. A multitude of difficulties prevented a frictionless assimilation of the new technologies by these firms. The requisite capital expenditures for purchasing equipment and training personnel were only the beginning. Enormous interface problems—choosing the correct equipment, linking the machines together, and bringing them into a compatible software system—left small firms dependent on outside consultants. Finally, as the production apparatus became more thoroughly integrated, the risk that a single small problem would halt the entire operation grew proportionately.[147]

For smaller firms, these risks meant that piecemeal adoption of automated machines was far more feasible than full-scale computerization of the entire production process. BMFT officials had originally hoped that the Programm Fertigungstechnik would, by ameliorating the financial risk, encourage roughly 50 percent of the firms in the mechanical engineering industries to incorporate CAD in their operations.[148] In fact, studies showed that about 20 percent of the firms had adopted CAD by the end of 1986, while approximately 20 percent planned to do so in 1987. Moreover, the distribution of firms adopting CAD was heavily skewed toward those with over one hundred employees. Of all the computer aided technologies, only separate CNC machine tools had been adopted by more than half the firms in mechanical engineering by the end of 1986. Most problematic of all were the internal connections; through 1986, only 12 percent of the mechanical engineering firms had internal networks to link machining processes with any of the other preliminary design or subsequent inspection processes.[149] The evidence was strong that smaller firms were automating in small steps.

The policy debate over strategies for automation was paralleled by a broader discussion over the changing role of skilled labor in the production process. Some observers argued that automation would marginalize labor in general and skilled workers in particular. Other observers argued that continued automation was compatible with and in many ways dependent on broadened responsibilities and expanded autonomy for skilled workers. This debate was never resolved in the German context, partly because there seemed to be no single optimal strategy for firms in all market segments and competitive conditions.[150] In the machine tool industry, however, it was clear that the introduction of CNC products was accompanied by an increase in the already high proportion of skilled workers in the industry's total employment numbers (from roughly 70 percent in 1973 to 85 percent in 1983).[151] Although they no longer controlled machines through physical manipulation, skilled workers nonetheless remained responsible for loading work, overseeing machine operations, altering preprogrammed operations when necessary, and solving quality control problems before they were exacerbated by the automated equipment. This effect was even more pronounced in smaller firms that opted for the "islands of automation" suggested by the proponents of decentralized production.

The advantages of decentralized, stepwise automation could only be realized if skilled machinists were prepared to acquire the computer skills needed to operate CNC machines. Since the famous *dual System* for industrial apprenticeships could be adjusted only through arduous negotiation among the social partners, it was not likely to supply the needed personnel quickly. Trade classifications in electronics and metalworking had been under review for ten years. The new classifications and curricula would come into effect in August 1987. The seriousness of the negotiations is suggested by the precision of the curricula for new apprentices. For most machine tool operators, the new trades required at least eight weeks learning to use CNC programs and machines. Additional periods for training on traditional or CNC machines depended on the specialization in question: sixteen weeks for mill operators, eighteen weeks for lathe operators, and nineteen weeks for operators of grinding machines![152] Since these apprenticeships lasted three and a half years in all, they clearly could not fill the immediate need.

The *dual System* had, however, already provided a reservoir of skilled workers who were solidly prepared to gain additional skills through further training. By 1986, the management press was calling for intensified efforts to provide such further training. One machine tool builder, Deckel, established a CNC academy for other company trainers as well as for instructors at the professional and technical schools. A variety of other training efforts in electronically guided machines were mounted by the VDI, the trade union association (DGB), the chambers of commerce, and local technical academies.[153]

The skilled machinists quickly sought to consolidate their autonomy within the new technological environment. The key question was who would program the tools. The earliest machine tool software was APT (automatic programmed tool), a highly mathematical language developed in the United States for machining aircraft parts. Since APT and its derivatives required advanced mathematical or engineering skills, they left machinists subordinate to central programmers and work planners.[154] Machinists in Germany as in the United States preferred programming languages structured in dialog form that specified operations in terms of traditional machining language. This kind of programming, which enabled machinists to intervene in the instructions without calling on programmers from outside software houses, became known as shop-floor programming (*Werkstattprogrammierung*), as opposed to office programming (*Büroprogrammierung*).[155]

The machinists' quest for enhanced autonomy through shop-floor programming soon gained wider support. Many German managers and experts in work organization saw advantages in shop-floor programming once they learned more about the process of assimilating automated production technologies. For the same reasons that stepwise automation was more appropriate to many firms than fully integrated automation, shop-floor programming was often more appropriate than office programming. First, the APT-derived languages were very unwieldy for all but the most complex metal parts. Studies in the early 1980s, for instance, had shown that shop-floor programming was more economical for almost all lathing operations than central, office programming. Second, the more complex languages left smaller and medium-sized firms dependent on outside software houses, who were generally not interested in tailoring their advice to the particular needs of smaller customers.[156]

The importance of skilled machinists in the decentralized approach to automation fed back into the further development of CNC technology. By the mid-1980s, the main market for CNC machine tools consisted of precisely those small and medium-sized firms for whom the decentralized approach seemed best suited. As a result, many major machine tool producers sought to adapt their CNC units to shop-floor programming.

The impulse toward shop-floor programming gained public imprimatur when the BMFT supported an elaborate joint project (*Verbundprojekt*) for that purpose in 1984. Many actors in Germany's dense institutional landscape were brought together in this project. Research support was provided by the Fraunhofer Institute for Work and Organization (Stuttgart), the Institute for Machine Tools at the University of Stuttgart, and the Institute for Automation at the University of Bochum. Software expertise was provided by four of the independent software houses that had begun proliferating.[157] Perhaps most important, programming sequences for particular operations were contributed by many of the country's most famous machine tool builders: Gildemeister and Traub for lathe operations; Blueco-Technik-Bluemle, Bosch, and Werner und Kolb for milling; Alfred Hermann and Behrens for sheet metal processing. Finally, major mechanical engineering firms, MTU and Brown, Boveri, provided additional software and test capabilities.[158]

The joint project in shop-floor programming was but one of several ambitious efforts coordinated by the BMFT during these years. Other efforts in robot technology or high-speed milling were quite compatible with more centralized models of automated production. The joint project in shop-floor programming was nonetheless important because of the type of expertise it brought together with the goal of developing technologies that would meet workers' needs. The participating firms were among the most technically advanced in the world. They brought the best experience available in the industry to bear on software that was being tailored to the needs of skilled machinists, whose practical experience remained one of the main assets of the small and medium-sized firms. This was precisely the kind of effort that experts in the CFDT had recommended in France several years earlier. Yet the enthusiasm among French policymakers and industrialists for machines without operators meant that such recommendations fell on deaf ears.

Similar initiatives occurred at other major machine tool producers without public subsidy. Trumpf, one of the leaders in sophisticated sheet metal cutting machinery, initially bought controller technology from a major electronics firm, only to find that the controllers were widely rejected by the machinists at the small and medium-sized firms that purchased equipment for Trumpf. After engaging Robert Bosch to help develop new CNC units with the participation of eventual users, Trumpf was once again able to meet the needs of its smallest firms. Maho, a pioneer in automated production for drilling and milling machinery, also placed great emphasis on technology that was appropriate to shop-floor personnel. Maho's chief, Werner Babel, argued at the time that the American machine tool firms had lost their most important asset by dismissing a third of their skilled workers. For his firm's early CNC technology, Babel undertook joint design in consultation with other firms and experts from IG Metall.[159]

The drive to increase the qualification of skilled workers was a rational business option, but the availability of the option depended on Germany's permeable hierarchy of professional groups. Since skilled workers could expect further training and advancement, their ranks were filled by capable and engaged individuals who gained the confidence of their employers.[160] These patterns of openness and advancement in career structure could not be sustained only at one level of the professional hierarchy. Within organized labor, providing autonomy for skilled workers risked splitting the upper ranks of the shop floor from the semiskilled and unskilled workers who comprised 80 percent of IG Metall's membership. In addition, "qualification" could be a management tactic for eroding labor's influence over job descriptions and trade classifications. The union's response was to support the norm of opportunity at all levels of the hierarchy through a campaign for "life-long learning."[161] There was also no uniformity among business on the preferred type of qualification. Particularly among larger firms that employed unskilled and semiskilled labor, however, management accepted the norms of "lifelong learning."

As the personnel chief of Volkswagen put it, "A large company like Volkswagen must reflect the social environment in its employment structure. We can't take the top-grade people and just send the others back home. At VW there will be no relentless selection process of the kind the unions fear. Each employee must be able to trust that he will not simply be dropped during hard times. Only under this premise can we maintain the skilled worker as a business resource."[162] The form of qualification would be continually debated, but there was wide recognition that experience-based skills needed to be replenished in order to safeguard the range of options they had opened for German business.

Consequences

There is much evidence that public policy substantially reinforced the ability of Germany's machine tool sector to make significant changes in technology and competition. In 1983 and 1984, German machine tool builders effected a dramatic turnaround in sector-wide indicators. Aggregate production began to rise, and employment losses were largely stemmed. Moreover, German policy supported precisely those resources—public know-how and trained personnel—that appeared most important for firm-level adjustment. By avoiding a centralization of resources and decision-making power in the national capital, German policymakers also created new institutions that served as common resources for machine tool builders as well as for their customers in the larger metalworking industry.

The problem is to link these policy results to the aggregate turnaround in the industry through a detailed analysis of mechanisms. It is always difficult, perhaps impossible, to assess the effectiveness of policy with exactitude. There is always the argument that the German machine tool sector possessed such internal dynamism that it reversed its own decline and made public policymakers look good in the process. There were, however, a number of specific mechanisms that support a policy-based explanation for the sector's resilience in the 1980s.

The sector-wide indicators in the mid-1980s show a clear recovery among German machine tool builders. When world markets turned upward after 1984, German producers were able to expand production and regain much of the business they had lost (see Table 4). From 1983 to 1986, German production rose from US$3,193.5 million to US$5,185.4 million, while French production rose only nominally from US$560.1 million to US$588.1 million. More important, Germany's producers increased their share of world production from 16.68 percent

Table 4. Market value of metal-shaping tools produced by selected countries, 1981–1986 (millions of U.S. dollars)

Country	1981			1983			1985			1986		
	Value	%	Rank	Value	%	Rank	Value	%	Rank	Value	%	Rank
FRG	$3,953.4	15.08%	3	$3,193.5	16.68%	2	$3,168.4	14.75%	2	$5,185.4	18.42%	2
USA	5,111.3	19.50	1	2,044.9	10.68	4	2,717.8	12.65	4	2,747.9	9.76	4
USSR	2,932.3	11.19	4	3,076.9	16.07	3	3,035.8	14.13	3	3,672.0	13.04	3
Japan	4,797.1	18.30	2	3,541.8	18.50	1	5,316.6	24.75	1	6,872.6	24.41	1
UK	720.7	2.75	9	400.7	2.09		417.8	1.95	9	550.0	1.95	9
Italy	1,539.4	5.87	5	1,037.0	5.42	5	1,115.5	5.19	5	1,624.6	5.77	5
France	809.5	3.09	8	560.1	2.93	8	444.7	2.07	8	588.1	2.09	8
Switzerland	846.2	3.23	6	766.5	4.00	7	822.1	3.83	6	1,223.0	4.34	6
E. Germany	827.7	3.16	7	829.0	4.33	6	730.4	3.40	7	1,000.7	3.55	7
Sweden	210.9	0.80		142.8	0.75		161.4	0.75		236.7	0.84	
PR China	440.0	1.68		475.5[a]	2.48[a]		341.2	1.59		363.7[b]	1.29[b]	
Yugoslavia	276.7	1.06		231.0	1.21		239.2	1.11		390.4	1.39	
Brazil	305.0	1.16		98.1	0.51		265.0	1.23		370.0[b]	1.31[b]	
Romania	624.9	2.38		438.9[b]	2.29[b]		324.1	1.51		307.0[b]	1.09[b]	
Taiwan	249.4	0.95		211.0	1.10		276.2	1.29		356.7	1.27	
Total	$23,644.5	90.20%		$17,047.7	89.03%		$19,376.2	90.21%		$25,488.8	90.53%	
Other	2,565.0	9.79		2,099.5	10.97		2,103.9	9.79		2,665.9	9.47	
All countries	$26,209.5	99.99%		$19,147.2	100.00%		$21,480.1	100.00%		$28,154.7	100.00%	

[a] Unrevised figure.
[b] Estimated from fragmentary data.
SOURCES: National Machine Tool Builders Association, *Economic Handbook*, various years.

in 1983 to 18.42 percent in 1986, while France's share dropped from the already low figure of 2.93 percent to 2.09 percent over the same period.

The contrast is even more marked in employment. Both Germany and France shed employment steeply in the early 1980s. When the upturn came in 1984, however, German firms were able to respond efficaciously while French firms continued to shed employment even more rapidly than before (see Table 3). The German industry hit a low point in employment, 83,000, at the beginning of 1984. By 1986 it had regained 10,000 workers to total 93,000. In France, employment fell from 18,984 in 1981 to 15,502 in 1983. Its rapid descent continued, however, so that only 11,450 Frenchmen were employed in machine tools in 1986.

Sector demographics between 1975 and 1985 also suggest that German policy supported the sector's recovery. During these years, the number of German firms shrank 7.6 percent, from 460 firms to 425 (see Table 2). As in the French case, however, small size appeared to make firms more viable. In France, the clear dividing line in the data was 20 employees. Firms with fewer than 20 employees were the only category that increased in number from 1975 to 1985. In Germany, small firms with fewer than 50 employees dipped from 165 in 1975 to 155 in 1980, but then increased to 169 in 1985. The viability of the smaller firms is also reflected in the nearly constant number of firms with 51 to 100 employees. Firms in this category dropped from 81 in 1975 to 75 in 1980 before returning to 81 in 1985. For firms with more than 100 employees, however, the trend started downward, from 224 firms in 1975 to 220 in 1980, and then dropped steeply to 175 in 1985. Those firms that as a group appeared to recover well were precisely those whose needs were consciously addressed by public policy. Such data cannot prove beyond a doubt that policy was a positive factor in Germany, but they clearly contradict the view that policy was systematically hurting the sector.

Evidence of the participants' assessment comes from the further course of policy. In 1987, the Programm Fertigungstechnik was renewed for another five years. The official goal was to strengthen the enterprises' initiative so that they could promptly join "the process of future-oriented structural adjustment."[163] Officials apparently believed that the first program was successful but that more could be done. The first year of the extended program apparently did produce the "bandwagon effect" that BMFT officials had expected a few years earlier. Project administrators in Karlsruhe were flooded with applications, and funds available for indirect-specific measures were quickly oversubscribed.[164]

Statements of the larger machine tool producers indicate clearly that they also anticipated a bandwagon effect in their business. By late 1988 executives at these firms were anxiously advertising their commitment to technology designed for the skilled machinist. The vice president of Trumpf said his firm had seen explosive business in shop-floor programmable tools since 1983. The marketing director of Traub stated flatly that "only shop-floor programming processes have a future." The executive director at Gildemeister reported similar gains in sales of shop-floor programmable tools, and argued that they were leading to transformations in the hierarchy of many enterprises. The management press pronounced that CNC technology was making the human element "more central" in enterprise philosophy than ever.[165]

As in France, the patterns established in the 1970 and 1980s continued to characterize the way managers and policymakers responded to the turbulence of the 1990s. The cyclical downturn of the early 1990s prompted an investment decline that was severely amplified in the machine tool sector. Combined with renewed competition from Japanese producers in Europe, declining domestic demand drove German machine tool production down by 38 percent between 1991 and 1993. Large firms were not immune to the cutbacks. Maho and Deckel, two of Germany's best-known producers, merged in 1992 and were subsequently absorbed by Gildemeister. Even as the number of firms in the sector declined, the proportion of those with more than 500 employees declined from 20 percent in 1990 to 12 percent in 1993. During these years, German machine tool firms continued to emphasize custom and semicustom products. Firms such as Trumpf and Gildemeister began to produce their standardized tools abroad while retaining more knowledge-intensive parts of their production in Germany. As employment dropped to 70,000 in 1993, in industry leaders voiced growing concern about the loss of skilled workers.[166] When the German Machine Tool Association (VDW) and IG Metall jointly lobbied for state assistance, they asked not only for investment subsidies for their customers but also for permission to reduce working hours to continue in-plant training programs.[167] As in earlier decades, the industry's commitment to skill upgrading helped small and large firms weather cyclical downturns and rebuild capacity when demand returned.

These comparisons of French and German policy efforts to promote machine tool technologies illuminate the pivotal role of intermediary organizations for linking the administrative elites who formulated policy and the occupational groups responsible for implementing it. As argued elsewhere in this book, the quality of these links depends not only on formally prescribed organizational procedures, but also on the visions and convictions of the occupational groups that inhabit those organizations. In the machine tools sector, policy formulation was guided by the inherited outlook of central policymakers. Policy implementation depended heavily on the ability, or the willingness, of those policymakers to elicit the cooperation of sectoral elites with technical knowledge pertinent to the industry.

In France, policy discussion was guided by the predisposition of Parisian officials for centralized, state-led planning. This predisposition led to policies aimed at industrial concentration, investment, export promotion, and radical advances in technology through state-coordinated projects. If these ideational predispositions determined the way policy was formulated, however, they did not guarantee that it could be implemented. The several plans for machine tools represented typical cases of mission-oriented policy strategy. Yet in a sector where expertise was distributed in mostly small firms through a highly dispersed industrial structure, there was no clear way to implement such a strategy. The historical weakness of the mechanical engineering profession in France and the fragmentation of skilled workers in the labor movement meant there were no sectoral elites that Parisian policymakers could easily mobilize to provide information or assistance. Industrial restructuring through financial interventions was the only policy instrument that could be effectively exercised. Yet, as policymakers eventually observed, these financial interventions could by themselves do little to upgrade the technological levels that prevailed in the industry.

This account suggests that policy strategies are not likely to work if there are no organizational means to implement them. Yet, in the period analyzed here, French institutions showed every sign of reproducing a set of policies doomed to futility. Such a tendency toward self-reproducing policies requires interpretive as well as organizational explanation. Even when industry experts argued on the front page of *Le Monde* that concentration was not the solution for the machine tools sector, policymakers persisted in using their old recipes. Even when policymakers began to see that the lack of qualified personnel was a major obstacle to sectoral recovery, they continued to talk as if reductions in employment were an important policy achievement. Finally, despite the pockets of dynamism in the small-firm segment of the industry, policymakers persisted in their preference for dealing with larger enterprises. These tendencies are difficult to explain without reference to the highly rationalist approach to technology that prevailed among policymakers in Paris. The weakness of French mechanical engineers or skilled machinists may have prevented French policymakers from recruiting them as partners in the implementation of policy for machine tools. Yet, their understanding of technology as the logical unfolding of scientific knowledge also prevented Parisian policymakers from grasping the centrality of the more practically oriented professions or recognizing the importance of experience-based know-how in manufacturing industries.

This pattern of self-reproducing policies was not immutable. Indeed the apparent success of German educational institutions in the 1990s prompted efforts at explicit imitation in France. When Edith Cresson became Prime Minister in 1991, she prompted a high-profile effort to reform the French law on apprenticeships for skilled workers.[168] For technicians, the French government had already in the late 1970s established university-level departments (*institutes universitaires de technologie,* or IUTs) that provided two years of study beyond the baccalauréat. In 1991 the minister of education added twenty-five university-level departments for professional studies (*institutes universitaires professionelles,* or IUPs) that provided four years of study beyond the baccalauréat. The new IUPs, intended to train practical production engineers (*ingénieurs-maîtres),* were modeled explicitly on Germany's *Fachhochschulen.* Proponents hoped that graduates would immediately take operational responsibilities and be willing to "get their hands dirty"—in contrast, it was said, to the classically trained engineers from the grandes écoles. The new programs were, however, too late to help French machine tool producers amidst the crisis of the early 1990s. In 1993, moreover, expansion of the IUPs was limited by active resistance from the IUTs as well as the grandes écoles. By 1995, graduates of the IUPs were destined as much for the service sector as for manufacturing.[169]

In Germany, administrative and customary norms of consultation assured that policymakers would open the policy discussion to producer groups and academic experts. As a result, the debate between proponents of Strukturpolitik and Ordnungspolitik reflected the interests of the social groups favored by the different ministries in Bonn. The mixture of so-called indirect-specific measures and joint projects was clearly developed as a compromise between these two approaches to economic policy. The major difference from the French case, however, was that all the actors involved in formulating policy were able to help implement it. The extensive membership of the Association of German Engineers provided an ideal umbrella under which the Berlin Technologiezentrum implemented the first indirect-specific program. The Forschungskuratorium Maschinenbau was able to help policymakers in Bonn identify target groups for its key technologies with precision. And IG Metall provided an organizational conduit through which policymakers learned of the needs and capabilities of the skilled machinists, who became important figures in the assimilation of new production technologies.

As in the French case, however, the establishment of these organizational patterns cannot be explained without reference to shared visions and norms. The widely shared belief that important sources of competence lay outside the state played a crucial role. For it was this belief that enabled German policymakers to engage social interests in the process of policy formation without fear that they would capture policy and divert it toward their particular goals. Widespread acceptance of the VDI's competence in technical matters enabled the BMFT to involve industry and labor in policy formulation and to establish an independent agency for administering policies to promote the diffusion of microelectronics. Similarly, the important role of skilled machinists in the German case is difficult to explain from IG Metall's organizational clout alone. IG Metall's size and unity were a major factor in the union's political force, particularly when compared to the fragmented French labor organizations; yet many managers also supported the movement for more qualified machinists. In many cases, they were from small and medium sized firms, which required a stepwise path toward automation that could not be negotiated without highly skilled personnel. Yet this vision of automation—as a means of enhancing responsiveness to customer needs rather than reducing employment—was itself a choice. This choice was widely debated by the leaders of the Fraunhofer Society and widely discussed by the press in terms of power, autonomy, and even spirit.[170] Moreover, the goal of enhancing qualification received support from a variety of larger firms as well as public agencies. Once in place, a highly skilled industrial workforce became a collective good that served the interests of many actors. Yet, it was the widely shared recognition of experience-based knowledge that justified the social investment needed to create this public good and reproduce it from cohort to cohort.

The comparison of these cases from France and Germany illuminates the limits on state-led strategies for industrial innovation. action. It suggests that the structure of state agencies cannot explain the contours or the consequences of technology policy. State capacity does not result solely from the organizational resources within the direct control of public officials. It may also result from their ability to fashion policy strategies that can be implemented with societal resources. When the resource in question is technical knowledge distributed through small and medium-sized enterprises, the presence of highly concentrated state cadres may unexpectedly limit state capacity as much as bolster it. The answer turns on the ideational as well as the structural links among elites.

In the language of policy analysis, these two cases show that mission-oriented policy strategies do not work if professional gaps prevent public officials from mobilizing more broadly dispersed technical occupations. Given a broadly distributed pattern of technical expertise, diffusion-oriented policies are more likely to show results. The mission-oriented policies that worked so well in France's telecommunications sector were inadequate to mobilize or strengthen the more practical skill base that was essential to the machine tool sector. Conversely, the pattern of deliberate consultation with private-sector actors that limited the efforts of German officials to upgrade the country's telephone network proved to be quite well adapted to the challenges facing the machine tool industry.

CHAPTER FIVE

Searching for Industrial Sovereignty: Semiconductors

The policy challenge faced by French and Germany policymakers in promoting semiconductor technology went far deeper than the problems posed by the telecommunications or machine tool industries. Semiconductor devices, the basic components for microelectronics, opened new possibilities for transforming old industries and creating new ones. As a result, political leaders began to see semiconductors as part of a country's essential industrial base, having both military and commercial uses. Policy for semiconductor technology, therefore, became a major issue for public authorities in France and Germany during the 1970s. The interesting question is not simply why policymakers in these two countries tried to support their respective semiconductor producers, but why they did so in such different ways.

In both countries, officials sought to assemble the expertise involved in semiconductor design and production. In France, concern with semiconductor components grew out of the Plan Calcul, which was an attempt to launch a national computer industry. Starting in the mid 1970s, French officials prepared two successive Plans Composants. Technological self-sufficiency was a central objective of these policies. Both initiatives involved licensing technology from American firms, but the conditions of technology transfer were carefully monitored in bilateral discussions between French officials and each of the French firms. In Germany, the problem of computer technology was compounded by fears that legendary firms such as AEG, Grundig, Blaupunkt and Siemens were missing the microelectronics revolution in consumer and capital goods alike. Nonetheless full autarky in technology was less important in Germany than industrial vitality. The German government therefore left German firms freer to regulate their own technology transfer relationships with foreign firms. When the Bonn government did provide major funding for semiconductor development, it did so by requiring its main industrial partner, Siemens, to cooperate through a program known as Mega-Project with the Dutch firm Philips and later with other European companies as well. The result was a much more integrationist strategy in which public officials found it useful to make cross-national industrial cooperation a requirement for public support.

The implications of semiconductor technology for national sovereignty gave the semiconductor question great urgency. As a fundamentally new generic technology, semiconductor production represented a much larger technical leap than did the changes occurring in telecommunications and machine tools. As a result, part of the problem faced by French and German policymakers was that neither country had the technical expertise necessary to sustain large-scale commercial production. To be sure, both countries had first-rate solid-state physicists with the requisite scientific learning to make contributions in this field. Yet neither country had the combination of scientific knowledge and manufacturing expertise that was necessary for keeping pace in this industry. From the policy perspective therefore, the problem was not one of redeploying existing research resources but rather of importing new kinds of expertise from abroad, or generating it from scratch at home.

The observed differences in French and German approaches to semiconductors can be partly explained by the foreign policy objectives of the two countries. In France, the Gaullist objective of independence in world affairs put a high priority on access to important military technologies. For German officials however, autarky mattered less than industrial performance. Germany's position in the postwar world largely obviated the need for military self-sufficiency but made it essential that German industry remain competitive in an open world economy.

Yet the contours of policies for semiconductors cannot be explained by reference to foreign policy objectives alone. The challenge of the new technology involved more than importing specific types of scientific knowledge. It also required finding the organizational forms that would support continual progress in materials science and that would also enable firms to bring that knowledge into commercial products before it became obsolete. In order to participate in the evolving semiconductor industry, firms needed to build new organizational capabilities as much as master new knowledge.

This chapter argues that such a task does not fit easily into the categories of mission-oriented and diffusion-oriented policy. In tying new knowledge to evolving organizational forms, the policy task entailed deliberate experimentation with a range of organizational frameworks. This process of organizational experimentation is, like the other organizational challenges discussed in this book, informed by the outlooks and self-images of the professional groups involved. Because of France's order of state-created elites, French firms were not well equipped to link the high-powered scientific learning with the more practical manufacturing expertise which was necessary to enter this industry on their own. Yet the deductive outlook that characterized top French officials made them reluctant to accept the uncertainty that came with detailed collaboration between French and non-French development teams. Germany's order of state-certified professions made it far easier, by contrast, to assemble the scientific knowledge and technical production expertise that this industry required. Equally important, the ethos of qualification that characterized relations between administrative and technical elites in Germany engendered greater openness to policy experimentation, even if it meant cooperating with non-German firms.

THE ORGANIZATIONAL CHALLENGE

The organizational challenges posed by the semiconductor industry were defined by both the nature of the innovation itself and the changing competitive conditions that characterized the rapidly evolving industry. The initial development of semiconductor devices represented a qualitative advance over previous electronics technologies. The story of microelectronics began in 1947 and 1948, when scientists at Bell Laboratories developed the transistor, which used semiconducting materials such as germanium and silicon to produce an amplification effect with far less power than vacuum tubes required. Since the transistor was quickly recognized as an invention of fundamental significance, engineers and policymakers alike came to see this industry as one driven by radical innovation. Yet, as firms commercialized the new devices, they soon confronted a task more complex than a series of one-time breakthroughs. As engineers learned to combine several discrete electronic functions on a single "chip," or integrated circuit, they opened possibilities that posed a changing set of challenges for firms in the industry.[1]

Beginning in the early 1960s, the industry came to be characterized by its now-legendary increases in the density of the components that could be placed on a single silicon chip. As physicists and engineers learned more about the behavior of the silicon substrates, they moved from small-scale integration (ten components per circuit) to medium-scale integration (one hundred components per chip) until by the early 1970s they had learned to design and fabricate thousands of electronic components on a single integrated circuit (large-scale integration, LSI). The transition to LSI marked a fundamental turning point for the importance of semiconductors in the electronic equipment business. Once designers could pack electronics functions closely enough together, it was only a matter of time before someone perfected the circuitry that could perform most of the tasks of a computer on a single chip—data input, storage, processing, and output. Such a chip, or microprocessor, not only made the personal computer possible; it also enabled designers to place complex programs and subsystems inside all manner of products, from household appliances to machine tools to weapons-guidance systems. With LSI, integrated circuits became available for a "proliferating market of ever broadening applications."[2] While vastly increasing the market, however, LSI also imposed costly investments in new design and fabrication technologies. Since designers could no longer even hope to visualize LSI circuits, they developed special design tools known as CAD (computer aided design) packages. As LSI pushed forward the possibilities for digital signal processing, software writing came to play a major part in the design of components as well as final equipment goods.[3]

The steady increases in the density of electronic functions on a single integrated circuit gave the industry its relentless pace of change. Perhaps most important, the advent of the integrated circuit placed growing importance on the manufacturing process. As circuit densities increased, the requirements for materials and process equipment grew more exacting. Accordingly, the crucial tasks in this industry included not only designing the latest or smallest devices, but testing and improving the process technologies that produced them. Process improvements involved a combination of radical and incremental changes in the equipment that chipmakers used. Semiconductor production became an important case in which the dichotomy between radical and incremental innovation was not adequate to describe the challenge. As chip manufacturers came to rely on specialized suppliers for their manufacturing equipment, they had to learn how to combine these many types of equipment and materials to achieve a well-functioning process. These tasks introduced the challenge of so-called architectural innovation, which involved changing the relationship among separate elements in the manufacturing process.[4] The nature of architectural innovation posed quite specific organizational tasks for firms in the semiconductor industry, and for policymakers who sought to promote their innovation capabilities.

In the first instance, the importance of process technologies for semiconductor production meant that product designs had to be linked to specific manufacturing skills. Both France and Germany had their share of solid-state physicists who did research on the behavior of semiconducting materials. In order to link this research to the commercial tasks of chip design and production, however, managers had to ensure that the implications of this research reached their product development teams, manufacturing engineers, and quality control personnel. Once the microprocessor brought complex software to the level of single chips, all of these groups also needed a substantial understanding of the links between alternative circuit designs and their software requirements. In organizational terms, innovation was proceeding at such a rapid pace that a company could pursue its own development process only if these groups of technologists were in much closer contact with one another than had previously been necessary.

As the industry evolved, the demands of the architectural innovation in the chip manufacturing process extended from groups within a single firm to technical personnel in entirely different organizations. Once chipmakers could produce sophisticated devices for particular purposes, known as application-specific integrated circuits (ASICs), they needed to establish ongoing dialogs with their customers regarding the design and testing of new products. In some cases, sophisticated users or "lead customers" provided the impetus for important innovations in semiconductor technology.[5]

Another link between chipmakers and outside organizations became important in the 1980s. By this time, the requirements for manufacturing processes had become so demanding that chipmakers began to depend on a number of dedicated suppliers for the best performing manufacturing equipment. As circuit lines began to be measured in microns (thousandths of a millimeter), the many types of production equipment had to meet extremely demanding tolerances. The central piece of production equipment was the "stepper," which took silicon wafers through numerous steps of photolithography. Circuit lines were projected through masks onto the chip surface, to be "etched" into the silicon through a variety of ion implantation processes. In addition to the steppers, machines and materials for dozens of other parts of the

production process had to be properly attuned to the particular tolerances imposed by each new generation of semiconductor devices.[6]

Chip producers not only had to find individuals who had mastered
particular types of knowledge; they also had to find ways of coordinating
their contributions in designing semiconductor devices and perfecting
the production processes that would enable them to fulfill shifting market needs quickly. These tasks required a capacity for controlled organizational experimentation in which the links among established
occupational groups were central.

THE DISTRIBUTION OF EXPERTISE

In both France and Germany, the major obstacle to promoting semiconductor operations was the absence of people or organizations with
the combination of scientific knowledge and engineering expertise to
sustain a process of continually upgrading production lines. Part of the
problem was simply to promote training in those fields of expertise,
especially advanced production engineering, needed to build such production lines and to keep them up to date. A more difficult part of the
problem was rooted in the professional orders of the two countries.
Even when the specific types of expertise most relevant to a particular
technology were not abundantly available, established habits of consultation among technical occupations quickly came to govern patterns of
communication in emerging industries as well.

The distribution of specific expertise was in the first instance shaped
by the industrial structures that took hold in the semiconductor business.
Already in the 1950s, distinct patterns of industrial organization appeared among firms entering the industry in Europe, the United States,
and Japan.[7] In the United States, the new technology drew three types
of firms into the industry: equipment producers such as AT&T and
International Business Machines used semiconductor devices in their
own products; established firms such as General Electric, RCA, and
Sylvania recognized transistors as substitutes for the receiving tubes they
had used earlier in their products and moved into the new technologies.
Newcomers such as Fairchild, Texas Instruments, and Motorola entered
the business as specialized producers, or "merchant" firms, selling their
output on the open market.

In Europe and Japan, early efforts in chipmaking were led by established firms. In Europe, these were the older electrical conglomerates.
In Japan, they were the diversified electrical and machinery firms in

the postwar *keiretsu* groupings. Though these firms were well supported by their respective governments, they had never been organized to compete on a continually moving technological frontier. In neither case did conditions favor fast-moving merchant producers on the American model. Sources of venture capital were limited, and scientists seemed unwilling to risk their careers in such ventures. In addition, since American merchant firms had already assumed technological leadership in the industry, it was not easy for small European or Japanese producers to get started in the early years.

The early technological lead obtained by the Americans created a division of tasks in which the latest components were provided by the young American firms and were used for systems applications by the older European groups in electrical machinery.

In the late 1950s and early 1960s, as long as the business was dominated by transistors and other discrete devices, the European firms, particularly Philips of the Netherlands and Siemens of Germany, managed to retain leadership in their own markets.[8] As the prevailing scale of integration progressed, however, the European firms experienced longer lags in assimilating American-authored innovations. The American entrepreneurs gained economic rents through their technological monopoly—either in the form of licensing royalties or by selling directly to European customers—while the European firms used their knowledge of local markets and local needs to maintain their place in the larger equipment business as well as in specialty niches.

The geographical distribution of semiconductor production shows very clearly that European firms were following the lead of American and later Japanese concerns in introducing the new devices. In 1973, European facilities accounted for roughly 18 percent of total world semiconductor devices, but only 10 percent of the technologically more sophisticated integrated circuits. By 1984, Europe's shares had fallen to 8.3 percent of world semiconductor production and only 6 percent of IC production.[9] Moreover, of those semiconductor devices fabricated in Europe, a large portion were produced by subsidiaries of American firms, particularly Texas Instruments, Fairchild, and Motorola, which had built their own production plants in Europe in the mid 1960s.[10]

While European industries depended on the American merchant firms for the latest semiconductor devices, American technological leadership did not imply dominance over the entire electronics sector. As European firms steadily produced a smaller proportion of semiconductor components than their American and Japanese competitors, they were pushed increasingly into the business of manufacturing final equipment goods, for which Europe remained the world's second largest market. The introduction of microprocessors in the early 1970s enabled the American merchant firms (particularly Intel and Motorola) to extend their technological lead, but European firms promptly licensed the new technology and assimilated it into their product lines, thereby solidifying their position as systems vendors who incorporated the new microprocessor chips into electronic products for their traditional customers. As European firms fell behind in the race to develop and commercialize ever more advanced integrated circuits, they perfected their ability to assimilate the new components developed elsewhere into profitable end products.

While this emphasis on systems applications left many European companies with important markets, it did not necessarily please political authorities. From the viewpoint of public officials, profitability might be a sufficient goal at the level of the individual enterprise, but it could not satisfy countrywide goals that included security of supply, autarky, and long-term economic vitality. As the importance of microelectronics for industrial and military systems became evident, French and German policymakers faced a number of different options. The least tenable option was to do nothing and let the leading national firms fare as they might. The second option was to encourage the least costly path already adopted by many European firms; namely, to specialize in end-product applications. The third option involved protecting national markets through nontariff barriers and procurement preferences. And the fourth option was to fight the Americans head-to-head for technological leadership. In both France and Germany, there was a tendency to use a combination of different approaches. In each case, the inherited distribution of expertise gave policymakers a mix of resources and weaknesses as they responded to the challenges posed by competition in this new industry.

France

France's order of state-created elites was particularly ill-adapted to the needs of the semiconductor industry. This problem resulted more than anything else from the disjunction between the grandes écoles and other options open to French students for technical training. The deductive style of the polytechniciens did not prevail in all of the lesser known grandes écoles, but it was reflected in the overall preference of diploma holders for administrative rather than practical engineering roles.[11] In electronics as in other sectors, engineering careers in France showed a paradoxical pattern whereby those with the most rigorous training tended not to work as engineers, while those who lacked systematic training were promoted to engineering positions on the basis of seniority.

For the semiconductor industry, such a pattern was singularly problematic because of the high degree of scientific learning that had to be combined with practical engineering expertise in order to achieve success in the design and fabrication of microelectronic components. This problem became clear when the government commissioned a report on microelectronics in France from a leading software specialist in late 1979. The authors pointed out that only ten of the country's engineering schools were oriented toward electronics, and of them, only four had access to equipment which could provide their students with any practical familiarity in the design or fabrication of integrated circuits. The total cohort of graduates with such experience was ninety-five per year. The full gravity of the situation was only intimated by the report's numerous recommendations. The authors remarked on the unnecessarily theoretical education given to the product and production engineers who were needed to maintain fabrication facilities. They recommended more attention to practical experimentation, particularly in the physical chemistry of solids. They also pointed out that the scholarship committee of the Foreign Ministry had provided almost no opportunities for advanced students to study microelectronics abroad—partly because the committee had no members who could evaluate applicants in this field. Particularly for the elite or "polyvalent" schools—such as Polytechnique, Mines, and the Ecole Centrale—the authors suggested that more students be directed toward research and internships abroad.[12]

If the schools had largely failed to prepare specialists in semiconductor technologies, there was one institutional base that did foster expertise in semiconducting materials—the group of *grands organismes* for applied research. These special centers had played a major part in France's thrust toward independence in military technologies. Two of them— the Commissariat à l'Energie Atomique (CEA) and the Centre National d'Etudes de Télécommunications (CNET)—included units that concentrated a fair proportion of France's expertise in microelectronics. The Laboratoire d'Electronique et de Technologie de l'Informatique (LETI) in Grenoble was part of the CEA, while the Centre Norbert Segard (CNS), also in Grenoble, was part of the CNET. Each of these laboratories enjoyed a good deal of financial autonomy, and in the course of the 1980s, they each concluded technology transfer agreements with industrial enterprises.[13]

Based largely on the model of the other *grands organismes,* the LETI and the CNS were expected to provide technologies that the state could support through procurement— such as nuclear power plants, nuclear weapons, and space vehicles—as well as through research support. In microelectronics, however, where new knowledge in materials science had to be linked to a continuously moving frontier in production methods, the policy of concentrating scientific knowledge in applied research installations tended to insulate researchers instead of helping them orient their work to emerging commercial possibilities.

These patterns in the training and recruitment of technical personnel had far-reaching implications for the way French firms fared in semiconductors. The traditional reliance on in-house training for practical engineers greatly hampered French firms in sectors where technological change was so rapid. State-of-the-art expertise in semiconductors simply could not be transmitted from one generation to another on the basis of plant-specific knowledge alone. Supervisory personnel, with their "polyvalent" education, also had little chance to learn the basic elements of semiconductor production. French firms were not only limited to a terribly small supply of engineering graduates who possessed familiarity with semiconductor technologies; they also had a hierarchical organization that undermined their efforts to build upon the expertise that did exist among their employees. The result was that almost all factors of industrial organization and human resources militated against French efforts to develop an autonomous research program that could keep up with worldwide developments in semiconductor technologies.

Germany

German institutional resources were, like the French, far from well adapted to the needs of the semiconductor industry in 1970. Indeed, at first glance, the traditional strengths of the German technical community—precision engineering and mechanical ingenuity—seemed particularly inappropriate to the requirements of microelectronics technologies. The French, whose admiration for mathematics and abstract thought was so deeply rooted in institutions of secondary education, appeared to be in a far better position to take advantage of the new electronics technologies than their German counterparts. In fact, however, German educational institutions had certain features which allowed them considerably more flexibility in producing the kinds of technically trained personnel who could perform in a changing industrial world.

The absence of any German equivalent to the grandes écoles meant that there were fewer barriers to communication among scientists and engineers in Germany than in France. Solid-state physicists and materials engineers often attended the same universities in Munich, Stuttgart, Aachen, or Berlin. At the graduate level, they were also likely to follow developments in the same research community. To be sure, spokesmen for the semiconductor research community were not entirely satisfied with the supply of highly trained personnel available. In 1985, a report commissioned by the Ministry of Research and Technology said an additional 2500 research scientists and engineers were needed in order to pursue the many fields of research in the information industry.[14] The situation was, however, not so severe as in France. The major German technical institutions in Munich, Stuttgart, and Aachen could by 1985 each provide close to 100 graduates in semiconductor electronics per year. Additional students leaving smaller programs in Berlin, Darmstadt, Duisburg, Göttingen, Hannover, Karlsruhe, and Wuppertal would bring the total to roughly four times the number of French graduates with substantial training in semiconductor research or production.[15]

Another major difference between the German university system and the French grandes écoles resulted from Germany's regional administration of educational institutions. Whereas the grandes écoles were responsible to a national ministry and beholden to a homogeneous alumni body, German technical institutions and universities answered to the regional, Länder governments. There were long-standing relationships tying the curricula of the technical schools to the needs of local industry. For technology intensive sectors, the Länder governments also seized upon the universities as vehicles of regional economic competition. The two major regions for high-tech development, Baden-Württemberg and Bavaria, competed with one another to attract expertise as well as investment capital. In Bavaria, the Zentrum für angewandte Mikroelektronik (Center for Applied Microelectronics, Burghausen), financed by the *Land* and run by the universities, provided vocational training and retraining.[16] In Stuttgart, the Institute for Microelectronics was a more ambitious institution, with a world-known director and an expert staff of over fifty professionals who designed customized integrated circuits for small and medium-sized firms in Baden-Württemberg. Although the institute only got fully underway in November 1986, it relied on a network of regionally funded centers at technical schools which had existed within Baden-Württemberg for years.[17]

These local and regional relationships were reinforced by the national institutions of basic and applied research. Basic research was the mission of the Max Planck Society, which consisted of specialized laboratories in various cities. Although the separate Max Planck institutes were independent of the universities, their permanent researchers usually had close ties to university faculties and often recruited younger researchers directly from those universities. For the science of semiconductor materials, the Max Planck Institutes for Solid-State Research (*Festkörperforschung*) in Stuttgart and Plasma Physics (*Plasmaphysik*) in Munich were particularly important.

More directly significant for the semiconductor industry in Germany was the Fraunhofer Society, which paralleled the Max Planck Society in applied research.[18] The Fraunhofer Society was equipped and partly funded by the Ministry of Research in Bonn, but most of the individual institutes also relied on grants from regional governments and research contracts from local firms. In materials science, the Institute for Applied Solid-State Physics in Freiburg and the Institut for Solid-State Technology in Munich provided advanced training to the top graduates of neighboring universities and then sent them on to research careers or to positions in industry. By providing the regional labor supply, with relatively experienced specialists, the Fraunhofer Institutes effectively institutionalized the links between the universities and the major firms in the area. The Munich Institute in particular, which was closely linked to the Technical University, spawned several new Fraunhofer installations for solid-state research, including those in Erlangen and Berlin. These institutionalized relationships helped keep German firms well informed of new findings that could have influenced their business practices—both at the level of advanced, science-based technologies and at the level of incremental improvements in production methods.

As in France, the institutions for training and recruiting technical personnel in Germany had important implications for the capacity of individual firms to adjust to changing circumstances of the semiconductor industry. Most important, the country's best trained engineers were largely available for industry. They were not, as in France, skimmed off the top of each graduating cohort and recruited into administrative positions. Recruitment channels in Germany more typically led top engineering graduates from their institutions to the large industrial firms in the same region. In addition, the top engineers in Germany were better integrated into the production and maintenance operations of their companies than their counterparts in France.

For semiconductor operations, close cooperation among materials scientists, chip designers, and advanced production engineers was essential. Collegial relationships among these groups were made more possible by the large technical universities, particularly in Munich and Stuttgart, than at any of the grandes écoles. Within large electronics firms, including Siemens and Bosch, such links were maintained through the practice of rotating research scientists and engineers out of central R&D divisions and into product development groups which were attached to operating divisions.[19]

In both France and Germany, concern over manpower resources and policy efforts to encourage industrial development typically remained widely separate in the political arena. The social norms which underlay institutional arrangements for research and training only occasionally became visible topics of political debate. The resources that those institutional arrangements provided could only be altered over a long-term time horizon. Elected officials usually saw little political reward in attempting difficult institutional changes whose results were only likely to become apparent years later. Other instruments for technology promotion—large R&D grants, state-sponsored financial restructuring, government-to-government programs in technology cooperation, and strategic alliances among companies—frequently received more publicity than educational or manpower policies. When these kinds of instruments led to unambiguous policy failures, however, then the underlying capacities of the political order for reassessment and adjustment became more apparent. Precisely this kind of case was provided by French and Germany efforts over the last twenty-five years to promote domestic firms in the semiconductor industry.

POLICY FOR COMPUTERS

Political concerns about semiconductors only emerged gradually from both governments' experience with policy programs that supported domestic computer firms in the face of American competition. Well before the full range of semiconductor applications could be imagined, political authorities recognized the importance of computer technology for military as well as civil industrial uses. Particularly in France, national plans for computers were launched with great enthusiasm.[20] Through their largely unsuccessful efforts to support a viable national firm to compete with IBM in the 1960s and 1970s, officials in both countries began to see how important the components industry was and how inadequate their initial efforts to support it were.

169

France: The Plan Calcul

In the French case, misgivings over the computer industry appeared in the early sixties. The American presence in the French market was led by IBM, which manufactured over three-fifths of the computers sold in France. In 1964, the leading French computer maker, Compagnie des Machines Bull, encountered severe financial difficulties and ceded management control to General Electric—effectively putting another 20 percent of the French market in American hands.[21] The event that led to concerted intervention by the French state was the U.S. decision to bar the sale of two large Control Data computers to the French Commissariat à l'Energie Atomique in 1965. Since the French military wanted the machines for France's independent nuclear deterrent, the *force de frappe*, the American decision powerfully reinforced their argument for a fully independent computer capability. In July 1966, the French cabinet approved a plan by which the Compagnie Internationale pour l'Informatique (CII) would be formed by merging two existing French firms. The plan's strategic aims were aptly symbolized in 1967 when the new company took up residence outside Paris at the former NATO military headquarters in Louveciennes.[22]

From the outset, the new firm, CII, was expected to be the single French national champion in electronic data processing.[23] A second firm, Sperac, was formed to provide peripheral tapes and terminals. Initially, CII was to produce computers under license from the American firm, Scientific Data Resources, but the long term goal was an entirely French-designed and French-produced machine. This goal clearly necessitated a French supply of electronic components, and state aid of Fr 100 million was therefore allocated over five years to a third firm, COSEM, a subsidiary of CSF (Compagnie Générale de Télégraphie Sans Fils). During the first two years, 1966 and 1967, CII still expected to purchase about 30 percent of its components from subsidiaries of American firms, but in fact the components problem turned out to be one of the primary obstacles to genuine independence.[24] A major restructuring occurred in 1969 when two large electronics firms, Thomson and CSF, merged and combined their respective semiconductor subsidiaries, SESCO (Thomson) and COSEM (CSF), to form a new all-French chip producer, SESCOSEM. At the same time, the computer firm CII, which had been partially owned by CSF, now came under the control of the newly merged parent organization, Thomson-CSF. Remarkably enough, despite pressure from the state and from Thomson-CSF, the managers of CII still insisted on purchasing over half of their components from American firms because they could do so more economically than purchasing entirely from their sister firm SESCOSEM. It was particularly ironic that IBM, with its large French market share, proved to be a more important customer for SESCOSEM components than the French national champion firm, CII.

After 1971, when Intel Corporation introduced the microprocessor, French policymakers had even more trouble supporting a vital semiconductor producer that could make a national French computer independent of American innovations in integrated circuitry. The downturn in the semiconductor business of 1970–71 had hit all European firms including SESCOSEM particularly hard. In late 1971, the French Minister of Finance, Giscard d'Estaing, announced that Thomson-CSF would receive research aid of Fr 300 million over the next four years.[25] By this time, CII had managed to garner only 6 percent of the French computer market, mostly from government agencies and state-owned firms. The next five years displayed a pattern of ongoing state aid combined with increasingly intricate industrial machinations. The major French electronics firms maneuvered assiduously for state assistance, but none of them showed much desire to invest their own funds in electronic data processing.[26] These maneuvers reached a new configuration in 1976, when CII was merged with the old French firm Bull, in which GE's controlling interest had since been sold to the American firm, Honeywell. This type of constant financial restructuring did little to support an indigenous French semiconductor capability. Indeed, SESCOSEM made no investment in producing LSI microcircuits in the first half of the decade. Since the firm was not profitable, it was absorbed as an operational division of its parent, Thomson-CSF, in 1972.[27] Even so, its share of the French components market declined from roughly 20 percent in 1968 to 16 percent in 1978, while the share of the sophisticated microprocessor producers, Motorola and Intel, was on the upswing.[28]

Germany: The Data Processing Programs

In Germany, anxieties about data processing (*Datenverarbeitung*) also began to appear in the early 1960s. From the outset, public attention focused on the computer's implications for industrial performance and employment rather than on its consequences for military autarky.[29] German know-how in computing machines extended back to the work that Konrad Zuse had done before the Second World War, and additional work on digital techniques had been undertaken in the 1950s by AEG and Brown, Boveri and Company (BBC). Despite these early efforts, a

171

market study conducted by John Diebold showed that IBM accounted for over 60 percent of the machines installed or ordered in the Federal Republic by 1964, while German producers (Siemens, AEG, SEL, Zuse) together accounted for only 11 percent.[30]

From the very beginning, experts outside the state administration took more initiative in setting the terms of the policy discussion than did nonstate actors in France. Ministerial level discussions began in August 1965 on the basis of the Diebold study and a joint memorandum prepared by Siemens and AEG-Telefunken.[31] The memorandum from Siemens and AEG showed that the German proposal differed significantly from the national-champion strategy which had guided French deliberations.[32] The two industrial firms proposed a partnership (*Arbeitsgemeinschaft*) with the relevant government bureaus, for the purpose of conducting research and development in the field of electronic calculators. Beginning in August 1965 discussions began between the Ministry of Scientific Research and the Ministry of Defense and were then extended to include eight other departments. After further consideration by an expert advisory committee (*DV-Fachbeirat*), the resulting program was redrafted and released by the Federal Cabinet in March 1967.[33]

The implementation of the Data Processing Program showed further how it differed from the national-champion strategy embodied in the French Plan Calcul. Instead of merging existing firms into a single, new enterprise under state tutelage as the French had done, policymakers in Bonn relied on the existing industrial firms. Siemens and AEG-Telefunken received the lion's share of the funding (respectively, DM995 million and DM295 million over fifteen years) to finance independent development programs.[34] Four other firms—CGK (Computer Gesellschaft Konstanz), Nixdorf, Keinzle, and Philips—received over DM50 million each and another six received over DM10 million each. Moreover, the commercial strategies of the firms showed that technological independence was not as high a priority for the German program as was functional performance and market success. Indeed, data processing may be the first field where Siemens displayed what one commentator has called the strategy of the fast runner-up.[35] By licensing a computer design from RCA and contenting itself largely with market development through 1970, Siemens developed its capabilities more gradually but perhaps more steadily then the French national champion CII.[36] After RCA abandoned its commitment in computers in the early 1970s, Siemens started to market IBM compatible mainframes made by the Japanese firm, Fujitsu.

Although technological autarky did not have the same priority in Germany as in the French Plan Calcul, neither the firms nor the government wanted to ignore component technologies which promised wide applications for the future. Thus, the second five-year Data Processing Program (1971–1975) included funds for research on the new MOS semiconductors,[37] and the third funding period (1976–1979) designated funds for AEG to work on LSI components for high-speed computers.[38] Aside from the Data Processing Programs, the Federal Ministry for Research and Technology also began funding generic research in advanced components in the early 1970s. In 1972, Siemens received a three-year bloc grant of DM26 million to subsidize semiconductor research in general, and a year later the firm obtained an additional four-year grant of DM3.539 million specifically for LSI devices in MOS. Further funds for work on MOS circuits were allocated to AEG, Bosch, and other firms.[39]

In 1974, the Technology Ministry expanded its interest in electronic components by launching Europe's first coordinated program for integrated circuits. The program had little direct connection to the priorities of the Data Processing Programs, but rather supported the development of a semiconductor capability for its own sake. With funding of DM376 million, the effort was to extend over five years (1974 through 1978).[40] Siemens received specific grants to develop MOS memory chips as well as a family of high-speed chips in complimentary-MOS (CMOS). AEG, meanwhile, received specific funds for the computer-aided-design tools needed to support design of the increasingly complex components. Although the Technology Ministry supported work on technologies which promised foreseeable commercial applications, it also continued to fund research on more esoteric materials, such as gallium arsenide devices, whose market in the 1970s was minuscule compared to the market for silicon devices.[41]

Even while the ministry in Bonn encouraged firms to cultivate their internal semiconductor capabilities, these firms continued to go to outside sources for many of their commercial components. The ministry imposed no apparent restrictions on foreign-sourced components being used in products that were funded through the Data Processing Program. During the early 1970s, several of the German firms worked hard to accumulate know-how by combining their own research efforts with technology licensed from abroad. Owing mostly to their strengths in industrial electronics and discrete semiconductors (as opposed to integrated circuits), both Siemens and AEG-Telefunken already had semiconductor revenues of approximately $50 million each in 1973.[42] As in

France, firms in Germany refrained from any substantial commitment to commercial production of LSI devices until the second half of the 1970s. When microprocessors began to transform the microelectronics business in the 1970s, however, the German firms did not hesitate to go to the Americans for the new technology. For example, Siemens obtained public grants of almost DM12 million for microprocessor research in 1975, but the firm ensured its own access to commercial microprocessors by licensing Intel's 8080 chip in the same year. Similarly, AEG-Telefunken arranged to produce a Rockwell processor under license, and Nixdorf contracted to buy its microprocessors from Nitron, a subsidiary of McDonnell Douglas.[43]

The German openness to foreign-sourced technologies also made direct investment in the United States a logical method of keeping pace with state-of-the-art circuits. Already in 1974, Siemens bought the small American company, Dickson. Direct investment became even more attractive in 1975 when the Dutch giant, Philips, purchased Signetics outright. In 1977 Siemens bought another American semiconductor company Litronix and also purchased a 20 percent stake in one of the fastest growing American merchant houses, Advanced Micro Devices.[44] Meanwhile, the German specialist in automotive electronics, Bosch, purchased a 25 percent stake in American Microsystems to facilitate joint development of new semiconductor materials, particularly MOS devices, and within a few years was producing many of the specialized circuits it needed for its own products.[45]

Whatever their results in microelectronic components, both French and German policymakers were obliged by the end of their computer plans in 1976 and 1979 to acknowledge the limits of their success. For France, the continuing lack of technological autonomy—which was symbolized most clearly by the merger in 1976 of the national champion, CII, with the mixed French-American firm Honeywell-Bull—clearly signified policy failure. The Nora-Minc Report, commissioned by the government in the mid 1970s, expressed explicitly France's renewed desire to become the third world power in electronics, after the United States and Japan.[46]

In Germany, despite substantial investments in knowledge of advanced components, the major firms had never attempted to achieve full autarky. The problem for German policymakers was a persistent series of cases where the largest recipient of state aid, Siemens, proved unable to supply satisfactory computers. By the late 1970s, Siemens had not developed its own mainframe model and the firm continued to market a Fujitsu machine for the top of its line. Further doubts were raised about the company's computer capability when it announced in early 1981—after five years of development work—that it was scaling back an ambitious computer control system for the national railway.[47] Along with its experience in semi-electronic telephone exchanges, the company's experience in the computer plan showed that the Siemens designers had not fully mastered the latest semiconductor devices. Whether they developed the components in-house or licensed them from external sources, German firms were no better prepared than their French counterparts to incorporate the chip technology they needed for their larger systems products.

POLICY FOR COMPONENTS

In devising further policies to support their semiconductor firms in the late 1970s and 1980s, officials in Paris and Bonn showed quite different abilities to learn from the lessons of the earlier computer plans. For the French, the main lesson of the computer experience was that French firms needed ongoing access to state-of-the-art technology, even if it meant developing closer ties to the leading non-French firms. Unfortunately, the view that technological applications could be deduced from correct principles prevented French policymakers, especially those in the military, from embracing this lesson with great enthusiasm. When they began to accept it, there remained great pressure to monitor technical licensing agreements at the highest political levels. From their attempt to promote German computer manufacturers, German policymakers began to aim at persuading firms to expand their semiconductor research in closer connection with their overall commercial strategies. Rather than monitoring their industrial partners directly, however, German policymakers found ways to share the risks of R&D with a number of industrial partners while encouraging the firms themselves to monitor one another.

France

In France discussion of renewed funding for microelectronic components first reached the political arena in the spring of 1976. Prompted by the minister of the Post and Telecommunications Service (PTT), an interministerial committee outlined a plan to encourage French firms to propose credible strategies in integrated circuits and microprocessors. Formulated under ascendance of Giscard d'Estaing's liberal concept of industrial redeployment (*redéploiement industriel*) the Plan Composants assumed that French firms would fit their strategies to the opportunities offered by the world economy. It quickly became clear that the state wanted to encourage international technology transfer agreements of precisely the kind that French firms had thus far avoided. Although German firms had begun looking for American technology in integrated circuits several years previously, the French firms only started searching abroad for new technology in May 1977, when the state approved Fr 600 million for the purpose.[48]

In a significant modification of the national champion philosophy that had typified the Plan Calcul and the other grands projets, the Plan Composants was to provide inducements to more than a single firm. Over the next two years, five separate agreements were concluded, four with French firms and one with the French subsidiary of Philips. The competitive dynamic was presumably designed to dissuade firms from using more public investment funds than could be justified by the likely commercial returns. A fascinating interplay between the firms and the state arose as each ministry sought to have firms adopt strategies that would support its particular mission.[49] The PTT, for example, favored at least some foreign production in France, so that the PTT and its equipment suppliers (especially CGE, the Compagnie Générale d'Electricité) would not be wholly dependent on French suppliers for integrated circuits. The Ministry of Defense was equally interested in state-of-the-art circuits, but preferred to obtain them through licensing agreements which would make the foreign technology available to dependable French companies, preferably to Thomson, the largest French supplier of defense electronics. Although the Directorate of Electronic Industries (DIELE) in the Ministry of Industry administered the funding, the most knowledgeable members of the interministerial coordinating committee were usually from the Ministry of Defense.[50] In particular, the *Sous-Chargé* for components in the DIELI was traditionally chosen from the elite engineers of the Corps d'Armements—which effectively guaranteed that defense priorities would get a full hearing in the Ministry of Industry. The regional development agency, DATAR, added to the complexity by providing funds to firms which would locate production facilities in poorer regions.

Only in 1978, when interministerial bargaining reached a plateau, could the firms finalize contracts to receive public funds in exchange for bringing certain technologies into France.[51] In keeping with the interests of the different ministries, each of the five agreements was intended to serve a different purpose.[52]

In April 1978, the Philips subsidiary Radiotechnique-Compelec (RTC) signed an agreement to provide bipolar integrated circuits intended for use in computers and computer equipment. RTC agreed to provide customized components for CII-Honeywell-Bull and was designated by its parent, Philips, to become a specialized European fabrication center for certain other components.[53] In exchange, the firm was to receive Fr 100 million over five years.

In a second agreement, Thomson-CSF's semiconductor division, Thomson Composants (still sometimes known by its old name, SESCO-SEM), received a commitment for Fr 100 million over five years to support its own efforts in bipolar circuits. These components, intended for consumer electronics, were to be based upon technology provided by the American firm, Motorola.

The third agreement, between Thomson-CSF and Motorola, created a new firm, EFCIS, to be held half by Thomson-CSF and half by the French Commissariat for Atomic Studies. Under this accord, EFCIS was to establish production facilities near Grenoble for a variety of MOS circuits, which were quickly becoming the fastest growing product lines in the semiconductor industry. In order to gain mastery of this important branch of semiconductor technology, EFCIS would receive technical assistance and process technology from Motorola.[54] Motorola received an undisclosed amount, presumably drawn from the grant of Fr 200 million that EFCIS was to receive from the state, while the two French parent houses, Thomson-CSF and the Commissariat for Atomic Studies, each agreed to invest Fr 108 Million in EFCIS over five years.

The fourth agreement enabled the well-known glassmaker Saint-Gobain-Pont-à-Mousson to enter the microelectronics sector. Saint-Gobain was to receive Fr 200 million from DATAR to establish a joint venture with the American firm National Semiconductor for the production of MOS circuits. Saint-Gobain was to invest Fr 300 million of its own, while National Semiconductor would obtain a 49 percent equity stake for its know-how (valued at approximately Fr 100 million) in MOS technology. This accord grew out of the inability of the large component users CII-Honeywell Bull and CGE to develop their own agreement regarding MOS components[55]—allowing the widely respected industrial firm, Saint-Gobain, to step into the breach. The new joint venture, to be called Eurotechnique, was to set up production in Rousset, near Aix-en-Provence.

The fifth agreement supported the aeronautics and ordnance specialist Marta in establishing a joint venture with the U.S. firm Harris in CMOS circuits.[56] Matra was to invest Fr 80 million while the state would provide Fr 120 million in a combination of direct subsidies and loans. Public financing came, again, from DATAR, which required Matra to locate its production facilities near Nantes. In exchange for licensing its design technology and providing production processes (valued at approximately Fr 48 million), Harris was to receive a 49 percent equity stake and take a role in managing the new firm, to be called Matra-Harris-Semiconductors, or MHS.

The last two agreements illuminated the new government's efforts to temper the older, coordinated policies centered around national champions. This centrally coordinated approach—evident in French programs for nuclear power, aerospace, and defense electronics—had also provided the initial incentive for Thomson-CSF to invest in its semiconductor subsidiary, SESCOSEM. Since Thomson-CSF was capable of moving without warning into telecommunications, computers, or additional markets in defense electronics, France's other major electronics firms wanted alternative suppliers for their semiconductor needs. Such firms—most notably CGE and CII-Honeywell-Bull—found that their interests suddenly coincided with the Giscard government's desire to inject more competition into the French semiconductor industry. It was no accident that these firms supported the new activities of RTC, Saint-Gobain, and Matra in the French semiconductor business.[57]

Once the Socialist party came into power, the electronics sector again became a focal point for an ambitious program of economic modernization. The notion of the economic *filière*—a vertically coordinated group of producers whose output ranged from capital goods and components to consumer products—became one of the guiding concepts for industrial policy. Public policy for semiconductor components was henceforth incorporated within the integrated plan for the electronics sector, the *programme d'action en filière électronique,* which became a major Socialist policy showcase.[58] Under this program, the Socialists effectively replaced the previous government's liberal policy of promoting competition with something closer to the national-champion strategy of the pre-Giscard period.[59]

In line with the new policy, the government forced Saint-Gobain to transfer its assets in microelectronics to the designated electronics leader, Thomson. A full return to the national-champion strategy was neither possible nor desirable, however, because Matra had strengthened its position in components very quickly. In late 1980, Matra had agreed with its American partner, Harris, to expand its joint products from CMOS chips to include bipolar chips. Shortly thereafter, Matra and Intel, the American microprocessor leader, began talks that eventually led to three types of cooperation. First, Matra's semiconductor subsidiary, MHS, participated in an agreement by which Harris would convert several advanced Intel circuit designs in NMOS technology to the CMOS technology in which Harris specialized. Second, MHS obtained an agreement directly with Intel to produce Intel NMOS microprocessors in Nantes for sales worldwide. Third, MHS and Intel agreed to establish a joint venture—to be called CIMATEL—to provide special design and support services for devices tailored to European markets, particularly in automotive electronics and telecommunications.[60]

Although the agreements between MHS and Intel were recognized as major additions to the technology base available within France, they disrupted any hopes among French policymakers for coordinated allocation of the country's markets. Matra's president, Jean-Luc Lagardère, was a well-known maverick in French business and his firm was regarded cautiously by other industrialists. By expanding into the market for bipolar circuits, MHS had already signalled its intention to compete with RTC and Thomson Composants. Now, by concluding an agreement with one of the world's leading NMOS producers, MHS also threatened to make incursions into the markets that were to be the preserve of Eurotechnique. Well aware of Intel's reputation for dynamism, the Ministry of Industry at one point suggested that the American firm invest $40 million to gain access to the French market—an entry fee which Intel steadfastly refused to pay.[61]

Within a few years, MHS established itself as an important supplier of telecommunications and other components. Although the Socialist government recognized MHS's performance in semiconductors, Matra was clearly an outsider in the government's plans for the electronics sector.[62] Neither MHS nor its parent, Matra, received any of the major capital infusions that the Socialist ministries made available to Thomson and Machines Bull (also nationalized) in 1983 and 1984.[63] From the viewpoint of the Defense Ministry, the problem with MHS was precisely the fluidity of its technology-sharing arrangements with Harris and Intel, combined with the uncertainty of its ownership. Matra held a controlling interest in MHS, but because Matra was itself only 50 percent nationalized, the military could never be certain of controlling the semiconductor subsidiary.

The reticence of the French defense establishment toward Matra's semiconductor activities demonstrated the obstacles in the way of French firms' efforts to bring outside talent and resources to the country's technology base. There was no lack of awareness in policy circles of the need for more engineering talent. At least in rhetoric, research and training were high among the priorities of the Socialist government's Plan Filière. An official in the Ministry of Research and Industry said that the entire sector needed eleven hundred additional engineers per year and asserted, "Education is one of the main bottlenecks in the industry."[64] In their efforts to implement the Plan Composants, the semiconductor producers alone reported a shortfall of 1,500 fully trained engineers, including 500 highly sought-after specialists in integrated circuits. Three and a half years later, industry sources estimated the demand for semiconductor engineers at over 2,500—nine times the supply.[65] Given the priority of technological autarky in France's defense policy, it was hardly surprising that the Ministry of Defense hesitated to make its equipment dependent on technology that Matra had licensed from American firms. Nonetheless, blanket resistance to MHS products clearly militated against opening the French semiconductor industry more widely to foreign technology sources. Indeed, this was a case where the pursuit of technological autonomy by a mission-oriented agency undercut the wider diffusion of precisely that resource—expert manpower—which would have enhanced France's technological independence in the longer term.

The state's main entrant in the components field—and the French military's primary supplier for defense electronics—was Thomson. Under the Minister for Research and Industry, Jean-Pierre Chevènement, Thomson was to lead the "reconquest of the internal market" and to project France's export capability abroad. Toward this end, Thomson adopted a mass-production strategy which was intended to gain 3 percent of the world semiconductor market by 1990, but which would also require huge investments from the firm's new shareholder, the French state. The components division accounted for a substantial portion of the state's capital grants, which totalled approximately Fr 1.5 billion for 1983 and 1984 combined, and reached Fr 1.7 billion in 1985. At that point, the firm made known its view that continuing investments of roughly Fr 1 billion per year would be needed to realize its plan of garnering 3 percent of the world semiconductor market by 1990. The company extended its agreement with Motorola in 1984 in order to assure access to the upcoming generation of 32-bit microprocessors and signed an additional licensing agreement with the Japanese firm, Oki, in order to obtain certain additional CMOS technologies.[66]

Despite its magnitude, the state's support for Thomson did not appear to strengthen the country's technological base any more than Matra's strategy of establishing full, joint ventures with foreign partners. Thomson ran substantial deficits on semiconductors in 1982 and 1983, as it was absorbing the operations of Eurotechnique, but it also continued to lose on components in 1985 when the rest of the firm turned a net profit.[67] Intent as ever on the advantages of scale, French officials underwrote Thomson's efforts to expand market share as much as to build in-house capabilities. French officials applied an approach familiar from the machine tool sector when they approved Thomson's acquisition of the former U.S. technology leader, Mostek, which was by 1985 in severe financial straits. The Mostek acquisition helped Thomson eclipse Siemens in the European market for integrated circuits in 1986, but it appeared to be a one-time gain rather than a lasting improvement in Thomson's in-house technology base. Over 90 percent of Thomson's R&D continued to occur in the operational branches, which were dominated by the division for defense electronics. Thomson's continuing difficulties in securing expertise for integrated circuits also became clear in 1986, when the firm reported that it had gone to Italy, the UK, and Portugal to recruit semiconductor engineers.[68]

Subsequent events revealed the underlying logic of France's official policy. By underwriting market share and requiring public approval for Thomson's technology strategy, French policymakers undermined precisely those organizational processes by which Thomson managers might have identified market opportunities that would reinforce the firm's existing technology resources. Ironically, by aiming at more technological self-sufficiency than appeared realistic by the mid-1980s, French policy perpetuated Thomson's dependence on foreign sources of expertise. In April 1987, Thomson's president, Alain Gomez, made the astonishing announcement that Thomson was merging its nonmilitary semiconductor operations with an Italian firm, Società Generale Semiconduttori (SGS).[69] The agreement was justified on the grounds of a worldwide rationalization in the industry and the need to achieve 3 percent of the worldwide market. Based on an even 50–50 equity participation between Thomson and SGS, the agreement indicated unprecedented acceptance of the view that international market share was important enough to justify dilution of national control.

Germany

In Germany as in France, the early 1980s witnessed major policy efforts to reinforce industrial levels in advanced components. Because German firms had already developed extensive agreements for acquiring technology from abroad, German policymakers could concentrate on ways of prompting German firms to develop their know-how and integrate it

into their commercial activities. Unlike France, where the major enterprises had neglected developments abroad in the 1970s, the problem
in Germany seemed to be that the major firms had become too good
at adapting foreign technologies and too cautious about launching their
own development programs. By the early 1980s, the German press took
Siemens to task for adopting a "banker's mentality" and letting others
do the experimenting.[70] The dilemma faced by policymakers was therefore to push industrial firms to maintain mutually beneficial links with
the best foreign producers, but not to purchase those technologies which
the country's larger interests suggested should be developed
domestically.

Officials in Bonn adopted an integrationist strategy by inducing Siemens to develop a cooperative research program with the only larger
European-based semiconductor firm, Philips, of the Netherlands. The
program had a very specific goal: to leapfrog into the market for the
next generation of memory circuits—the so-called megabit chip—which
would store over one million bits of information. The cooperation with
Philips had two parts. First, the total subsidy offered by the Ministry for
Research and Technology in Bonn was split between Siemens (to receive
about DM 243 million over several years) and Valvo, the Philips subsidiary
in Germany (to receive about DM 77 million). Second, the Dutch government itself agreed to contribute approximately DM 160 million directly
for research done by Philips at its main research center in Eindhoven.
The firms themselves planned to invest roughly twice as much as their
respective governments for the research, and additional funds for the
associated fabrication facilities.

The initiative for this unusual arrangement came in large part from
the Technology Ministry in Bonn. It was clear that Siemens would invest
in semiconductor technology with or without the ministry's support,
though the firm might not have located production facilities within the
Federal Republic.[71] Part of the ministry's concern stemmed from a visit
to Japan in June 1982 by a Ministry official, Uwe Thomas, and Professor
Ingolf Ruge of Munich's Technical University to observe Japanese semiconductor firms.[72] They concluded that innovations leading to ever
smaller and more complex chips threatened to leave Germany's industrial plant thoroughly outmoded.

The Japanese example provided a rationale for public funding to
promote semiconductor development. As Germany's largest electronics
concern, Siemens was the natural candidate for any large-scale funding.
Yet the Technology Ministry needed a mechanism to make sure that
any publicly funded research done by Siemens would remain competitive

at world standards in this volatile and rapidly changing sector. The joint venture with Philips had several advantages from the policymakers' point of view. First, it provided a powerful incentive to Siemens to develop expertise in very advanced submicron technologies and to develop that expertise inside Germany. Second, by insisting on cooperation with a non-German firm, the program simultaneously forced Siemens to keep abreast of important technologies outside Germany. In practical terms, since the firms were required to send their research teams on reciprocal visits to one another's labs, the program provided an external reference point for each firm, which amounted to a built-in monitoring mechanism that also helped the government assess each firm's progress. Third, the competitive relationship between Siemens and Philips forced each firm to keep its research focused on commercial applications.[73]

Glimpses of earlier policy problems nonetheless arose when Siemens realized it had been too sanguine about the pace of the competition. Originally, Siemens had aimed at producing a 1-megabit DRAM chip by late 1986 and a 4-megabit DRAM chip in 1989, while Philips had planned to produce a 1-megabit version of the more complex SRAM in late 1988.[74] In mid 1985, however, the Japanese firms NEC and Toshiba were distributing samples of their own megabit DRAMs. Siemens realized that its own development teams were not keeping pace.[75] Without consulting its supporters in Bonn,[76] Siemens announced an extensive licensing deal with Toshiba. Siemens paid an undisclosed sum in exchange for design, testing, and production data on Toshiba's 1-megabit DRAM, which Siemens expected to start producing in Germany in 1986. The deal infuriated the Megaproject's critics, who claimed that Siemens was only using public funds to buy foreign technology[77]—which, for better or worse, was exactly what the French state had been cajoling its major firms to do only a few years earlier.

The controversy over the Toshiba agreement was significant because it revealed the delicacy of the promotional tasks in such a quickly moving industry. The BMFT had little choice but to work with Siemens on a project of this magnitude. Yet Siemens had little choice but to maintain access to current technologies for its commercial divisions, even in areas where it received substantial public subsidies.[78] The Ministry of Research and Technology was only willing to continue funding the Megaproject after hearing from an international advisory group specially convened to reassess the program.[79] The Toshiba deal also prompted a significant change in Siemens's statements about the project. Instead of espousing the notion that Siemens and Philips would leapfrog their way into the competitive markets for commodity chips, Siemens spokesmen now argued that the public research program would be a learning platform for developing the new generations of logic chips necessary for systems applications in telecommunications and factory automation.[80] As circuit densities increased relentlessly, however, even systems specialists needed a staggering concentration of in-house expertise in the new VLSI technologies. The head of Siemens components division explained his view of the Megaproject by saying, "If you accept the slogan that the system is the chip, . . . this is the only response to the challenge."[81]

While Siemens hardly had a trouble-free entry into the realm of VLSI components, later events nonetheless suggest that the firm's basic strategy for development of semiconductor technology was working.[82] By 1985, Siemens had developed a major commitment to strengthening its own expertise in very-large-scale-integration devices. Despite some delays in commercial shipments of the megabit memory chip, the firm was making demonstrable progress on the next generation of 4-megabit chips. By the beginning of 1988, Siemens started mass-producing 1-megabit memory chips in Regensburg. Although still lagging its Japanese competitors, Siemens had achieved a foothold in precisely the same market from which American firms had been dislodged by Japanese competitors. Until the Korean firm Samsung provided another alternative supplier, Siemens was the only non-Japanese producer selling DRAMs on the open market.[83] The firm had secured its foundation for participating in a new range of research collaborations in the 1990s. Equally important, through a combination of in-house development and external licensing, Siemens had established sufficient capability in the all-important manufacturing processes it needed for the broad range of application-specific chips it wanted to sell.[84]

From the viewpoint of policymakers in Bonn, the Siemens efforts were part of a larger policy objective of promoting technological capabilities throughout the economy. Individual firms in Germany therefore did not face the stark choice confronted by their counterparts in France between cooperating with state strategies or becoming outsiders. In the semiconductor sector, the Megaproject was the single most important R&D effort in the Federal Republic. There were several other cases where very significant technological capabilities were achieved. In a cooperative research project (*Verbundprojekt*) of the kind used in the machine building sector, Siemens joined efforts with Telefunken, the Fraunhofer Institute, and a number of small firms in order to perfect prototypes for a process known as X-ray lithography. This technique was then believed to be the most promising method of producing chips so small that the circuit lines became too narrow to be etched with normal light waves. By 1987, German teams in Berlin had reported orders of precision clearly superior to their nearest competitors in the United States and Japan.[85] The broader range of technology promotion with which the German government supplemented the Megaproject helped prepare a large number of firms and institutes to contribute to the industry's increasingly international technology base in the 1990s.

INTERNATIONALIZATION AND THE EUROPEAN ARENA

Competitive conditions in the industry had changed in several unexpected ways during the course of the 1980s. In so doing they altered the nature of the challenge facing policymakers who wished to promote domestic capabilities. As the industry experienced intensifying competition, it also became one of the main battlegrounds for disagreements over trade policy among the advanced countries. Even as trade issues grew in visibility, however, the distinctive national approaches that governments refined in their efforts to promote domestic technological capabilities remained decisive.

The underlying change that drove the industry's evolution was a dramatic increase in the organizational and capital requirements for new fabrication facilities. As the industry moved into the 4- and 16-megabit generations of memory chips, the costs of equipping new plants became daunting for even the largest producers in the industry. Much of the problem lay in the ever more exacting requirements for the materials and production equipment, and the costly testing necessary to perfect their use in each new product generation. Small imperfections in any of the numerous steps in the production process could lower the yield of defect-free chips. The entire process had to be enclosed in specifically equipped "clean" rooms. Seemingly mundane tasks—from polishing silicon wafers to characterizing the gases and fluids with which they were treated—became limiting factors that required the support of highly specialized suppliers.[86]

In the 1980s, Japanese producers were the first to master the new levels of exactitude and complexity in memory chip production. With their great production expertise, continuously refined through feedback from in-house users, Japanese firms achieved new quality levels in mass-produced chips. In so doing, they also supported continuous improvement among their own suppliers, thereby generating an unsurpassed "industry infrastructure" of semiconductor equipment and materials suppliers. By the mid-1980s, the domination of Japanese firms sparked fears that they could restrict the supply of memory chips. In the later 1980s, these fears focused less on memory chips themselves than on the production equipment needed by chip manufacturers. American and European chip producers alike were becoming increasingly dependent on Japanese suppliers for equipment, materials, and the systems know-how to assemble semiconductor plants.[87] The importance of systems know-how was brought home when IBM chose Shimizu America, the subsidiary of a Japanese construction firm experienced in building clean rooms, to design IBM's newest fabrication facility in East Fishkill, New York.[88]

The success of Japanese chip producers prompted two responses in the United States. Many of the U.S. merchant firms argued that Japanese firms were gaining market share in the United States by selling their chips under cost. After lengthy investigation and negotiation, the United States and Japan concluded a bilateral agreement to regulate semiconductor trade in July 1986. The agreement stipulated that the U.S. Commerce Department and the Japanese Ministry of International Trade and Industry should establish rules to determine fair market values at which Japanese chips could be sold in the United States. When in 1987 U.S. officials became dissatisfied with MITI's implementation of the pact, the United States took the highly unusual step of applying retaliatory tariffs to a range of consumer appliances manufactured by the main Japanese chip-producing firms.[89]

While many people in the United States called for trade sanctions against Japanese producers, a slightly different coalition proposed a national institute for applied research on process technologies. Most industry observers agreed that Japanese firms had greatly improved their manufacturing capabilities during the 1980s. An important boost to their efforts came from a Japanese government program to promote manufacturing technologies for very-large-scale-integration devices. Since the VLSI program focused on just those manufacturing technologies where U.S. suppliers had grown weaker in the 1980s, the Defense Science board supported the proposal for a similar effort in the United States. The Pentagon began funding such an institute, called Sematech, in 1988.[90]

Yet another coalition of younger U.S-based firms opposed Sematach on the grounds that it helped only the larger producers whose strategies were based on outmoded conceptions of mass production and stable markets. These newcomers, particularly in Silicon Valley, emphasized flexibility and specialization. By forming cooperative relationships with other nearby firms, they were able to specialist in just a few aspects of the production process. While the "new-wave" firms in Silicon Valley developed a uniquely open and innovative ethos, their strategies illustrated a more general split in the industry. While process requirements for high-volume production were growing more demanding, the market possibilities for customized and semicustomized chips were growing. Accordingly, a new strategy that emphasized application-specific integrated circuits, or ASICs, was becoming increasingly popular for new entrants in the chip sector.[91]

These developments made the semiconductor industry a natural candidate for pan-European promotion in the 1980s. Not only had the U.S.-Japan trade agreement threatened to encourage predatory pricing in European markets, but the Sematech project threatened to exclude European firms from a major cooperative effort in manufacturing technologies. If semiconductor policy were elevated from a national to a European concern, however, it remained unclear whether that policy would focus on efforts to alter the terms of trade or on efforts to deepen Europe's technology infrastructure for semiconductor manufacturing.

Discussion of pan-European cooperation in semiconductor production emerged in 1986 in talks between Siemens and Philips about ways of continuing work begun in the Megaproject. Dubbed the Joint European Silicon Structures Initiatives (JESSI), the initial idea was to seek support from several European governments in developing future generations of semiconductor products. This proposal quickly encountered resistance from some of Germany's most prominent semiconductor users who argued that earlier aid to Siemens had only made the firm less responsive to the needs of German chip users.[92] The Nixdorf Computer company took the lead in arguing that public support for microelectronics ought not subsidize large chip producers in making components for their own use, but should push those producers to satisfy the needs of large chip users as well.[93]

Throughout the 1980's, Germany Ministry for Research and Technology had been receptive to the argument that no single firm could fully represent the public interest in matters of technology. As JESSI took shape, this ministry became the coordinating agency for the planning group, which included representatives from firms and national governments in five countries (France, Germany, Italy, the Netherlands, and the United Kingdom). The ministry sought to make JESSI something much broader than a collaborative project among Siemens, Philips, and SGS-Thomson. Largely at the ministry's urging, the planning group made four broad categories of projects eligible for JESSI support. Only the first category would include the submicron designs and devices of interest to the three large chip producers. Upstream linkages were to be strengthened through projects including materials and equipment suppliers. Downstream linkages were also to be strengthened by supporting custom and semicustom chip users who increasingly wanted their applications designed on single circuits. Finally, longer-term research into materials and techniques was to be supported through a number of European institutes. The national government representatives required that industrial participants provide at least half the funding for JESSI projects. In providing the other half, government representatives indicated that 29 percent would go into the submicron chip development, 15 percent into materials and equipment supply, 34 percent into user applications, and 22 percent into basic research.[94]

In its role as the initial coordinating agency, the Ministry for Research and Technology in Bonn had successfully pushed JESSI away from concentrated subsidies of a few large projects toward a much broader framework for diffusing know-how across a larger number of firms. The continuing role of the national governments was also apparent in their ability to prevent the European Community from taking primary administrative control of JESSI. The national governments as well as the firms wanted to involve the European Community as an additional source of public funds. In order to circumvent direct EC supervision, the planning group put JESSI under the umbrella of a different European program, EUREKA. Under the EUREKA framework, national governments disbursed funds on a case-by-case basis. The Commission of the European Community could participate in EUREKA, but only as one of the twenty participating governments, not as a supervising body.[95]

Soon after the initial discussions for JESSI got underway, the merged French-Italian firm SGS-Thomson sought entry, but Siemens and Philips were reluctant to make their prior development work available to a potential competitor.[96] The dispute was resolved in two ways. First, the JESSI framework adopted a complex structure of subordinate boards in which industry representatives gained access only to the results of projects within their division. In addition, in May 1990, more flexible conditions on intellectual property were added to JESSI's rules so that participants could request that certain background information be exempted from the usual requirements for disclosure.[97]

JESSI's eventual structure was noteworthy for its flexibility. With no more than a small administrative office in Munich, JESSI became an excellent example of technology promotion through interorganizational networks. The JESSI board consisted of eight members, all from industrial firms, while governments were represented only in an advisory committee. Each of the four subprograms—technology, materials and equipment, applications, and long-term research—also had a management board. Projects could be proposed by any group of participants, providing they represented at least two different countries. The subprogram boards approved projects for inclusion. But approval did not guarantee public funds; it only enabled participants to go to their national governments to apply for funds that had been earmarked for projects with the JESSI label. This board structure linked together a porous group of firms that determined their own partners without giving government any binding voice. Officials in the national ministries thus exercised discretion only over the specific projects they would fund. In effect, national governments gave up hierarchical control over the technical guidelines of the program in exchange for the opportunity to promote a broader network of firms operating in Europe.[98]

Not all participants favored such a complex structure. Several of Germany's leading research authorities in the industry argued that JESSI's many programs drained resources and attention from the central tasks of refining process technology for high-volume devices.[99] The French side also saw JESSI's structure as inadequate for the kind of promotion it envisioned. SGS-Thomson was controlled in equal parts by the French state through the nationalized firm, Thomson-CSF, and by the Italian state through the nationalized holding, IRI-Finmeccanica. While the French Ministry of Industry prided itself on allowing the firm managerial discretion, SGS-Thomson's French owners at Thomson-CSF were in ongoing contact with the ministries.[100] The semiconductor firm decided to approach Siemens in early 1990 to propose joint production of memory chips. When direct contacts with Siemens yielded no results, the French side tried working through the European Community. Accustomed to its status as a national champion in defense materiel within France, Thomson-CSF sought to make its semiconductor operation a "European champion" with the help of Brussels.[101] In April 1991, the President of the Commission of the European Community, Jacques Delors, met with the chief executives of Siemens, Philips, SGS-Thomson, and Olivetti in Western France to revive the proposal for a joint European chip producer.[102]

By this time, Siemens was beginning to reassess the link between its European and global strategies. While the firm positioned itself as Europe's leading producer of commodity chips, it pursued continuing technology partnerships with non-European producers. Both goals became explicit when Siemens announced that it would coproduce the 16-megabit DRAM with IBM at a fabrication facility in Essones, France, and that the two companies would cooperate in developing process technology for next-generation, or 64-megabit, DRAM. In France, unsurprisingly, the alliance with IBM was seen as a repudiation of European cooperation and became a subject of discussion between President Mitterrand and Chancellor Kohl shortly thereafter.[103]

Within a year, however, Siemens acknowledged that its commodity chip business had to be justified as much on grounds of technological capability as on those of commercial profitability. Siemens increasingly emphasized application-specific integrated circuits (ACISs) in its commercial strategy, while it continued to invest heavily in technology partnerships to keep up with state-of-the-art process technology. More and more, excellence in semiconductor technology meant participating in the world's leading consortia rather than developing technology alone. This was one of the reasons that JESSI's managing board had allowed IBM to participate in JESSI projects through the firm's German and French subsidiaries. In 1992 Siemens and IBM expanded their joint development agreement and included Toshiba in work on the 256-megabit DRAM.[104] Such development projects enabled Siemens to invest aggressively in DRAM production when the circumstances seemed propitious, while otherwise using its growing process expertise to expand its product lines in application-specific chips.

Meanwhile, the JESSI program also broadened its focus. High-volume production remained important for JESSI because equipment and materials suppliers could test their products only by using them in such serial-production, or so-called Beta, test sites. One of JESSI's main functions became the coordination of arrangements by which European equipment suppliers gained access to the test sites that European chip manufacturers could provide.[105] About the same time, JESSI shifted the organization of its funding priorities from particular projects to larger "flagship" efforts that included downstream applications, such as automotive electronics and telecommunications, as well as upstream linkages, such as lithography systems. One particularly important example of the upstream linkages was the work on a new line of steppers by the Dutch firm ASM Lithography through the JESSI flagship project headed by IBM Deutschland.[106]

As it did during JESSI's planning phase, the German federal government reinforced the broadening of JESSI's goals away from specific semiconductor devices to the industry's technology infrastructure as a whole. As German firms became more interested in application-specific devices, the Ministry for Research and Technology found it natural to convene the major users to plot broad guidelines for the German industry's evolution.[107] A different approach was made possible by Germany's unification, after which Siemens announced plans to build a center for semiconductor research and production near Dresden, in the former East German region of Saxony. The new center was slated first for research and for production of application-specific chips, and eventually for production of the 64-megabit and 256-megabit DRAMs that Siemens was developing in partnership with IBM and Toshiba.[108]

Arrangements for Siemens's center in Dresden again cast BMFT in a facilitating role. Public assistance for the investment in Dresden came almost entirely from the structural funds of the European Union. When pressed to provide details, the BMFT insisted that it was providing no assistance for investment purposes, but said it might well extend its "smart fab" R&D program, begun under the JESSI framework, to the center in Dresden. The ministry had effectively coordinated its research plans with agencies at the supranational level in Brussels and the subnational level in Saxony, without taking on any of the political risks or financial obligations incurred by those other agencies.[109]

The changing contours of the industry also forced French officials to reassess their policy strategies in the 1990s. Once Thomson had combined its semiconductor operations with the Italian firm SGS in 1987, the merged firm began to exercise much more managerial autonomy. The new entity gained a binational identity by appointing an Italian, Pasquale Pistorio, as chief executive and locating the new headquarters in Paris. Known as SGS-Thomson Microelectronics, or STM, the Franco-Italian firm focused entirely on commercial production. Under Pistorio's leadership, STM concentrated on semicustomized chips and cultivated downstream relationships with important suppliers. Since Pistorio had earlier gained marketing expertise with Motorola, the U.S. producer decided to withhold the design technology for the 32-bit microprocessor that it had earlier licensed to Thomson Components. The new firm also lost access to certain French technologies when French defense officials assigned production of more specialized military chips to Thomson-CSF. Without these technologies, the new Franco-Italian firm was obliged to build a product portfolio around its new emphasis on sophisticated sales efforts and application-specific integrated circuits.

STM's changing product strategy did not, however, preclude all sources of state support. Along with its growing emphasis on ASICs, STM maintained a commitment in the high-volume market for electronically programmable read-only memories, or EPROMS. According to some observers, the firm benefited in this segment from the U.S.-Japan semiconductor agreement, because it led Japanese producers to leave EPROM production to their competitors.[110] More direct assistance came from the French state in 1992, when the government induced two other state-owned enterprises, France Telecom and the commercial branch of the Center for Atomic Studies, CEA-Industrie, to take a stake in the chip-maker. One goal was to provide additional capital for STM, but another goal was to tighten STM's links to the public laboratories in Grenoble, the LETI and the CNS.[111] Finally, STM benefited from participation in a range of JESSI projects, where, as one of Europe's major high-volume producers, it played much the same role as did Siemens.

Even as STM benefited from public support, however, its strategy hinged primarily on downstream relationships that remained largely beyond the influence of French policymakers. The main state-owned shareholder, Thomson-CSF, monitored STM's strategy carefully, but vigorously resisted any pressure to help STM through preferential procurement of STM chips for its own operating divisions. STM relied increasingly on its identity as Europe's main independent merchant supplier. Some of the firm's larger customers—Bosch, Alcatel, Thomson Consumer Electronics, and Northern Telecom—had a clear interest in purchasing ASICs from a European firm that was not linked to any of the major American or Japanese electronics firms.[112] By developing new process technologies as cheaply as possible and broadening its client list as quickly as possible, STM refined a strategy that made it gradually resistant to the fluctuations in demand that affected most other merchant chip producers. In 1994, both the French and the Italian sides diluted their stakes to roughly 35 percent each through a successful flotation of STM's shares on the stock exchanges in Paris and New York. Rather than remaining a national champion, STM was becoming a well-recognized and broad-based niche producer.[113]

Like Siemens, STM had substantially tempered its commitment to commercial success in high-volume commodity chips. French policymakers had encouraged the shift by allowing STM greater latitude in building customer relations. Rather than experimenting with new methods of technology promotion as their German counterparts had done, however, French policymakers experimented mainly by giving STM more autonomy to match its product strategy to the technological capabilities that seemed most easily within reach.

This chapter argues that the nature of the innovations required for competition in the semiconductor industry were quite different from the challenges posed by the telecommunications or machine tool sectors. For this reason, the semiconductor sector illustrates what happens when familiar approaches to public policy require dramatic reassessment.

Given the novelty and magnitude of the tasks involved in semiconductor production, it is not surprising that European firms and policymakers eventually abandoned their hopes of linking commercial success with full autarky in chipmaking technologies. By the mid-1990s, the leading firms in France and Germany had found remarkably effective ways of fitting into an industry where international competition forced participants to conclude a range of technology partnerships. Yet the distinctive policy strategies by which French and German officials promoted their firms remained central even as these firms defined their own responses to the changing imperatives of the international market.

As in the other industries analyzed in this book, firm-level strategies in semiconductors were shaped by the institutional arrangements that governed the production and the use of technical expertise in France and Germany. In the early years, these arrangements imposed limitations on firm-level strategies quite directly by limiting the number of design and production engineers available to firms in the industry. Subsequently, institutional arrangements continued to affect competitive strategies because the processes of organizational experimentation that drove competition in the industry were shaped by the received norms of communication among technical occupations in the two countries.

The importance of semiconductor technology was first brought home to public officials in France and Germany by anxieties over possible dependence on American-made computers. To ward off this threatening possibility, both countries mounted public programs that bore many of the hallmarks of mission-oriented policies. In France's Plan Calcul, policymakers strove as much for military autarky as for commercial success. In Germany, where commercial goals were paramount, policymakers tempered the simple mission-oriented goals of the program by pushing Siemens to work with other firms to develop computer technology. With time, policymakers in both countries came to see that semiconductors were more than components for computers or other systems that particular state agencies might need. Semiconductors were becoming a generic technology that promised to reshape entire industries. As policymakers defined plans to promote chipmaking capabilities within their own borders, their distinctive national approaches to technology promotion grew clearer.

In France, public officials experimented with greater or lesser degrees of state intervention, but found it difficult to devise alternative methods of bolstering the in-house technological capabilities of French firms. Since the policy elites and the business elites were so closely tied together, the relevant question was how much influence public officials should exert over firm-level strategy. The possibility of providing industrywide public goods remained, as in the machine tool case, subordinate to more narrowly defined efforts to ensure that firm-level strategies matched specific policy goals. Thus the state alternated between efforts to cultivate competition during the presidency of Valéry Giscard d'Estaing and efforts to build a single national champion during the first presidency of François Mitterrand. The options open to firms were exemplified by Matra and Thomson. By committing itself to a strategy of international technology alliances, Matra rendered its semiconductor subsidiaries ineligible for a crucial source of public funding. By committing itself to a strategy of mass production and national control, Thomson secured its eligibility for military research and contracts but was unable to build the internal linkages it needed in order to strengthen both its technology base and its commercial networks. The outcome in 1987 was an unprecedented merger of the company's chipmaking operations with the Italian firm SGS.

In Germany, by contrast, policymakers pushed their main industrial partner, Siemens, to share semiconductor technology with other German firms. When the scale required for chip development grew too large to follow this approach, German policymakers applied the logic of diffusion-oriented policy to international cooperation, through the Megachip project with Philips. At the same time, officials in the BMFT imposed few restriction on the technology partnerships that Siemens concluded with other firms. This way of defining the task meant that German officials found it quite acceptable to support Siemens in work that deepened the country's technology base without limiting management's autonomy in choosing product strategies or technology partners.

These distinctive policy tendencies were accentuated rather than attenuated by the increasing internationalization that gripped the semiconductor industry in the late 1980s. As firms all over the world pushed manufacturing capabilities to new levels of precision and quality, the requisite innovations began to involve much more than radical breakthroughs in chip design or incremental improvements in manufacturing equipment. Increasingly, chip producers also had to master the challenge of architectural innovation, in which the links among different elements in the manufacturing process were reconfigured. This challenge also entailed a task of great interroganizational complexity inasmuch as it meant managing a range of varied relationships with suppliers, competitors, and users.

In confronting the tasks of architectural innovation, German policymakers adapted the instruments of diffusion-oriented policy and relied on the ethos of qualification that characterized managerial approaches to innovation in German firms. This combination of policy instruments and firm-level expectations turned out to be surprisingly appropriate for the new competitive conditions. German policymakers took the lead in pushing the pan-European JESSI framework toward a porous network of suppliers, producers, and users. Although critics complained about JESSI's complexity, this complexity seemed well suited for the web of linkages that were required in order to deepen Europe's technology infrastructure.[114]

The French approach required much greater adjustment in order to fit the changing requirements of international competition. The combination of mission-oriented policy instruments and a deductive epistemological style among technologists had to be decisively revised before French entrants could easily participate in the interfirm networks that were becoming central to the industry. After the merger of Thomson Components with SGS, the new firm's strategy emphasized downstream linkages with a diversified customer base rather than upstream linkages with equipment and materials suppliers. As successful as the merged firm's strategy eventually became, it starkly illuminated the limitations of France's public strategies for technology promotion. Only by diluting national control and allowing Italian management to build a strong customer base could French policymakers enable their main domestic chip producer to become more competitive.

The planning and elaboration of the JESSI framework showed that both French and German officials were willing to embrace European frameworks of cooperation. In both cases, however, they used JESSI as an instrument to advance the conceptions of technology promotion that accorded best with the professional outlooks of policymakers and technologists in their home countries. As in earlier iterations of policy, German policymakers achieved more by aiming for less. They were able to define a realm in which they could promote the German public's interest in domestic technological capabilities even if they could not control the market opportunities to which those capabilities might be applied. By so doing, they helped Siemens maintain its place in the world's leading research consortia. French policymakers learned only belatedly to subordinate national goals to the increasingly international scale of technology development. Even after they relinquished control of Thomson's component division to joint Franco-Italian ownership, their mission-oriented approach limited the repertoire of instruments that seemed appropriate. They saw the state's role in terms of protecting national—or later European— sovereignty. When those goals could not be achieved by the traditional instruments of dirigiste planning and public ownership, French policymakers could promote France's efforts in this sector only by abandoning earlier conceptions of policy and reducing the state's direct stake in the sector.

Chapter Six

Conclusion

This book began with the observation that French and German policymakers exhibited remarkably persistent approaches to the task of encouraging technological change in industry, but that these approaches had quite different consequences in different sectors. Unlike many explanations of national policy patterns—which emphasize either the legal capabilities of the state or interest group configurations in society—this study emphasizes the professional identities of policymakers and technical elites. Unlike most explanations of technological change—which emphasize either market structures or the allocation of resources within the firm—this book emphasizes the way institutional resources external to the firm can shape the options open to managers. The three sectoral comparisons analyzed in this book all show how public policies helped shape the broad patterns of technological change that characterized industrial adjustment in the two countries. In none of these cases, however, did public officials dictate competitive outcomes. Instead they defined the public's stake in technological advance and, in so doing, created conditions that made it more or less rational for firms to adopt distinctive innovation strategies.

This argument—that public policies exert an indirect but pervasive influence on the way firms approach the innovation task—runs counter to conventional debates about government's proper role in promoting industrial technologies. These debates are largely dominated by proponents of state-led or market-driven adjustment. This book claims that the dichotomy of state versus market, while always an oversimplification, has been rendered even more inadequate by the shift from scale-based to knowledge-based competition. The proponents of state-led adjustment neglect the degree to which public officials depend on nonstate sources of expertise for purposes of promoting industrial change. The proponents of market-driven adjustment neglect the ways in which knowledge resides in groups with strong professional identities and complex networks of relationships that confound any simple description based only on market forces. To elaborate my alternative perspective, this conclusion reviews the mechanisms by which public policymakers influenced the conditions for technological advance in each industry. It then explores the broader implications of a perspective that explains state action as a function of elite networks and professional identities.

SECTORAL OUTCOMES

In each of the three sectors compared in this book, the possibilities for technological change were significantly shaped by public policy—but the consequences of those policies depended on a legacy of elite relations that could not be altered within the confines of any single policy program or initiative. In France, policymakers consistently defined programs in terms of public missions implemented through high-visibility programs and concentrated resources. This approach made it rational for firms to seek both the prestige and the resources that would result from capturing a leading role in public efforts to achieve radical or breakthrough innovations. In Germany, by contrast, policymakers relied on structured consultation and diffusion-oriented programs, making public resources available in smaller amounts that were typically tied to cooperation among firms and research organizations. This form of public support pushed German firms toward less dramatic and less risky technology strategies aimed at incremental innovation.

The sectors compared here also reinforce the view that the dichotomy between radical and incremental innovation strategies no longer represents the range of alternatives available to firms. More complex changes in technology may also require some degree of architectural innovation, by which firms seek to improve relationships among components of a product (or elements of a process) without necessarily altering the components (or elements) themselves.[1] All three types of innovation are likely to occur to some extent in most settings. Whichever kind of innovation became central in the industries compared here, however, all three sectors showed how the links between administrative and technical elites became critical in formulating as well as implementing public strategies for change.

198

Of the three sectors examined in this book, telecommunications represented the clearest case of state-orchestrated industrial development.
The puzzle posed by this sector was that the mission-oriented approach
succeeded in France but not in Germany. In both countries, the jump
from electromechanical to digital telephone exchanges entailed radical
redesign of the product on the basis of fundamentally new componentry.
In addition, the organizational configuration of state agencies and industrial partners displayed remarkably similar structures in France and
Germany. Within these similar organizational structures, however, the
relative influence of administrative and technical elites drove policy
outcomes in quite different directions.

In France, the ingénieurs des télécommunications gave the state a
major research capability that enabled public officials to set the timing
and the precise specifications of the technologies to be developed. These
technical specialists also provided the means through which a mission-
oriented strategy could be implemented. They played the key role in
developing and deploying France's digital technologies and did so more
quickly than other countries could effect similar changes. Yet, the prestige and self-image of the ingénieurs des télécommunications provided
more than an organizational resource. They provided such a cohesive
force within the industry that the Direction Générale des Télécommunications (DGT) had trouble devolving discretion over technical specifications to the firms. Even during the Giscardian experiment with domestic
competition, firms found it difficult to determine their own technical
agenda.

Although the successor to the DGT—France Telecom—was organized
as an enterprise rather than as a public administration, ongoing control
of new technologies for television broadcasting and other services remained central to the organization's strategy. The general trend toward
privatization began to lead France's elite civil servants into the private
sector at a younger age, but there was ample resistance to a rapid
reduction of the public sector's role.[2] In telecommunications, France
Telecom became more reluctant to share technology with its traditional
suppliers such as Alcatel, and the control of technical information largely
controlled by the ingénieurs des télécommunications remained central
to France Telecom's strategies for a more open market.[3] There is little
question that France Telecom's growing independence from the French
state implies greater reliance on market mechanisms as a framework
for organizing growth in telecommunications. The politics of setting
the rules to regulate the new competitors will, however, continue to
depend heavily on the ingénieurs des télécommunications and the way

they choose to exert their influence within the sector's changing organization.

In Germany, the record was almost the reverse. The Bundespost's technical specialists in the Fernmeldetechnisches Zentralamt (FTZ) had long regarded the industrial suppliers, led by Siemens, as the country's main source of expertise in the field. From the 1920s, they had allowed Siemens, working in consortium with the other court suppliers, to set the pace and many of the specifications for technological renovations of the telephone network. Only after prolonged and expensive efforts to develop a semi-electronic switch in the 1970s, did the Bundespost abandon the principle of joint development. Germany's policy approach was not well suited to the vertical coordination of planned innovation and publicly funded infrastructure development that the tight linkages of the French elites made possible.

By ceding technology leadership to Siemens, this approach left the Bundespost's successor, Deutsche Telekom, with a set of challenges quite different from those faced by France Telecom. As the processes of liberalization and privatization began to transform the European telecommunications industry in the early 1990s, they also weakened Deutsche Telekom's ties to its traditional suppliers. Accordingly the company urgently needed to deepen its internal sources of R&D capability. If only to monitor and evaluate the offerings of other suppliers, Deutsche Telekom needed to develop news ways of attracting and keeping top technical specialists who, in Germany, had traditionally gone to the main industrial firms such as Siemens and Bosch.

If the telecommunications sector showed that elite linkages in Germany were less well adapted than in France for implementing mission-oriented policies, the machine tool sector showed how much better Germany's elite linkages served the purposes of diffusion-oriented policies. In this sector, the advent of computer numerical control required steady adaptation of traditional metal-cutting and metal-forming processes to the improved calibration and precise guidance that the new technology made possible. The structure of the machine tool industry—dominated by smaller traditional firms—posed the challenge of disseminating a variety of computer technologies for controlling machine operations. For this task, the ability to create robust intermediary organizations became critical.

In France, however, even where industry structure made diffusion-oriented policy appear appropriate, policymakers repeatedly conceived of state action in terms of centrally coordinated plans and industrial restructuring. Parisian policymakers clearly had little confidence in the smaller firms' ability to implement sophisticated technologies, and they tended to avoid advice from the firms. Instead, they worked with management consultants to specify the employment plans and the product strategies on which state aid was conditioned. There were some efforts to bolster the sector's joint research centers—CETIM and CERMO—but they were undercut by the "growth contracts" and financial mergers that the ministry negotiated directly with the larger firms. Perhaps most important, the Ministry of Industry did little to bolster the shop-floor manpower resources available to firms in this sector. Only in 1985 did ministry officials express much awareness that the skills required to implement the technologies envisioned were simply not present in many French firms. In the 1990s, national leaders began serious efforts to define more practically oriented educational tracks, but it was far from clear that the new degrees would lead to genuine prospects for recognized careers. The result was a drastic fall in the sector's employment, acquisition of major firms by foreign competitors, and a sharply declining position among world producers.

In this sector as elsewhere, German officials adopted a more diffusion-oriented approach than their French counterparts. They devised a set of indirect-specific measures which made funds available to small firms without direct state supervision. In order to distribute funds without disrupting the sector's self-regulatory links, the BMFT delegated a great deal of discretionary responsibility to an independent consulting bureau in Berlin under the auspices of the German Engineering Association (VDI). In dramatic contrast to Paris, the Technology Ministry relied heavily on intermediary organizations and thereby enabled the industry to respond more readily to signals from labor as well as from management that human resources required more investment.

To be sure, the German machine tool industry had long been larger and better organized than the French industry. German policymakers could rely on many resources that the French industry did not have— the industry association's own active research bureau (the Forschungs-kuratorium Maschinenbau), the metalworkers' extensive knowledge of the industry, and the Fraunhofer Institutes for mechanical engineering. Yet, these differences in prior position cannot account for the outcomes observed. If anything, the divergence in policies coincided with an ever growing gulf in the vitality of the two national industries. Public officials in Bonn deliberately reinforced the know-how and organizational resources available to firms in the sector, while French policymakers tried to fit the firms into their familiar centrally coordinated framework. By the mid-1980s, the German industry had largely assimilated the new microelectronic technologies, had reversed its decline in employment, and began recouping its relative position against new competitors. Public policy was not the only factor that explained this result; yet the evidence shows clearly that German policymakers reinforced their industry's resilience while French officials unwittingly undermined their industry's capabilities.

In the semiconductor industry, French and German policymakers again confronted similar industrial structures, but they faced a task quite different from the other two sectors. Rather than mobilizing expertise for a major development project as in telecommunications or disseminating new technologies throughout a sector as in machine tools, the task in semiconductors was more architectural in nature. In this sector, relentless miniaturization of the product depended on an ever more demanding manufacturing process in which the multiple linkages among different types of equipment and materials became a critical dimension of competition. Political objectives were somewhat different in the two countries. Paris sought full self-sufficiency for military reasons while German officials sought to maintain a semiconductor capability for purposes of general industrial vitality. To achieve these goals, policymakers in each country nonetheless faced much the same challenge: how to identify the specific expertise needed to bring national firms into the expensive business of chip production and how to combine the types of knowledge necessary to make the development process a self-sustaining one. These similarities aside, French and German officials pursued the task quite differently.

French policymakers specified the timing and much of the content for the technology licensing agreements of the late 1970s. In the 1980s, the Socialist government streamlined the plan and restricted public investments to Thomson's program for becoming a substantial world player in the industry. When one of the state's earlier partners, Matra, showed an independent determination to remain in the sector without allowing the state much influence over its technology agreements, public officials refrained from offering support. Instead, the state effectively built a mission-oriented plan around Thomson, its main source for defense electronics, only to learn in 1987 that the firm could not survive in the sector unless it merged its chip-making division with the Italian national champion, SGS. Even after the cross-national merger, however, French officials used their share of ownership to continue a mission-oriented policy strategy in which the state sought to concentrate resources to achieve very specific outcomes.

German policymakers chose a quite different route. They started supporting semiconductor research in the early 1970s, but without any effort to specify the technology agreements that German firms concluded with foreign (mostly American) suppliers. In the early 1980s, German policymakers pushed Siemens to invest in the most competitive industry segment, memory chips, but they did so through a very novel arrangement. Even when the state's objective was a measure of industrial autonomy in semiconductors, policymakers in Bonn trusted a set of instruments that would diffuse technology rather than concentrate it in the hands of a single firm. The Megaproject required Siemens to work with the Dutch electronics giant Philips on the submicron circuit technologies necessary for advanced memory chips. Policymakers in Bonn eschewed a direct role in monitoring such complex R&D, preferring to exercise a check on their own industrial partner by requiring cooperation with a non-German firm. In effect, when the magnitude of the task meant that only one German firm could pursue it, officials applied the logic of diffusion-oriented policy to the German subsidiary of a non-German firm. Through the JESSI framework, German officials similarly raised a diffusion-oriented approach to the European level by supporting the technology infrastructure for the broader electronics industry while allowing the major firms great discretion in choosing commercial investments.

In all six of these policy histories, the consequences of policy rested on the ability of public officials to mobilize resources and also on their ability to channel those resources to the firms and research organizations that could undertake the desired innovations. The tasks of gathering information about suitable research partners and distributing resources in ways that facilitated successful innovation were far from trivial. They hinged not only on the legal powers of public officials, but also on the formal and informal networks that linked these officials to technical specialists in specific industrial settings. The state's ability to mobilize expertise in the service of technological change therefore involved both the legal discretion and the professional authority exercised by public officials. In this sense, these cases illustrated how the two meanings of competence—professional competence as recognized expertise and legal competence as delegated authority—came together in the role of the public official. The importance of these professional relations shows why a largely unexamined type of politics—the politics of competence—is central to public efforts to bolster industrial competitiveness through technological change.

POLICY ADAPTATION

While especially useful in explaining why inherited policy approaches persist, the politics of competence also illuminates the conditions under which policymakers adapt and try new approaches.[4] In this book I have argued that policy consequences result both from historically inherited policy approaches and from the challenges posed by changing circumstances in specific industries. Since the interaction of these factors cannot be predicted with any precision, public technology policies are rich in uncertainties and unintended consequences.

Such uncertainties and unintended consequences are central to the possibilities for policy learning. The first requirement for policy learning is that policymakers have the ability to assess past policy efforts and adjust future efforts accordingly. In the case of technology policy, this feedback requirement entails communication between specialists who understand the content of particular technological challenges and the policymakers who are responsible for maintaining or changing future policies.[5]

The possibilities for learning therefore hinge on the vertical and horizontal links among occupational groups. The vertical relations that link superordinate public agencies to private-sector organizations can be facilitated by interpersonal, horizontal linkages between members of the same professional group. Such links were crucial for the one example of a successful mission-oriented policy, namely, the French efforts in digital switching technologies. But vertical links between members of distinct occupational groups are equally important. As shown in the comparison of French and German policy for machine tools, misguided policies could only be improved when the channels between different levels in an occupational hierarchy allowed important information to move back and forth so that new policies could be devised and old ones adjusted.

By examining these varied links among occupational groups, this book advances a new perspective on the role of ideas and interests in policy change. Many scholars have examined the possibilities for deliberate and reflective change in public policies. In most of these accounts, ideas are sources of change, while interest groups impose constraints on the actions of policymakers.[6] This book supports the view that ideas matter. But it does so by emphasizing a different type of ideas—namely, the ideas that occupational groups use over time in order to justify their claim to a privileged voice. These ideas are sometimes made quite explicit, particularly at the early stages of a group's "professionalization project," but at other times they become a more diffuse and implicit part of the group's identity. Because the identities taken on by knowledge-bearing elites are society's way of reconciling expertise and authority, these identities become an important part of the culture of policymaking. Drawing on his comparative study of policies for railway development in the nineteenth century, Frank Dobbin argues similarly that countries have a policymaking culture that "shapes the sorts of means people can envision when they first think about solving a problem."[7]

The content of these professional identities can either broaden or narrow the range of options that policymakers can realistically entertain. Since policy learning depends on experimentation as well as feedback, professional identities impinge quite directly on the range of that experimentation. Knowledge-bearing elites have an interest in adapting their methods to new problems, but they also seek to define those problems in ways that emphasize their own established claims to competence and jurisdiction.

The deductive epistemological style of French elites, for example, introduced a consistent rigidity into French policymaking. This style expressed the way French elites reconciled the competing claims of expertise and authority: according to the French elites, these two claims had to coincide. Since French officials were expected to know the procedures and formulae that would lead to successful outcomes, their own deductive approach made it difficult for them to acknowledge unsuccessful policies or learn from their experience.

This style of policymaking fit closely with the French state's centralized and unitary structure, which located legal discretion in the central ministries. Yet, even when policymakers attempted to decentralize their agencies or bolster intermediary institutions, they encountered great difficulties.[8] For example, the regional research centers for metalworking technologies, CERMO and CETIM, look similar on paper to the German *Trägerorganisationen* that administered the indirect-specific measures for disseminating microelectronics. Yet CERMO and CETIM never quite became self-sustaining organizations as did the VDI Technology Center in Berlin or the Forschungskuratorium in Frankfurt. The key difference was the amount of esteem in which policymakers and industry groups held the different organizations. In France the regional centers were modest entities which were never given the priority that public officials accorded the instruments of central control, particularly the "growth contracts" and mergers arranged by ministerial staffs and management consultants. In Germany, on the other hand, the Trägerorganisationen were regarded as important sources of expertise to which officials in Bonn quite readily ceded discretion over the implementation of policy.

The German policy approach, with its ethos of qualification, assumed a certain division of expertise among different knowledge-bearing groups. This policy style reconciled the competing claims of expertise and authority by suggesting that public officials needed the procedural expertise, not to formulate policy by themselves, but rather to engage the occupational groups that could best act in the broader public interest on any particular policy issue.

THE CHANGING ROLE OF THE STATE

The cases examined in this book illustrate an unmistakable shift in the role played by the state in industrial development. In the early decades after World War II, national governments in Europe rebuilt important industrial capabilities by planning sectoral development and by allocating public resources to power that development forward. The French state, with its elite civil servants, became the model for this type of activist or dirigiste public strategy. From the mid 1970s onward, however, the state's most effective tools for industrial development shifted from the allocation of resources to the construction of institutions for accumulating and sharing knowledge. Of the cases examined in this study, French policy toward telephone switching exchanges was the only example where the old recipe of state-directed innovation worked well.

As the dimensions of industrial competition shifted from scale-driven economies toward knowledge-driven advantages, public authorities had to rely increasingly on intangible resources that were inherently difficult to control directly or to allocate precisely. Under these competitive conditions, the German state's spectrum of tools for strengthening and shaping the flow of knowledge became the more admired model for industrial promotion. Rather than creating industrial capabilities through state action alone, public servants in Germany learned how to work in partnership with other actors in order to promote new industrial capabilities and make those capabilities more widely available to firms throughout the economy.

Given this shift in the policy instruments that prove effective under the conditions of knowledge-based competition, policy adaptation becomes a crucial concern. Earlier literature on industrial development stressed the state's ability to control and coordinate the use of resources by insulating parts of the national economy from market outcomes. Much of the policy debate on managed trade remains focused around these same debates about government's capabilities for strategic action.[9]

Subsequent literature in political economy has shifted its emphasis from the location of the public-private boundary to the nature of that boundary. This shift is evident in several efforts to illuminate the institutional features that help policymakers as well as managers in adjusting to changing economic conditions. Some authors focus on the larger institutional arrangements that condition national policies for wage levels, money supply, and currency rate.[10] Other authors focus on more localized institutional arrangements—such as supplier networks, regional labor organizations, and industrial orders—with more direct effects on particular firms.[11]

This book shows that the occupational identities of knowledge-bearing elites are themselves a critical part the institutional infrastructure that underpins or undermines the adjustment capabilities of different countries. Where these professional identities facilitate the exchange of different types of knowledge—scientific research, organizational expertise, technical engineering knowledge, marketing insights, and practical skill—the possibilities for innovation will be increased. Where these identities make it difficult for knowledge-bearing elites to exchange expertise, the possibilities for innovation will be narrowed. Since neither policymakers nor managers have much influence over the content of professional identities, however, both need to allow room for some degree of experimentation. Only with such experimentation can they discover which policies or strategies are well adapted to the legacy of occupational identities within which they work.

These conclusions are most directly relevant to policy areas where there is high uncertainty and where implementation hinges on a combination of abstract and practical knowledge. Yet there are many reasons to think that the salience of occupational identities and professional networks extends well beyond the spheres of technology-driven changes in France and Germany. In the United States, the trend toward corporate downsizing is forcing white-collar employees to rely increasingly on their formal professional credentials and informal professional networks. In Japan, economic pressures are undercutting the hitherto unquestioned norm of lifetime employment in large firms, opening the possibility that professional associations and networks will begin to take a more visible role. In Eastern Europe and the former Soviet Union, networks of former state administrators remain an important repository of organizational and technical expertise, a situation which has in several cases helped former party elites regain political influence under altered names.

More generally, as rigid hierarchical forms of organization give way to more flexible forms, the interpersonal links fostered by professional affinities begin to rival organizationally programmed contacts and routines in their ability to influence the success of both company strategies and public policies. From management's perspective, professional networks help inspire trust and loyal service to firms that cannot guarantee long-term job security. From the policymaker's perspective, these same occupational identities become more salient as traditional methods of macroeconomic management give way to firm- and industry-level recipes for supporting competitive performance.

TECHNOLOGY AND INTERNATIONAL COMPETITION

This book trains its focus on one type of publicly provided resource—scientific and technical knowledge. There are of course many other resources—from the cost of capital to the quality of managerial cadres—that affect the performance of firms in international competition. If new technologies are as important as prevailing opinion suggests, however, then the role of knowledge and the institutions that shape it in different countries should have significant implications for future patterns of competition.

My analysis moves strongly against the hypothesis that national institutional arrangements are converging around some "best" or most competitive set of institutions. Even as different countries seek to imitate the institutions of their competitors, the professional groups that animate these institutions are likely to retain distinctive outlooks and self-images. As competition comes to hinge increasingly on different kinds of knowledge, these knowledge-bearing groups become increasingly important as carriers of the intangible resources that firms need. In this sense, professional identities reinforce the distinctive national character of institutions that bear directly on the kinds of resources available to firms operating in different countries.

Explicit international agreements such as the Maastricht Treaty in Europe, NAFTA in North America, or the Structural Impediments Initiative in U.S.-Japan relations, can go only so far in achieving institutional symmetry across nations.[12] These frameworks have proved largely unable to harmonize institutional arrangements such as rules of access to retail distribution systems. It can only be more difficult to negotiate the content of occupational identities in different countries precisely because these identities rest on historically derived jurisdictions and informal prestige hierarchies. The analysis presented in this book shows that the jurisdictions and prestige granted to similar occupational groups in different countries can be as important for knowledge-based economic competition as other, more easily negotiated, institutional features.

The likely persistence of national differences in occupational identities and professional networks is in no way contradicted by the increasing importance of multinational corporations in trade and cross-border investment. Far from homogenizing world markets, multinational firms are increasingly intent upon exploiting local variations in skills and knowledge bases. That is to say, the economic rationale for multinationals rests not only on their ability to exploit economies of scale and imperfections in product markets, but increasingly on their ability to exploit cross-border differentials in intangible knowledge inputs.[13]

In the European Union, there have been several efforts to harmonize licensing standards for professionals, but their implementation has been quite limited.[14] There are, to be sure, some occupations where European and even global elites are coalescing. This development may be clearest for upper management in multinational firms. Also in some important new specialties, such as software writing, the norms of professional certification may be receding before a group of worldwide employers who constitute a transnational labor market. For the longer-established professions, however, national norms remain important. Large employers may be able to create a reliable market for software code writers, but wider populations are reluctant to give up such requirements as familiar building codes for construction engineers or known university certificates for health professionals.

These developments, like the cases analyzed in this study, show that the links between authority and expertise are deeply rooted in the national histories of different countries. The differences among advanced industrial economies have, for much of the postwar period, been thought to rest primarily on differences in large and readily codified institutions such as labor organizations, central banks, and welfare legislation. These were the institutions where, as John Ruggie's concept of embedded liberalism suggested, countries could follow their own paths as long as they accepted the rules of open markets in international transactions. The cases compared here show that occupational identities and professional networks are becoming similarly important in international competition. As companies continue to compete on the basis of resources available in different locations, countries compete on the basis of the knowledge-based capabilities provided by their domestic institutional arrangements. If the analysis presented in this book is correct, then this competition will continue to depend broadly and often decisively on the ways in which knowledge-bearing elites define themselves and their relationship to the public sphere.

Notes

1. Technology and the Politics of Knowledge-Based Competition

1. For representative views, see Laura d'Andrea Tyson, *Who's Bashing Whom?* (Washington, D.C.: International Institute of Economics, 1992); and Linda R. Cohen and Roger G. Noll, *The Technology Pork Barrel* (Washington, D.C.: Brookings, 1991).

2. Signal examples of this view include Andrew Shonfield, *Modern Capitalism* (London: Oxford University Press, 1965); Peter J. Katzenstein, "Introduction" and "Conclusion," in Katzenstein, ed., *Between Power and Plenty* (Madison: University of Wisconsin Press, 1977); and John Zysman, *Governments, Markets, and Growth: Financial Systems and the Politics of Industrial Change* (Ithaca: Cornell University Press, 1983).

3. See, for example, Michel Albert, *Capitalism contre capitalisme* (Paris: Seuil, 1991), and David Soskice, "Germany and Japan: Industry-Coordinated versus Group-Coordinated Market Economies" (Paper presented at the Cornell Conference on the Political Economy of the New Germany, Ithaca, New York, 14–16 October 1994).

4. See especially Paul Hirst, *Associative Democracy: New Forms of Economic and Social Governance* (Amherst: University of Massachusetts Press, 1994).

5. See John L. Campbell and Leon N. Lindberg, "The Evolution of Governance Regimes," in J. L. Campbell, J. R. Hollingsworth, and L. N. Lindberg, eds., *Governance of the American Economy* (New York: Cambridge University Press, 1991); and J. Rogers Hollingsworth, Philippe Schmitter, and Wolfgang Streeck, eds., *Governing Capitalist Economies: Performance and Control of Economic Sectors* (New York: Oxford University Press, 1994).

6. See especially Robert O. Keohane, *After Hegemony: Cooperation and Discord in the World Political Economy* (Princeton: Princeton University Press, 1984); and, for technology, Robert Gilpin, *Political Economy of International Relations* (Princeton: Princeton University Press, 1987), chap. 9.

7. The classic statement of "hegemonic stability theory" is Charles P. Kindleberger, *The World in Depression, 1929–1939* (Berkeley: University of California Press, 1973).

8. Kindleberger, *World in Depression;* John Gerard Ruggie, "International Re-

gimes, Transactions, and Change: Embedded Liberalism in the Postwar Economic Order," in Stephen D. Krasner, ed., *International Regimes* (Ithaca: Cornell University Press, 1983).

9. Robert O. Keohane, "The World Economy and the Crisis of Embedded Liberalism," in John H. Goldthorpe, ed., *Order and Conflict in Contemporary Capitalism* (New York: Oxford University Press, 1984).

10. Raymond Vernon, "International Investment and International Trade in the Product Cycle," *Quarterly Journal of Economics* 80 (1966): 190–207.

11. Birger Wernerfelt, "A Resource-Based View of the Firm," *Strategic Management Journal* 5 (April/June 1984): 171–180; Michael Best, *The New Competition* (Cambridge: Harvard University Press, 1990); and Margaret A. Peteraf, "The Cornerstones of Competitive Advantage: A Resource-Based View," *Strategic Management Journal* 14 (1993): 179–192.

12. For the development of this subject, see F. M. Scherer, *International High-Technology Competition* (Cambridge: Harvard University Press, 1992), chap. 2. For recent interest in these questions, see also Paul Romer, "Endogenous Technical Change," *Journal of Political Economy* 98, no. 5, pt. 2 (October 1990): S71–S102; and Gene Grossman and Elhanan Helpman, *Innovation and Growth in the Global Economy* (Cambridge: MIT Press, 1991).

13. For example, Bruce Kogut, ed., *Country Competitiveness: Technology and the Organizing of Work* (New York: Oxford University Press, 1993); Michael Porter, *The Competitive Advantage of Nations* (New York: Free Press, 1990); Robert Reich, *The Work of Nations* (New York: Random House, 1991); and Lester Thurow, *Head to Head* (New York: Morrow, 1991).

14. This point is discussed in Keohane, *After Hegemony*. For the diffusion of technology, see also Robert Gilpin, *U.S. Power and the Multinational Corporation: The Political Economy of Foreign Direct Investment* (New York: Basic Books, 1975); and Gilpin, *Political Economy of International Relations* (Princeton: Princeton University Press, 1987), chap. 9.

15. This view is based on a substantial body of theoretical and empirical work on what is known as the resource-based view of the firm, summarized in Peteraf, "Cornerstones of Competitive Advantage," and in David J. Collis and Cynthia A. Montgomery, "Competing on Resources: Strategy in the 1990s," *Harvard Business Review*, July–August 1995, 118–129.

16. On the boundaries of politics, see Charles Maier, ed., *Changing Boundaries of the Political* (New York: Cambridge University Press, 1987). Yaron Ezrahi also deals with these issues in *The Descent of Icarus: Science and the Transformation of Contemporary Democracy* (Cambridge: Harvard University Press, 1990).

17. See Alfred North Whitehead, *Science and the Modern World* (New York: Simon & Schuster, 1925). Political scientists have increasingly appreciated the role of broad ideas, including worldviews in political affairs. See Judith Goldstein and Robert O. Keohane, "Ideas and Foreign Policy: An Analytical Framework," in Goldstein and Keohane, eds., *Ideas and Foreign Policy: Beliefs, Institutions, and Political Change* (Ithaca: Cornell University Press, 1993), p. 8.

18. Emanuel Adler, *The Power of Ideology: The Quest for Technological Autonomy in Argentina and Brazil* (Berkeley: University of California Press, 1987); Frank Dobbin, *Forging Industrial Policy: The United States, Britain, and France in the Railway Age* (New York: Cambridge University Press, 1994).

19. Articles that established this view include Kenneth J. Arrow, "Economic Welfare and the Allocation of Resources for Invention," and other essays in National Bureau of Economic Research, *The Rate and Direction of Inventive Activity: Economic and Social Factors* (Princeton: Princeton University Press, 1962); Richard R. Nelson, Merton J. Peck, and Edward D. Kalacheck, *Technology, Growth, and Public Policy* (Washington, D.C.: Brookings, 1967); and Edwin Mansfield, *The Economics of Technological Change* (New York: Norton, 1968).

20. Cohen and Noll, *Technology Pork Barrel*, 378–385.

21. Don Price, *The Scientific Estate* (New York: Oxford University Press, 1965), 86–87, 272, and Price, *America's Unwritten Constitution: Science, Religion, and Political Responsibility* (Cambridge: Harvard University Press, 1985).

22. It is important to note that events in seventeenth-century England grew out of specific and highly contingent circumstances. As Michael Walzer has shown, the Calvinist revolt in England was a radical attack upon the traditional hierarchies and orders of the neo-Platonic worldview. It may have paved the way for capitalism and political pluralism, but not directly or doctrinally. Puritan congregations were extremely disciplined communities and they foreshadowed none of the optimism or the regard for individual privacy that came to characterize theories of political liberalism. Furthermore, science was not a natural or logical concomitant of Puritanism. It was incorporated into this novel constellation of ideas, as Robert Merton has shown, primarily because of its utility in the arts of war and extractive industry. Later in the seventeenth century, when science became what Merton calls an "autonomous" activity (i.e., valued in its own right), the Puritan revolt had lost its radical force. Science provided a path for those who wished to escape closed philosophies for an open, more secular worldview based on Baconian empiricism.

For Walzer's study of the Calvinist revolt, see his *Revolution of the Saints: A Study in the Origins of Radical Politics* (Cambridge: Harvard University Press, 1965), esp. 151–152, 301–303. Robert Merton's original analysis appeared as vol. 4, pt. 2, of *Osiris: Studies on the History and Philosophy of Science and on the History of Learning and Culture* (1938) and was reprinted in book form as *Science, Technology, and Society in Seventeenth-Century England* (New York: Harper & Row, 1970). Don Price also treats these issues, with commentary and further evidence regarding Walzer's thesis, in *America's Unwritten Constitution*, esp. 21, 32, and 159n. For the adoption of Baconian empiricism, see also Joseph Ben-David, *The Scientist's Role in Society* (Englewood Cliffs, N.J.: Prentice-Hall, 1971), 72–73. For the way these doctrinal conflicts fed into struggles for institutional change, see John Ferejohn, "Structure and Ideology: Change in Parliament in Early Stuart England," in Goldstein and Keohane, *Ideas and Foreign Policy*, 207–231.

23. See Michael Burrage and Rolf Torstendahl, eds., *Professions in Theory and History: Rethinking the Study of the Professions* (London: Sage, 1990), and Rolf Torstendahl and Michael Burrage, eds., *The Formation of Professions: Knowledge, State and Strategy* (London: Sage, 1990).

24. For an overview of such institutionalist perspectives, see James P. March and Johan P. Olson, "The New Institutionalism," *American Political Science Review* 78 (September 1984): 734–749, and Kathleen Thelen and Sven Steinmo, "Historical Institutionalism in Comparative Politics," in Sven Steinmo, Kathleen Thelen, and Frank Longstreth, eds., *Structuring Politics: Historical Institutionalism in Comparative Analysis* (New York: Cambridge University Press, 1992).

25. Theda Skocpol, "Bringing the State Back In: Strategies of Analysis in Current Research," in Peter Evans, Dietrich Reuschemeyer, and Theda Skocpol, eds., *Bringing the State Back In* (New York: Cambridge University Press, 1985), 3–37, as well as the editors' introduction to Part I in the same book, 39–43.

26. See, for example, Max Weber, *From Max Weber: Essays in Sociology*, ed. and trans. by H. Gerth and C. Wright Mills (New York: Oxford University Press, 1972), esp. 211, 212, 214. As important as rational-legal forms of authority may have been in Weber's work, their emphasis at the expense of other aspects of Weber's sociology gave the state-centered institutionalists a pronounced tilt toward structural determination of political outcomes. An important corrective attempt to retrieve Weber's complex view of structure and the pluralism of motives is provided by Stephen Kalberg, *Mex Weber's Comparative Historical Sociology* (Chicago: University of Chicago Press, 1994), 3–9 and 23–49.

27. Katzenstein, "Introduction" and "Conclusion," in *Between Power and Plenty;* and Zysman, *Governments, Markets, and Growth.*

28. Theda Skocpol, "Bringing the State Back In," p. 16.

29. Theda Skocpol and Margaret Weir, "Keynesian Responses to the Great Depression," in *Bringing the State Back In,* esp. 119.

30. Peter Hall, *Governing the Economy: The Politics of State Intervention in Britain and France* (New York: Oxford University Press, 1986), 16.

31. Peter B. Evans, Dietrich Rueschemeyer, and Theda Skocpol, "On the Road toward a More Adequate Understanding of the State," in *Bringing the State Back In,* 351, 359.

32. Harvey B. Feigenbaum, *The Politics of Public Enterprise* (Princeton: Princeton University Press, 1985), and Richard J. Samuels, *The Business of the Japanese State: Energy Markets in Comparative and Historical Perspective* (Ithaca: Cornell University Press, 1987).

33. David Vogel, *National Styles of Regulation: Environmental Policy in Great Britain and the United States* (Ithaca: Cornell University Press, 1986), esp. 284, and Samuels, *Business of the Japanese State.*

34. See the articles in Philippe Schmitter and Gerhard Lehmbruch, eds., *Trends toward Corporatist Intermediation* (Beverly Hills, Calif.: Sage, 1979); Gerhard Lehmbruch and Philippe Schmitter, eds., *Patterns of Corporatist Policy-Making* (Beverly Hills, Calif.: Sage, 1982); Suzanne Berger, ed., *Organizing Interests in Western Europe: Pluralism, Corporatism, and the Transformation of Politics* (New York: Cambridge University Press, 1981).

35. See Fritz W. Scharpf, *Crisis and Choice in European Social Democracy,* trans. Ruth Crowley and Fred Thompson (Ithaca: Cornell University Press, 1991), as well as the articles by Claus Offe in Berger, *Organizing Interests in Western Europe,* and David Cameron in John Goldthorpe, ed., *Order and Crisis in Contemporary Capitalism: Studies in the Political Economy of Western European Nations* (New York: Oxford University Press, 1984).

36. For an interesting attempt to solve this problem through the concept of "meso-corporatism," see Alan Cawson, ed., *Organized Interests and the State: Studies in Meso-Corporatism* (Beverly Hills, Calif.: Sage, 1985). This approach acknowledges the particularies of each sector. By attributing outcomes to the particular interest configurations in that sector, however, it risks merging explanations with its descriptions. In many accounts, this approach could explain almost any outcome in any sector.

37. See William H. Sewell, Jr., *Work and Revolution in France: The Language of Labor from the Old Regime to 1848* (New York: Cambridge University Press, 1980). The unofficial persistence of occupational solidarity among nineteenth-century French craftworkers, well after the French Revolution had outlawed guilds and workers' associations, was apparently one of the main inspirations for Emile Durkheim's view of the division of labor. See Emile Durkheim, *Durkheim on Politics and the State,* ed. Anthony Giddens, trans. W. D. Hall (Cambridge: Polity, 1986), 73–77.

2. Professional Identities and Policy Strategies

1. In this book, many types of knowledge are discussed. Without attempting an exhaustive typology, I use the terms "knowledge" and "technical knowledge" as general labels. I use "scientific learning" to designate systematic knowledge, usually developed in the pursuit of basic research results. "Expertise" is, by contrast, applied knowledge used by problem-solving professionals—physicians, lawyers, architects, and engineers. "Technical expertise" is based on knowledge of natural science and used most commonly in engineering tasks rather than medical or legal ones. "Craft-based skill" refers to fairly specific types of knowledge generated through experience in particular production processes. Skill often includes manual or other tactile aspects and is usually transmitted as much through practical supervision as through book learning. The term "practical know-how" refers to problem-specific knowledge that is not written down. Know-how is usually connected with skill, but is in principle no different from other types of "tacit" or "idiosyncratic" knowledge that are also resistant to written transmission. For more detail, see Richard R. Nelson and S. G. Winter, *An Evolutionary Theory of Economic Change* (Cambridge: Harvard University Press, 1982), and Michael Polanyi, *The Tacit Dimension* (Garden City, N.Y.: Doubleday, 1966).

2. Philip Selznick, *Leadership in Administration* (New York: Harper & Row, 1959), 17. For Selznick's discussion of leadership and true commitments in institutions, see ibid., chaps. 2 and 3.

3. This concept of worldview is drawn from Clifford Geertz, *The Interpretation of Cultures* (New York: Basic Books, 1973). For the importance of worldviews as cultural constructs that help occupational groups adjust to industrial change, see Charles Sabel, *Work and Politics* (New York: Cambridge University Press, 1982).

4. This is the central argument in Selznick's book, as described in Charles Perrow, *Complex Organizations,* 3d ed. (New York: Random House, 1986), 167.

5. Paul DiMaggio and Walter Powell, "Introduction," in DiMaggio and Powell, eds., *The New Institutionalism in Organizational Analysis* (Chicago: University of Chicago Press, 1991), 1–38. For Selznick's view of recent developments, see Philip Selznick, "Institutionalism 'Old' and 'New,'" *Administrative Science Quarterly* 41 (1996): 270–277.

6. This formulation elaborates on Williamson's dichotomy between market and hierarchy, developed in *Markets and Hierarchies* (New York: Free Press, 1975), where he derived different organizational forms from a combination of environmental factors and transaction factors. In 1985, he dropped the environmental factors and built his theory more strictly on the basis of the attributes of transactions. Thus, he writes, "efficiency purposes are served by matching governance structures to the attributes of transactions in a discriminating way" (Williamson, *The Economic Institu-*

tions of Capitalism [New York: Free Press, 1985], 68). Subsequent citations refer to the latter work.

7. For the property-rights approach, see Sanford Grossman and Oliver Hart, "The Costs and Benefits of Ownership: A Theory of Vertical and Lateral Integration," *Journal of Political Economy* 94 (1986): 691–719; Oliver Hart and John Moore, "Property Rights and the Nature of the Firm," *Journal of Political Economy* 98 (1990): 1119–1158; and Oliver Hart, *Firms, Contracts, and Financial Structure* (Oxford: Clarendon, 1995). For a comparison of this approach with other types of institutionalist analysis, see Peter A. Hall and Rosemary C. R. Taylor, "Political Science and the Four New Institutionalisms" (Paper delivered at the American Political Science Association, New York, September 1994).

8. Mark Granovetter, "Economic Action and Social Structure: The Problem of Embeddedness," *American Journal of Sociology* 91, no. 3 (November 1985): 481–510.

9. See, for example, Frank Dobbin, *Forging Industrial Policy: The United States, Britain, and France in the Railway Age* (New York: Cambridge University Press, 1994); Victoria Hattam, *Labor Visions and State Power: The Origins of Business Unionism in the United States* (Princeton: Princeton University Press, 1993); Gary Herrigel, *Industrial Constructions: The Sources of German Industrial Power* (New York: Cambridge University Press, 1996); and AnnaLee Saxenian, *Regional Advantage: Culture and Competition in Silicon Valley and Route 128* (Cambridge: Harvard University Press, 1994). The problem of combining structural and interpretive analysis through contextualized comparison is addressed in Richard Locke and Kathleen Thelen, "Apples and Oranges Revisited: Contextualized Comparisons and the Study of Comparative Labor Politics," *Politics and Society* 23, no. 3 (September 1995): 337–367.

10. James March and Herbert Simon, *Organizations* (New York: Wiley, 1958), 165, quoted in Perrow, *Complex Organizations*, 125.

11. Selznick, *Leadership in Administration*, 121–122.

12. See DiMaggio and Powell, "Introduction."

13. James March and Johan Olsen, *Rediscovering Institutions: The Organizational Basis of Politics* (New York: Free Press, 1989), 160–162.

14. See *Daedalus*, special issue "The Professions" (Fall 1963), for an excellent overview of the earlier period. See Robert Dingwall and Philip Lewis, eds., *The Sociology of the Professions: Lawyers, Doctors, and Others* (New York: St. Martin's Press, 1983), for the critical reassessment.

15. Bernard Barber, "Some Problems in the Sociology of the Professions," *Daedalus*, Fall 1963, 672.

16. Everett Hughes, "Professions," *Daedalus*, Fall 1963, 655–668, esp. 657.

17. Ibid., 658; Barber, "Some Problems," 671, 676.

18. Andrew Abbott, *The System of Professions: An Essay on the Division of Expert Labor* (Chicago: University of Chicago Press, 1988).

19. Magali Sarfatti Larson, *The Rise of Professionalism* (Berkeley: University of California Press, 1977), esp. 50–52.

20. John Van Maanen and Stephen R. Barley, "Occupational Communities: Culture and Control in Organizations," *Research in Organizational Behavior* 6 (1984): 287, 316 (for quoted items). See also 316–317 for a review of the critical literature.

21. Abbott, *System of Professions*, esp. 59–62.

22. See the essays in Rolf Torstendahl and Michael Burrage, eds., *The Formation of Professions: Knowledge, State and Strategy* (London: Sage, 1990), and Michael Burrage and Rolf Torstendahl, eds., *Professions in Theory and History: Rethinking the Study of the*

Professions (London: Sage, 1990).

23. Donald J. Treiman, *Occupational Prestige in Comparative Perspective* (New York: Academic Press, 1977).

24. The influence of the legal profession is a major part of Tocqueville's analysis in *Democracy in America*. For a more recent discussion, see Laurent Cohen-Tanugi, *Le Droit sans l'État: Sur la démocratie en France et en Amérique* (Paris: Presses Universitaires de France, 1985).

25. Leon Trilling, "Technological Elites in France and the United States," *Minerva* 17, no. 2 (Summer 1979): 225–243, esp. 240.

26. Hughes, "Professions," 657.

27. John Campbell discusses ideas as programs of action and legitimizing frames in "Institutional Analysis and the Role of Ideas in Political Economy" (paper delivered at the Center for European Studies, Harvard University, 13 October 1995).

28. Abbott, *System of Professions,* 193.

29. Ibid.

30. Differences between scientific inquiry and engineering are forcefully pointed out in Thomas J. Allen, *Managing the Flow of Technology* (Cambridge: MIT Press, 1977), chap. 3, and Nathan Rosenberg, "The Path Dependent Aspects of Technological Change," in his *Exploring the Black Box: Technology, Economics, and History* (New York: Cambridge University Press, 1994), 9–24.

31. Peter Hall, "Policy Paradigms, Social Learning, and the State: The Case of Economic Policymaking in Britain," *Comparative Politics* 25 (April 1993) 275–296.

32. Other political scientists have focused on more formal or codified ideas in demonstrating the political salience of cultural factors. For example, Peter Hall uses academic schools of thought or "paradigms" to explain patterns in British economic policy in his "Policy Paradigms," while Peter J. Katzenstein uses norms in legal discourse to explain patterns in Japanese security policies in his *Cultural Norms and National Security: Police and Military in Postwar Japan* (Ithaca: Cornell University Press, 1996). Richard J. Samuels uses more diffuse views of economic community to explain the "protocols" that guide Japanese policies in *"Rich Nation, Strong Army": National Security and the Technological Transformation of Japan* (Ithaca: Cornell University Press, 1994).

33. Ann Swidler, "Culture in Action: Symbols and Strategies," *American Sociological Review* (April 1986): 273–286.

34. John Ferejon, "Structure and Ideology: Change in Parliament in Early Stuart England," in Judith Goldstein and Robert O. Keohane, eds., *Ideas and Foreign Policy: Beliefs, Institutions, and Political Change* (Ithaca: Cornell University Press, 1993), 207–231.

35. Stanley Hoffmann, "Conclusion," in W. G. Andrews and S. Hoffmann, eds., *The Fifth Republic at Twenty* (Albany: State University of New York Press, 1981), 482–382.

36. Such an approach is suggested by the strategic definition of culture as a set of symbolic tools, offered in Ann Swidler, "Culture in Action." For the lag between organizational and ideational change, see also John A. Hall, "Ideas and the Social Sciences," in Goldstein and Keohane, *Ideas and Foreign Policy,* 31–54, esp. 46.

37. This relationship has been called the global-sectoral link (*rapport global-sectoriel*) in French agricultural policies in Pierre Muller, "Pour une analyse des politiques sectorielles," *Cahiers de l'Animation* 5, no. 53 (1985).

38. This term is developed in Ezra Suleiman, *Elites in France: The Politics of Survival* (Princeton: Princeton University Press, 1978).

39. Joseph Ben-David, *The Scientist's Role in Society* (Englewood Cliffs, N.J.: Prentice-Hall, 1971), 82–84, quotation on 84. See also Roger Hahn, *The Anatomy of a Scientific Institution: The Paris Academy of Science, 1661–1803* (Berkeley: University of California Press, 1971).

40. Louis Liard, *L'Enseignement supérieur en France,* vol. 2 (Paris: Armand Colin, 1894), 34, cited in Suleiman, *Elites in France,* 19.

41. This is the main argument in Terry Shinn, "Reactionary Technologists: The Struggle over the Ecole Polytechnique, 1880–1914," *Minerva* 22, nos. 3/4 (Autumn–Winter 1984): 329–345.

42. James M. Edmondson, *From Mécanicien to Ingénieur: Technical Education and the Machine Building Industry in Nineteenth-Century France* (New York: Garland, 1987).

43. Jürgen Schriewer, "Intermediäre Instanzen, Selbstverwaltung und berufliche Ausbildungsstrukturen im historischen Vergleich," *Zeitschrift für Pädagogik* 32, no. 1 (1986): esp. 75, 76, 82.

44. Stanley Hoffmann, "Paradoxes of the French Political Community," in his *In Search of France* (Cambridge: Harvard University Press, 1963), 73.

45. Richard F. Kuisel, *Capitalism and the State in Modern France* (New York: Cambridge University Press, 1981), 255–256.

46. Discussion of the grands corps is provided in Ezra Suleiman, *Politics, Power, and Bureaucracy in France* (Princeton: Princeton University Press, 1974), 50; and Suleiman, *Elites in France,* 97–101. For a discussion of the postwar adaptation of one of the grands corps, see Jean-Claude Thoenig, *L'Ère des technocrats: Le Cas des ponts et chaussées* (Paris: Editions d'Organisations, 1973.) The corps and the services are not coextensive, for the young corps member, after an initial training period, never loses the association with his corps, even if he is detached to another ministry or administrative service. The importance of this distinction is explained in detail in Suleiman's works. For detailed information regarding the postwar accommodation between ENA and the Polytechnique, see Suleiman, *Elites in France,* 101–108, and Pierre Birnbaum et al., *La Classe dirigeante française: Dissociation, interpénétration, intégration* (Paris: Presses Universitaires de France, 1987), 121–125, 143–145.

47. Michalina Vaughan, "Education: Cultural Persistence and Institutional Change," in Patrick McCarthy, ed., *The French Socialists in Power, 1981–1986* (Westport, Conn.: Greenwood, 1987).

48. A helpful summary and descriptive source is H. D. Lewis, *The French Education System* (New York: St. Martin's Press, 1985). The lesser known engineering schools are also, strictly speaking, members of the association of grandes écoles, although they are colloquially known as petites écoles. These fine-grained status distinctions are discussed in Elliott A. Krause, *Death of the Guilds: Professions, States, and the Advance of Capitalism, 1930 to the Present* (New Haven: Yale University Press, 1996), 154–156.

49. Suleiman, *Elites in France,* 167.

50. Emmanuelle Pautler, "The Links between Secondary and Higher Education in France," *European Journal of Education* 16, no. 2 (1981): 186; Michalina Vaughan, "Education," 79. Students wishing to enter the elite among the grandes écoles d'ingénieurs generally take their baccalauréat in section C (math and physics), a necessity for entrance to two further years of competitive preparatory classes in the intensive math section (*option forte M'*) or the intensive physics section (*option forte*

P'). The tracking systems and examination families are detailed in many guides, of which CEFI, *Guide 86: Formations d'ingenieurs* (Paris, 1986) is a good example.

Pierre Bourdieux, the foremost critic of French institutions for elite production, notes the importance of the "classes préparatoires" in *La Noblese d'État: Grandes écoles et esprit de corps* (Paris: Minuit, 1989), 176–181. The elaborate system of competitive preparatory classes for the leading schools goes back to at least the beginning of this century. See R. R. Locke, *The End of the Practical Man: Entrepreneurship and Higher Education in Germany, France, and Great Britain, 1880–1940* (Greenwich, Conn.: JAI Press, 1984), 45. The curriculum of the Ecole Polytechnique strongly reinforced the emphasis on rational analysis. CEFI's *Guide 86* gave the curriculum at Polytechnique as follows: After a year of military training, the next two years consisted of mathematics (3 modules), physics (3 modules), mechanics (2 modules), applied mathematics (2 modules), economics (1 module), chemistry (1 module), some training in general culture, and three elective modules.

51. See Suleiman, *Elites in France,* 166–175, for several forceful examples of this view.

52. For a concerted indictment of the research efforts of the universities as well as the grandes écoles, see Pierre Papon, *Le Pouvoir et la science en France* (Paris: Centurion, 1978), 90–95, 181–185.

53. See ibid., chap. 3. For Polanyi's description of the scientific enterprise, see his article "The Republic of Science: Its Political and Economic Theory," *Minerva* 1, no. 1 (Autumn 1962): 54–73.

54. Pierre Papon, *Pour une prospective de la science* (Paris: Seghers, 1983), 318.

55. See ibid., 342 ff., for Papon's "plaidoyer pour un néo-colbertisme."

56. For details, see Papon, *Pouvoir et la science,* 40–74.

57. Marc Maurice, François Sellier, and Jean-Jacques Silvestre, *The Social Foundations of Industrial Power: A Comparison of France and Germany,* trans. A. Goldhammer (Cambridge: MIT Press, 1986), 35, 36, 38.

58. Pautler, "Links between Secondary and Higher Education," 193; Jacqueline de Linares, *L'Express,* 17–23 December 1973, as cited in Guy Ratouly, "Les Instituts universitaires de technologie: Avantages et inconvenients," *Paedagogica Europaea* (old ser.) 10, no. 1 (1975): 41.

59. This is part of Leonard Krieger's main argument in *The German Idea of Freedom* (Chicago: University of Chicago Press, 1957).

60. Hans Rosenberg, *Bureaucracy, Aristocracy, and Autocracy: The Prussian Experience, 1660–1815* (Boston: Beacon, 1958), 210–211.

61. From Wilhelm von Humboldt's *Gesammelte Schriften,* vol. 10 (Berlin: Behr, 1903), 255, as quoted in Robert Nisbet, "Max Weber and the Roots of Academic Freedom," in Charles Frankel, ed., *Controversies and Decisions* (New York: Russell Sage, 1976).

62. The contrast between Humboldt's plans for the University of Berlin and the Napoleonic model is made explicit by the authoritative historian of German education Friedrich Paulsen in *The German Universities and University Study* (New York, 1906), quoted in Gordon Craig, *Germany, 1866–1945* (New York: Oxford University Press, 1978), 193.

63. Schriewer, "Intermediäre Instanzen," 77.

64. Ibid., 83.

65. For the German reaction to the prestigious Ecole Polytechnique as an example of technical education, see Lars U. Scholl, "Der Ingenieur im Ausbildung, Beruf und Gesellschaft, 1856 bis 1881," in Karl Heinz Ludwig, ed., *Technik, Ingenieure und Gesellschaft: Geschichte des Vereins Deutscher Ingenieure, 1856–1981* (Düsseldorf: VDI–Verlag, 1981), esp.-6–9.

66. Ben-David argues in *Scientist's Role in Society* that scientific leadership moved distinctly from Paris to Berlin in the 1830s.

67. The phrase in German—"ein inniges Zusammenwirken der geistigen Kräfte deutscher Technik zur gegenseitigen Anregung und Fortbildung im Interesse der gesamten Industrie Deutschlands"—is analyzed in context in Peter Lundgreen, "Die Vertretung technischer Expertise 'im Interesse der gesamten Industrie Deutschlands' durch den VDI 1856 bis 1890," in Ludwig, *Technik, Ingenieure und Gesellschaft*, 67 ff., quotation on 68.

68. For "parapublic institutions," or non-state bodies that performed public functions, see Peter J. Katzenstein, "Germany as Number Two: Reflections on the German Model," in Andrei S. Markovits, ed., *The Political Economy of West Germany: Modell Deutschland* (New York: Praeger, 1982).

69. Lundgreen, "Vertretung Technischer Expertise," 80–81, 92.

70. Wilfried Laatz, *Ingenieure in der Bundesrepublik Deutschland* (Frankfurt: Campus, 1979), 100.

71. Locke, *End of the Practical Man*, 51, 52.

72. For a useful analytic distinction between the terms "ethos" and "world view," see Clifford Geertz, "Ethos, World View, and the Analysis of Sacred Symbols," in *The Interpretation of Cultures* (New York: Basic Books, 1973). My term "ethos of qualification" has, to my knowledge, not been used before. In using it, I have drawn on Kenneth Dyson's emphasis on objective expertise in West Germany's policy style. See Kenneth Dyson, "West Germany: The Search for a Rationalist Consensus," in Jeremy Richardson, ed., *Policy Styles in Western Europe* (London: Allen & Unwin, 1982), 17–46.

73. Peter J. Katzenstein, *Policy and Politics in West Germany: The Growth of a Semisovereign State* (Philadelphia: Temple University Press, 1983), 298 and chap. 7 (which provides an excellent discussion of university reform).

74. Burkart Lutz and Guido Kammerer, *Das Ende des graduierten Ingenieurs?* (Frankfurt: Europäische Verlagsanstalt, 1975). For the relationship between graduate engineers, university engineers, and the classical ideal of nineteenth-century learning, see Konrad Jarausch, *The Unfree Professions: German Lawyers, Teachers, and Engineers* (New York: Oxford University Press, 1990), 19–22; and Krause, *Death of the Guilds*, 241–242.

75. See Maurice et al., *Social Foundations*, 101–107, for cases of this fruitful tension. Michael Crozier's results are presented in *The Bureaucratic Phenomenon* (Chicago: University of Chicago Press, 1964), 69.

76. For the process of specifying vocational curricula, see Wolfgang Streeck, Josef Hilbert, K. H. van Kevelaer, Friederike Maier, and Hajo Weber, *The Role of the Social Partners in Vocational Training and Further Training in the Federal Republic of Germany,* (Berlin: CEDEFOP, 1987), and Karlwilhelm Stratmann, "Curricular and Organizational Problems in Modernizing the Educational Systems in West Germany, with Emphasis on the Needs of Small and Medium-Sized Enterprises in the Metal and Electronics Sectors" (Conference on Worker Skills in the U.S. and the FRG, Goethe Institute, Boston, 27–28 May 1987).

77. Maurice et al., *Social Foundations*, 32–57 provides statistics on upward mobility within the occupational structure. For the nature of the links among occupational groups in Germany, see Arndt Sorge and Wolfgang Streeck, "Industrial Relations and Technical Change: The Case for an Extended Perspective," in R. Hyman and W. Streeck, eds., *New Technology and Industrial Relations* (Oxford: Blackwell, 1988), 19–47.

78. Burkart Lutz and P. Veltz, "Maschinenbauer versus Informatiker," in K. Düll and B. Lutz, eds., *Technikentwicklung und Arbeitsteilung im internationalen Vergleich* (Frankfurt and New York: Campus, 1989).

79. Henry Ergas introduced the distinction between "mission-oriented" and "diffusion-oriented" policies in "Does Technology Policy Matter?" in Bruce R. Guile and Harvey Brooks, *Technology and Global Industry: Companies and Nations in the World Economy* (Washington, D.C.: National Academy Press, 1987).

80. Hall, "Policy Paradigms," 279.

3. DIGITIZING THE PUBLIC TELEPHONE NETWORK: TELECOMMUNICATIONS

1. Throughout this book, I focus on the Federal Republic of Germany, which included West Germany until 1990 and unified Germany from that date onward. Unless the context requires further specification, I therefore use the term "Germany" in this sense.

2. Simon Nora and Alain Minc, *L'Informatisation de la société* (Paris: Documentation française, 1978), published in English as *The Computerization of Society* (Cambridge: MIT Press, 1980). For Germany, see *Regierungsprogramm zur Förderung von Forschung und Entwicklung im Bereich der Technischen Kommunikation, 1978–1982* (Bonn: BMFT, 1979).

3. Henry Ergas, "Does Technology Policy Matter?" in Bruce R. Guile and Harvey Brooks, eds., *Technology and Global Industry* (Washington, D.C.: National Academy Press, 1987), 191–245.

4. Elie Cohen, *Le Colbertisme "high tech": Economie des télécommunications et du grand project* (Paris: Hachette, 1992).

5. For the transaction-cost approach, see Oliver Williamson, *The Economic Institutions of Capitalism* (New York: Free Press, 1985), 61–63; for property rights, see Oliver Hart, *Firms, Contracts and Financial Structure* (Oxford: Clarendon, 1995).

6. For comparisons with the procurement and manufacture of switches in North America and Japan, see F. M. Scherer, *International High-Technology Competition* (Cambridge: Harvard University Press, 1992), 86–91; and Martin Fransman, *Japan's Computer and Communications Industry* (Oxford: Oxford University Press, 1995).

7. A. N. Holcombe, *Public Ownership of Telephones on the Continent of Europe* (Boston: Houghton Mifflin, 1911), 6, 12; Catherine Bertho, *Télégraphes et téléphones: De Valmy au microprocesseur* (Paris: Livre de Poche, 1981), 16. See also Catherine Bertho ed., *Histoire des télécommunications en France* (Toulouse: Erès, 1984), 19–23.

8. At certain times, the administrative unit dealing with communications was an autonomous ministry, while at other times it was part of another ministry and directed by a secretary of state with cabinet rank. The name "Postes et Télégraphes" or "P et T" was used until 1925, when the abbreviation "PTT" was officially adopted to signify "Postes, Télégraphes et Téléphones." In 1959 the ministry was redesignated "Postes et Télécommunications," although the abbreviation "PTT" was retained. In

1980 the full name was revised again when the ministry was also granted jurisdiction over television, and the PTT became officially known as the Ministère des Postes et Télécommunications et de la Télédiffusion (Louis-Joseph Libois, *Genèse et croissance des télécommunications* [Paris: Masson, 1983], 196, 202).

9. Rugès, *Le Téléphone pour tous* (Paris: Seuil, 1970), 54, and for employment figures, 56.

10. For details on the DGT's access to capital, see ibid. and Bertho, *Télégraphes et téléphones*, 476–477.

11. For a good analysis of relations between the DGT and the Planning Commission, see Libois, *Genèse et croissance,* 247. For the role of the Planning Commission, see Peter Hall, *Governing the Economy* (New York: Oxford University Press, 1986), 141–146.

12. Henri Jannès, *Le Dossier secret du téléphone* (Paris: Flammarion, 1970).

13. Bertho, *Télégraphes et téléphones,* 296, 412.

14. Ibid., 287.

15. Ibid., 443.

16. Catherine Bertho, "La Recherche publique en télécommunication, 1880–1941," *Télécommunications hors série,* October 1983, 72; Bertho, *Télégraphes et téléphones,* 418, 423, 444; Rugès, *Téléphone pour tous,* 86.

17. Art. 73, no. 7 and arts. 123 and 124, in conformity with the Law on Telecommunications Facilities, FAG, Gesetz über Fernmeldeanlagen (Fernmeldeanlagengesetz) of 14 January 1928.

18. Holcombe, *Public Ownership,* 23–25.

19. Ibid., 25, 26.

20. Information on the early development of telegraphy and telephony in Germany is taken from Holcombe, *Public Ownership;* Sigfrid von Weiher and Herbert Goetzler, *The Siemens Company: Its Historical Role in the Progress of Electrical Engineering . . . , 1847–1977* (Berlin: Siemens, 1977); Georg Siemens, *Geschichte des Hauses Siemens,* 3 vols. (Munich: Karl Alber, 1947–1953), and the revised edition of the same history, also by Georg Siemens, *Der Weg der Elektrotechnik* (Freiburg: Alber, 1961). For network growth, see also Frank Thomas, "The Politics of Growth: The German Telephone System," in Renate Mayntz and Thomas Hughes, eds., *The Development of Large Technical Systems* (Frankfurt/Boulder: Campus/Westview, 1988), 179ff.

21. The qualifications involved, first, any area where the Reichspost did not itself provide telephone service. And second, it involved three types of telephone links where approval from the Reichspost was waived (*Genehmigungsfreiheit*): those built by regional and municipal administrations for their own internal use; those built for transportation enterprises (mostly railroads) for their own use; and those built on a single private property or on jointly owned properties which were not separated by more than twenty-five kilometers. See the Gesetz über das Telegraphenwesen des Deutschen Reichs of 6 April 1892, *Reichs-Gesetzblatt,* 1892, 467, and the Gesetz über Fernmeldeanlagen of 14 January 1928, *Reichs-Gesetzblatt,* 1928, pt. I. p. 8.

22. Douglas Webber, "The Assault on the 'Fortress on the Rhine': The Politics of Telecommunications Deregulation in the Federal Republic of Germany," paper delivered at the Conference of Europeanists, Washington, D.C., 30 October–1 November 1987, published under collective authorship in Alan Cawson et al., *Hostile Brothers: Competition and Closure in the European Electronics Industry* (Oxford: Clarendon, 1990).

23. Renate Mayntz and Fritz W. Scharpf, *Policymaking in the German Federal Republic* (New York: Elsevier, 1975).

24. Webber, "Assault." 5.

25. G. Siemens, *Geschichte des Hauses Siemens,* 3:38.

26. The first of these joint ventures was FAEBAG (Fernsprech-Ämterbau G.m.b.H.), formed in 1920 for the provision of small local switches and transit switches. It had four members, including DeTeWe, Mix and Genest, C. Lorenz, Süddeutsche Telefon und Kabel. The second was Autofabag (Automatisiche Fernsprech-Anlagen-Bau-Gesellschaft m.b.H.), founded in 1922, for automatic exchanges. Its members were DeTeWe of Berlin, C. Lorenz of Berlin-Tempelhof, and Telephonfabrik Berliner of Berlin-Steglitz. See Karl-Heinz Loesche and Dieter Leuthold, *DeTeWe Chronik: Technisch-historisch Betrachtung des Firmengeschehens* (Berlin: Deutsche Telephonwerke und Kabelindustrie, 1970), 131, 199n.

27. Ibid.; Siemens, *Geschichte des Hauses Siemens,* 3:41, and *Der Elektrotechnik,* 2:79.

28. Loesche and Leuthold, *DeTeWe Chronik,* 53–54, 134.

29. George Washington Polk, "Siemens' Road to Rebirth: The Early Reconstruction Years of a German Industry" (undergraduate thesis, Harvard University, 1976), esp. 81–85.

30. Not until 1955, for example, did the firm modernize certain features of the rotary technology that were developed by AT&T just after World War I. See Godefroy Dang Nguyen, "Telecommunications: A Challenge to the Old Order," in Margaret Sharp, ed., *Europe and the New Technologies* (Ithaca: Cornell University Press, 1986), 130n.

31. Webber, "Assault"; R. J. Raggett, "Making the Digital Switch," *Telephony,* 5 May 1980. Market shares are reliable estimates for 1978 from Ernst Eggers, "Darstellung und wettbewerbspolitische Würdigung des Nachfrageverhaltens der Deutschen Bundespost im Fernmeldebereich," Gutachten im Auftrag der Monopolkommission (Bonn, March 1980), 20.

32. For switching technology, see Nguyen, "Telecommunications."

33. Ibid., 108.

34. Ibid., 101.

35. Thierry Vedel, "Les Ingénieurs des télécommunications," *Culture technique,* no. 12 (March 1984). Except where noted, the following is drawn from Vedel.

36. Libois, *Genèse et croissance,* 201–202; Vedel, "Ingénieurs des télécommunications," 67.

37. Libois, *Genèse et croissance,* 202, 226.

38. Bertho, "Recherche publique," 72.

39. Ibid., 73.

40. Ibid., 76–77.

41. Ibid., 78.

42. Libois, *Genèse et croissance,* 226–229.

43. Bertho, *Télégraphes et téléphones,* 440–441; Libois, *Genèse et croissance,* 99.

44. Rugès, *Téléphone pour tous;* Bertho, *Télégraphes et téléphones,* 417.

45. Rugès, *Téléphone pour tous,* 81–82.

46. Libois, *Genèse et croissance, Le Monde,* 20 November 1985.

47. Vedel, "Ingénieurs des télécommunications," 67; Libois, *Genèse et croissance,* 235.

48. Quoted in Vedel, "Ingénieurs des télécommunications," 68.

49. Ezra N. Suleiman, *Elites in France,* (Princeton: Princeton University Press, 1978), 167.

50. Bertho, *Télégraphes et téléphones,* 466. For a documentary review by the protagonist, see Henri Jannès, *Le Dossier secret du téléphone* (Paris: Flammarion, 1970).

51. Rugès, *Téléphone pour tous,* was the reverse spelling for the PTT's street address, Avenue du Ségur, by which the ministry was colloquially known.

52. Ibid. For penetration and financing figures, see also Bertho, *Télégraphes et téléphones,* 410, 450.

53. Rugès, *Téléphone pour tous,* 69.

54. The aggressively ambitious administrators, such as Giscard d'Estaing, who proceeded from Polytechnique to ENA were the exception rather than the rule.

55. Rugès, *Téléphone pour tous,* 62.

56. Ibid., 90–92, 96–97.

57. Ibid., 110.

58. Ibid., 111–112.

59. Jürgen Kocka, *Unternehmensverwaltung und Angestelltenschaft am Beispiel Siemens 1847–1914: Zum Verhältnis von Kapitalismus und Bürokratie in der deutschen Industrialisierung* (Stuttgart: Ernst Klett, 1969), 58. Siemens, *Geschichte des Hauses Siemens,* 1:101–102. Weiher and Goetzler, *Siemens Company,* 38.

60. The degree to which Stock relied on Swedish designs was unclear. Georg von Siemens emphasized Stock's dependence while Loesche and Leuthold in *DeTeWe Chronik* merely acknowledged a relationship of some kind.

61. Siemens, *Geschichte des Hauses Siemens,* 1:203–204.

62. Ibid., 2:84–85. For corroboration, see the official history of the Postal Ministry, Karl Sautter, *Geschichte der Deutschen Reichspost, 1871–1945* (Frankfurt: Bundesdruckerei, 1951).

63. Weiher and Goetzler, *Siemens Company,* 68.

64. Kocka, *Unternehmensverwaltung,* 148–192, esp. 155–156, 191–192.

65. Ibid., 173–174.

66. Siemens, *Geschichte des Hauses Siemens,* 3:33.

67. Ibid., 1:209.

68. Ibid., 3:38–39.

69. These enterprises were the Deutsche Fernkabelgesellschaft and the Automatische-Fernsprechanlagen-Baugesellschaft.

70. Ralf Dahrendorf, *Society and Democracy* (Garden City, N.Y.: Doubleday, 1967), gives many examples of the resilience of the prewar social elites.

71. Webber, "Assault," 4, 6.

72. Interviews, Bundesministerium fur das Post und Fernmeldewesen, Bonn, summer 1986; Deutsche Bundespost, *Geschäftsbericht,* 1982, 1983, 1984; Wolfgang Niopek, *Innovationsverhalten öffentlicher Unternehmen: Determinanten, Typen und Funktionen* (Baden-Baden: Nomos, 1986), 179, 181.

73. "Ingenieure im öffentlichen Dienst: Magere Bezahlung für Ingenieure schreckt ab," *VDI Nachrichten,* 28 March 1986, 1; Dietrich Bendfeldt, "Ingenieur-Mangel bei der DBP," *Der Ingenieur der Deutschen Bundespost* 2 (April 1986): 69–71.

74. Webber, "Assault," 12ff.

75. See ibid., 16, and Peter Bruce, "The High Price of a State Monopoly," *Financial Times,* 11 July 1985.

76. Interviews, VDMA, Frankfurt, August 1986.

77. Interviews, ZVEI and VDMA, Frankfurt, August 1986, and Nixdorf, Bonn, August 1986. Information from these interviews agrees well with the results reported by Webber, "Assault," and Bruce, "High Price of a State Monopoly."

78. Webber, "Assault," 17.

79. For the development of digital switching technologies in the United States and Japan, see especially Scherer, *International High-Technology Competition*, 86–91, and Fransman, *Japan's Computer and Communications Industry*, 49–73.

80. Libois, *Genèse et croissance*, esp. 159ff.

81. See above for the difference between semi-electronic and fully-electronic switching technologies.

82. Libois, *Genèse et croissance*, 163; Bertho, *Télégraphes et téléphones*, 489–490.

83. The most detailed account of the projet PLATON is given by Libois, who helped supervise it. See also Nguyen, "Telecommunications," 106.

84. Bertho, *Télégraphes et téléphones*, 488; Libois, *Genèse et croissance*, 167.

85. Bertho, *Télégraphes et téléphones*, 480; J.-H. Lorenzi and Eric Le Boucher, *Mémoires volées* (Paris: Ramsay, 1979), 120; Libois, *Genèse et croissance*, 262.

86. Bertho, *Télégraphes et téléphones*, 490; Lorenzi and Le Boucher, *Mémoires volées*.

87. Jannès, *Dossier secret*, and Rugès, *Téléphone pour tous*, both report on these practices. See also Lorenzi and Le Boucher, *Mémoires volées*, and Jean-Michel Quatrepoint and Alain Faujas, "Le Gouvernement organise l'industrie des télécommunications autour des groupes C.G.E. et Thomson," *Le Monde*, 15 May 1976.

88. This discussion is based on Bertho, *Télégraphes et téléphones;* Lorenzi and Le Boucher, *Mémoires volées;* and Quatrepoint and Faujas, "Le Gouvernement organise l'industrie."

89. Bertho, *Télégraphes et téléphones*, 489; *Le Monde*, 2 February, 21 April, and 15 May 1976.

90. Jean-Michel Quatrepoint in *Le Monde*, 14 May 1976.

91. Bertho, *Télégraphes et téléphones*, 490.

92. Ibid., 491.

93. Ibid. See also *Financial Times*, 15 December 1978; Lorenzi and Le Boucher, *Mémoires volées*, 123; and Alan Cawson, Peter Holmes, and Anne Stevens, "The Interaction between Firms and the State in France: The Telecommunications and Consumer Electronics Sectors," in Stephen Wilks and Maurice Wright, eds., *Comparative Government-Industry Relations: Western Europe, the U.S., and Japan* (Oxford: Clarendon, 1987), 10ff.

94. Interviews, Paris, July 1986. See also Cawson et al., "Interaction"; *Le Monde*, 11 January and 2 March 1983; *Financial Times*, 4 February 1983.

95. "Digital Switching: The French Connection," *Telecom France*, December 1981, 23.

96. Jean-Michel Quatrepoint, "Thomson et la C.G.E. négocient un nouveau partage de leurs activités," *Le Monde*, 9 September 1983: 1; *Le Point*, 25 September 1983.

97. For the agreement between Thomson and CGE, see *Le Monde*, 22 September and 4 October 1983; *Le Point*, (25 September 1983). The distinction between ownership and management under socialist auspices is stressed in Elie Cohen and Michel Bauer, *Les Grandes Manoeuvres industrielles* (Paris: Belfond, 1985).

98. *Le Monde*, 9 July 1982.

99. Barbara Jenkins and George Lodge, "French Telecommunications in the 1980s," case 9-388-160 (case study, Harvard Business School, 1988).

100. *Le Monde*, 23 September 1983. 32.

101. A report by A. D. Little which stated that a supplier needed at least 3% of the world switching market to survive was widely circulated about this time. See, for example, Nguyen, "Telecommunications," 107.

102. For details, see *Le Monde*, 22 September 1983, and Georges Pebereau's open letter to shareholders published ibid., 19 October 1983.

103. Interview, Alcatel, Vélizy, summer 1986. See also Cawson et al., "Interaction," 22.

104. See Eric Le Boucher, "La CGE et Thomson créent une société commune d'études de télécommunications," *Le Monde*, 2 December 1983, and articles by Pierre Laurent in *l'Humanité*, 15, 17, and 25 October 1985.

105. See Vedel, "Ingénieurs des télécommunications."

106. *Le Monde*, 8 July 1983; *Le Matin*, 8 July 1983; "On trouve tout dans les labos des Télécom," *Quotidien de Paris*, 9 October 1985.

107. For deregulation in telecommunications, see Steven K. Vogel, *Freer Markets, More Rules: Regulatory Reform in Advanced Industrial Countries* (Ithaca: Cornell University Press, 1995). The European Community's policies can be traced through Commission of the European Community, *Towards a Dynamic Economy: Green Paper on the Development of the Common Market for Telecommunications Services and Equipment* (Brussels, 1987); Commission of the European Union, *Green Paper on the Liberalization of Telecommunications Infrastructure and Cable Television Networks* (Brussels, 1994).

108. *Wall Street Journal*, 30 December 1986; *Financial Times*, 8 January, 9 January, and 31 December 1987; *Le Monde*, 24 April 1987.

109. "Les Ingénieurs des télécommunications proposent d'abondonner le statut d'administration," *Le Monde*, 28 November 1985; "La DGT et la déréglementation" and "Vives reactions syndicales du projet de réform des PTT," *Le Monde*, 2 December 1985; *Libération*, 25 November 1985; Cohen, *Colbertisme "high tech,"* 254.

110. *Financial Times*, 20 July 1988; Cohen, *Colbertisme "high tech,"* 254.

111. "Neuf Mois apres la grève du personnel," *Le Monde*, 3 August 1994; "France Telecom est victime de son propre changement," *Le Monde*, 13 July 1995; "François Henrot succède a la tête de France Telecom," *Le Monde*, 1 September 1995.

112. Interview, Alcatel, N.V., Paris, July 1992; Razeen Sally, "Alcatel's Relations with the French State: The Political Economy of a Multinational Enterprise," *Communications et Stratégies* 9 (1993). For ATM switching, see "Sprint Forms Joint Venture with Alcatel," *New York Times*, 4 February 1993, and "ATM with a French Accent," *Byte* 19, no. 12 (December 1994): 130.

113. *Le Monde*, 28 December 1993 and 19 April 1995.

114. "Les ingénieurs télécom sont apellés à devenir de plus en plus polyvalente," *Le Monde*, 20 February 1996; "Les Ecoles d'ingénieurs de France Telecom vont changer de status," *Le Monde*, 29 October 1996.

115. Raggett, "Making the Digital Switch."

116. On the Sachverständigen Kommission and other major advisory efforts in telecommunications, see Edgar Grande, *Vom Monopol zum Wettbewerb? Die Neokonservative Reform der Telecommunikation in Großbritannien und der Bundesrepublik Deutschland* (Wiesbaden: Deutscher Universitäts Verlag, 1989); and Barbara Mettler-Meibom, *Breitbandtechnologie: Über die Chancen sozialer Vernunft in technologiepolitischen Entscheidungsprozessen* (Opladen: Westdeutscher Verlag, 1986).

117. Raggett, "Making the Digital Switch."

118. *Frankfurter Allgemeine Zeitung*, 19 December 1972; *Süddeutsche Zeitung*, 19 December 1972; *Die Zeit*, 22 December 1972.

119. Volker Hauff and Fritz Scharpf, *Modernisierung der Volkswirtschaft: Technologiepolitik als Strukturpolitik* (Frankfurt am Main: Europäische Verlagsanstalt, 1975), esp. 9, 17–19.

120. Mettler-Meibom, *Breitbandtechnologie*, 179, 208.

121. Ibid., 210ff, 230, 234ff.

122. *Financial Times*, 15 December 1978 and 22 August 1979; *Telecomm France*, 2 December 1981, 20.

123. "Alte Mechanik," *Der Spiegel*, 5 March 1979, 84–86.

124. Raggett, "Making the Digital Switch."

125. Interviews, FTZ, Darmstadt, November 1988. The EWS software, which totaled hundreds of thousands of lines, had to be written and debugged in assembler language. Later in the decade, when more storage capacity became standard through LSI components, so-called high-level compilers such as CHILL were developed specifically for telecommunications switching. My interviews at the Fernmeldetechnisches Zentralamt, confirmed the general view of the difficulties that Siemens and the Bundespost (like all other actors in the industry) experienced with software development at this time.

126. Internal Bundespost memo, quoted in Mettler-Meibom, *Breitband technologie*, 301–302.

127. "Schwarzer Freitag in München: Die entwicklung des elektronischen Wählsystems für das Telephon muß gestoppt werden," *Die Zeit*, 2 February 1979.

128. Interview, Siemens Unternehmensbereich Nachrichtentechnik, Munich, June 1986. See also "Schwarzer Freitag in München."

129. Interviews, Bundespost and former Bundespost officials, Bonn, November 1988.

130. "Alte Mechanik," and *Der Spiegel*, 10 September 1979, as cited in Nguyen, "Telecommunications," 102. See also "Die Post ist Frei," *Die Zeit*, 2 March 1979.

131. Interview, Deutsche Bundespost, Bonn, May 1986; Raggett, "Making the Digital Switch," 86.

132. Raggett, "Making the Digital Switch."

133. Figure based on interviews reported in *Financial Times*, 22 August 1979. The company's worldwide employment was 344,000, of whom 235,000 were located in Germany. Employees in R&D numbered approximately 25,000, according to Siemens' annual report, *Geschäftsbericht, 1979/1980*.

134. Siemens, *Geschäftsbericht*, 1982.

135. Interviews, SEL, Stuttgart.

136. Interviews. Raggett, "Making the Digital Switch."

137. Susanne K. Schmidt, "Taking the Long Road to Liberalization: Telecommunications Reform in the Federal Republic of Germany," *Telecommunications Policy* 15, no. 3 (June 1991): 209–22.

138. Schmidt, "Taking the Long Road." For the DPG's role in the processes of liberalization and privatization, see Owen Darbishire, "Switching Systems, Technological Change, Competition, and Privatisation," *Industrielle Beziehungen* 2, no. 3 (1995): 156–179, and "Germany," in Harry C. Katz, ed., *Telecommunications: Restructuring Work and Employment Relations Worldwide* (Ithaca: Cornell University Press, 1997) 189–227.

139. "Zustimmung des Bundestags zur Postreform," *Neue Zürcher Zeitung*, 30 June 1994, 22; "Kurzatmige Bonner Postreform: Wenn die Privatisierung vom Wettbewerb ablenkt," ibid., 9 July 1994, 23.

140. *New York Times*, 10 August 1992, and *Financial Times*, 4 September 1990.

141. Hariolf Grupp and Thomas Schnöring, "Research and Development in Telecommunications: National Systems under Pressure," *Telecommunications Policy*, January/February 1992, 46–66. Aggregate figures exclude military R&D for telecommunications.

142. Interview, Personnel Department, Deutsche Telekom, Bonn, January 1996; transcript of remarks by Eckart Raubold, "The Technology Centre in Darmstadt," Deutsche Telekom press conference, Bonn, February 1996; *Computerwoche*, 22 January 1993, 20.

143. Interviews, CGE, Paris, July, 1986.

4. Retooling the Industrial Plant: Machine Tools

1. From the voluminous literature on machine tolls, the following were particularly helpful in my research: Gary Herrigel, "Industrial Order and the Politics of Industrial Change: Mechanical Engineering," in Peter J. Katzenstein, ed., *Industry and Politics in West Germany: Toward the Third Republic* (Ithaca: Cornell University Press, 1989); Marc Maurice, Arndt Sorge and Malcolm Warner, "Societal Differences in Organizing Manufacturing Units: A Comparison of France, West Germany, and Great Britain," *Organization Studies* 1 (1980): 59–86; Nathan Rosenberg, *Perspectives on Technology* (London: Cambridge University Press, 1976); and Michael Schumann, Volker Baethge-Kinsky, Martin Kuhlmann, Constanze Kurz, and Uwe Neumann, *Trendreport Rationalisierung: Automobilindustrie, Werkzeugmaschinenbau, Chemische Industrie* (Berlin: Sigma, 1994). Comparative developments in Japan and the United States are presented in David Friedman, *The Misunderstood Miracle: Industrial Development and Political Change in Japan* (Ithaca: Cornell University Press, 1988), and David Finegold et al., *The Decline of the U.S. Machine Tool Industry and Prospects for Its Sustainable Recovery* (Santa Monica: Rand, 1994).

2. Renate Mayntz, "Implementation von regulativer Politik," in Mayntz, ed., *Implementation politischer Programme*, vol. 2, *Ansätze zur Theoriebildung* (Opladen: Westdeutscher Verlag, 1983), 50–74, esp. 56.

3. On tacit knowledge and its historical distribution in France and Germany, see Burkart Lutz and P. Veltz, "Maschinenbauer versus Informatiker," in K. Düll and B. Lutz, eds., *Technikentwicklung und Arbeitsteilung im internationalen Vergleich* (Frankfurt/New York: 1989).

4. James M. Edmonson, *From Mécanicien to Ingénieur: Technical Education and the Machine Building Industry in Nineteenth-Century France* (New York: Garland, 1987).

5. Ibid., 95ff.; Peter Lundgreen, "Engineering Education in Europe and the U.S.A., 1750–1930: The Rise to Dominance of School Culture and the Engineering Professions," *Annals of Science* 47 (1990): 33–75; Charles Rodney Day, "The Making of Mechanical Engineers in France: The Ecoles d'arts et métiers, 1803–1914," *French Historical Studies* 10 (Spring 1978): 439–460.

6. CEFI, "Débouches–Carrières: Ingénieurs diplômés et non-diplômés" (typescript report, Comité d'Etudes sur les Formations d'Ingénieurs, Paris, n.d.). The

number of engineers defined in terms of their work responsibilities (*ingénieurs au sens de la fonction*) is compiled by the national statistical service (INSEE).

7. Jürgen Schriewer, "Intermediäre Instanzen, Selbstverwaltung und berufliche Ausbildungsstrukturen im historischen Vergleich," *Zeitschrift für Pädagogik* 32, no. 1 (1986): 82; Marc Maurice, François Sellier, and Jean-Jacques Silvestre, *The Social Foundations of Industrial Power: A Comparison of France and Germany*, trans. A. Goldhammer (Cambridge: MIT Press, 1986), 35, 36.

8. The following discussion is based especially on Maurice et al., *Social Foundations*, and Michel Crozier, *The Bureaucratic Phenomenon* (Chicago: University of Chicago Press, 1964).

9. Max Leclerc, *La Formation des ingénieurs à l'étranger et en France* (Paris: 1917), 78, quoted in R. R. Locke, *The End of the Practical Man: Entrepreneurship and Higher Education in Germany, France, and Great Britain, 1880–1940* (Greenwich, Conn.: JAI Press, 1984), 44.

10. Crozier, *Bureaucratic Phenomenon*, 122.

11. Lundgreen, "Engineering Education," 51.

12. Ibid.

13. Schriewer, "Intermediäre Instanzen," 84.

14. For the role of the graduierte Ingenieure, see Maurice et al., *Social Foundations*, 100–104; Charles F. Sabel, *Work and Politics: The Division of Labor in Industry* (New York: Cambridge University Press, 1982), 87; and Claus Oppelt, *Ingenieure im Beruf* (Berlin: Max-Planck-Institut für Bildungsforschung, 1976), Preface.

15. Extrapolating from French census figures from 1975, the number of employees in engineering jobs in 1980 is estimated at approximately 292,000. See CEFI, "Débouches–Carrières." For Germany, *Statistisches Jahrbuch* (Stuttgart: Kohlhammer, 1982), 98.

16. See the essays in Karl-Heinz Ludwig, ed., *Technik, Ingenieure und Gesellschaft: Geschichte des Vereins Deutscher Ingenieure, 1856–1981* (Düsseldorf: VDI, 1981), 155, 249, 537.

17. On the Facharbeiter, see Horst Kern and Michael Schumann, *Das Ende der Arbeitsteilung?* (Munich: Beck, 1984). On the importance of the craft tradition in Germany, see Sabel, *Work and Politics*.

18. Maurice et al., *Social Foundations*, 37.

19. These developments are traced in Philippe Mioche, "Les Difficultés de la modernisation dans le cas de l'industrie française de la machine outil, 1941–1953," European University Institute Working Paper 85/168. Elie Cohen and Michael Bauer, *Les Grandes Manoeuvres industrielles* (Paris: Belfond, 1985), 127–128, summarizes the same developments.

20. Jean Chardonnet, *L'Economie française*, vol. 1, "Industrie," 2d rev. ed. (Paris: Dalloz, 1970), 376; Cohen and Bauer, *Grandes Manoeuvres industrielles*, 124.

21. The coexistence of liberal and dirigiste doctrine in French industrial policy is analyzed in Suzanne Berger, "Lame Ducks and National Champions: Industrial Policy in the Fifth Republic," in W. G. Andrews and S. Hoffmann, eds., *The Fifth Republic at Twenty* (Albany: State University of New York, 1981).

22. Andrew Shonfield, *Modern Capitalism* (London: Oxford University Press, 1965), 138; Chardonnet, *L'Economie française*, 125–156, 374. For government plans in this sector, the English-language trade press was often quicker than the French.

See, for example, *American Metal Market,* 9 December 1974; *American Metal Market,* 26 January 1976; as well as Cohen and Bauer, *Grandes Manoeuvres industrielles,* 116–117.

23. Cohen and Bauer, *Grandes Manoeuvres industrielles,* 122–123; Philippe Labarde in *Le Monde,* 13 January 1976, also notes the official preference for dealing with larger firms.

24. This account is based on Cohen and Bauer, *Grandes Manoeuvres industrielles;* "M. d'Ornano présente un petit plan de développement de l'industrie des machines-outils," *Le Monde,* 13 January 1976, 32; Bernard Réal, "Technical Change and Economic Policy: Sector Report and the Machine Tool Industry" (Paris: OECD, August 1980), 40; *Nouvel Economiste,* 3 August 1981, 28–29.

25. This dynamic is at the center of John Zysman's *Governments, Markets, and Growth: Financial Systems and the Politics of Industrial Change* (Ithaca: Cornell University Press, 1983).

26. For example, several already existing export associations were revivified—including the Alliance des Constructeurs Française de Machines-Outils (AFCMO), which was first founded in 1951 for cultivating markets in the Far East and the Western Hemisphere, and the Comité de Coordination des Constructeurs Français de Machines-Outils (CCCFMO), which was formed in 1972 for monitoring major calls for bids in the Eastern Bloc countries. Additional export associations formed under the Ornano plan to promote trade to particular regions included Mofir (Machine-Outil Française en Iran), Mofeg (Egypte), and Mofcor (Corée du Sud). Interestingly, these efforts were all coordinated through the existing industry trade association (SCFMO), whereas the anticipated state agency for financing exports, SOFIMO (Société pour le Financement de la Machine-Outil), never got off the ground. These examples are presented in Georges Le Gall, "Ceux qui exportent," *L'Usine nouvelle,* 22 May 1980, 139–140. SOFIMO is discussed on 136.

27. *Financial Times,* 7 June 1978; *Echos,* 30 March and 4 April 1979.

28. *Echos,* 3 December 1979, 5 December 1980; *L'Usine nouvelle,* 1 February 1979; and *Nouvel Economiste,* 1 June 1981, 53.

29. For different opinions in this discussion, see "Faible pénétration de la machine-outil à commande numérique," *Echos,* 4 June 1980; "Machines-outils à CN: Les PMI de la mécanique s'équipent plus rapidement," *L'Usine nouvelle,* 5 June 1980; "La Commande numérique en vedette," *L'Usine nouvelle,* 29 May 1980; "Lasers et paliers magnétiques adoptés par la machine-outil," *Echos,* 30 May 1980; and "Machine-outils: Des lendemains périlleux," *Le Monde,* 30 May 1980, 38.

30. "Machines-outils: Le défi japonais," *Nouvel Economiste,* 2 June 1980, 62.

31. Pierre Dacier, Jean-Louis Levet, and Jean-Claude Tourret, *Les Dossiers noirs de l'industrie française* (Paris: Fayard, 1985), 331–375. This source is a retrospective analysis by figures involved in policy under the Socialist government and is therefore most useful as a guide to the perceptions of the policymaking elite. Levet was a civil servant in the DIMME. Tourret was employed in one of the consulting firms, SRI Paris, with which the DIMME worked closely. Dacier is a pseudonym for a former official involved in implementing policy for the Socialist government.

32. The discussion in this paragraph is drawn largely from Dacier et al., *Dossiers noirs,* esp. 345, 348, 351–352.

33. Quoted in *L'Usine nouvelle,* 22 May 1980, 138.

34. "Cri d'alarme des industriels de la machine-outil," *Echos,* 5 December 1980; see also "La France veut-elle garder un secteur de la machine-outil?" *Le Monde,* 2 December 1980.

35. Dacier et. al., *Dossiers noirs,* 354. See also "Le gouvernement prêt à prendre des mesures pour la mécanique et la robotique," *Echos,* 10 March 1981.

36. Dacier et al., *Dossiers noirs,* 354; *Echos,* of 10 March 1981; *Nouvel Economiste,* 4 June 1979, 58. The remarks of Claude Billaud of Renault Machine-Outil are quoted in *Nouvel Economiste,* 1 June 1981, 55.

37. The principal French entrants included Télémécanique, the large engineering firm; CIT-Alcatel, the country's main telecommunications supplier; and Feutrier, a CNC specialist attached to Ratier-Forest and subsequently purchased by Télémécanique. See *Expansion,* November 1976, 202.

38. Interview, Ministry of Industry, Paris, July 1986.

39. Interviews, Société NUM, Nanterre, December 1988. For NUM's early international strategy, see "Commande numérique: NUM tisse sa toile à l'étranger," *L'Usine nouvelle,* 22 May 1980, 139, and "NUM: Un réseau européen crée en un an," *L'Usine nouvelle,* 26 March 1981, 141–142.

40. The Dufour story is related in *Echos,* 29 July 1980, 2; *Le Monde,* 11 November 1980, 29, and 2 December 1980, 42; and *L'Usine nouvelle,* 29 January 1981, 52.

41. "L'Accord H. Ernault-Somua-Toyoda entre dans les faits," *Echos,* 19 September 1980; "Ernault Somua devoile ses plans," *L'Usine nouvelle,* 23 April 1981, 64–65.

42. *L'Usine nouvelle,* 25 June 1981, 38; Dacier et al., *Dossiers noirs,* 362.

43. For relations between government and labor, see George Ross, "From One Left to Another," in George Ross, Stanley Hoffmann, and Sylvia Malzacher, eds., *The Mitterrand Experiment* (New York: Oxford University Press, 1987), 199–216, esp. 202.

44. The process of policy formulation was described to me in detail by two officials from the Ministry of Industry without any reference to labor's involvement (interviews, Ministry of Industry, Paris, July 1986, and former official at the DIMME, Paris, December 1988). Labor is conspicuously absent from the list of policy interlocutors mentioned by the Minister of Industry, Pierre Dreyfus, in "Le Programme machine-outil demarre," *L'Usine nouvelle,* 3 December 1981, 68.

45. Interview, Ministry of Industry, Paris, 1986. For background on the DIMME, see also Cohen and Bauer, *Grandes Manoeuvres industrielles,* 115–116.

46. This view of industrial policy was popularized in the United States by Ira Magaziner, the founder of Telesis, and Robert Reich in *Minding America's Business* (New York: Harcourt Brace, 1982).

47. Quoted in *L'Usine nouvelle,* 10 June 1982, 149.

48. Except as noted, sources for this account are from interviews at the Ministry of Industry, Paris, and with a former official at the DIMME, Paris, both in December 1988, as well as from "Machine-outil: Une Industrie refaçonnée," *L'Usine nouvelle,* 10 December 1981.

49. *Le Monde,* 3 December 1981, 1; *L'Usine nouvelle,* 3 December 1981, 67.

50. *L'Usine nouvelle,* 3 December 1981, 68; ibid., 10 December 1981, 82.

51. For figures and projections, see *Le Monde,* 3 December 1981, and *L'Usine nouvelle,* 10 December 1981, 66–67.

52. Quoted in *L'Usine nouvelle,* 3 December 1981, 67.

53. Dacier et al., *Dossiers noirs,* 359.

54. Jean-Claude Tarondeau, "Où en est l'industrie française de la machine-outil?" *Revue Française de Gestion,* September–October 1981, 59–70, esp. 64–67. See also "Le Plan machines-outils répond-il aux besoins?" *Le Monde,* 3 December 1981, 1, 17.

55. Liné's strategy can be followed in *Echos,* 7 May 1979, 7, 12 July 1979, 6; and 3 August 1979, 5. The firms it acquired included Gambin (Haute Savoie); Gendron (Villeurbanne); Albert-Machine-Outil; Adam; and the St.-Etienne facility of Ernault-Somua.

56. "Une Percée ratée," *Nouvel Economiste,* 1 June 1981, 52–53.

57. *Nouvel Economiste,* 3 August 1981, 28–29.

58. *L'Usine nouvelle,* 10 June 1982, 152.

59. *L'Usine nouvelle,* 8 July 1982, 25. See also *Echos,* 15 April 1982, 6; and *Le Monde,* 3 July 1982.

60. *Financial Times,* 11 October 1982.

61. The various discussions are reported in *L'Usine nouvelle,* 10 December 1981, 83, *Echos* 15 April 1982, 2; and *L'Usine nouvelle,* 10 June 1982, 148.

62. Interview, Ministry of Industry, Paris.

63. Financing difficulties were mentioned emphatically by interview subjects. See also Dacier et al., *Dossiers noirs.*

64. An unidentified observer quoted in *L'Usine nouvelle,* 10 June 1982, 147. In the first six months of 1982, bankruptcy filings included Armeca, Billaud, and LBM.

65. Suzanne Berger, "French Business from Transition to Transition," in Ross et al., *Mitterrand Experiment,* 187–198.

66. François Beaujolin, *Vouloir l'industrie: Pratique syndicale et politique industrielle* (Paris: Ouvrières, 1982), 152.

67. Ibid., 132–134.

68. Roger Ferrand, "Machine-outil: Tenir les engagements," *Economie et politique,* June 1983, 49.

69. Jean-Pierre Larçon of the SCFMO in 1978, quoted in *L'Usine nouvelle,* 10 June 1982, 154.

70. The report *Technologies d'information, enjeu stratégique pour la modernisation économique et sociale* (Paris: Documentation française, n.d.), by Philippe Lemoine of the DIELI, was summarized in *Le Monde,* 25 January 1983.

71. Ibid.

72. "De la mécanique traditionalle à la productique" report of the Groupe de Stratégie Industrielle, no. 11, Biens d'équipements, mécaniques, Commissariat Général du Plan, (Paris: April 1983). Group members included nine representatives of firms or industry associations, eight representatives of union organizations, ten civil servants from various state agencies, and four other experts.

73. *Le Monde,* 25 May 1983.

74. *Financial Times,* 6 October 1983.

75. Eric Le Boucher, "La Crise de la machine-outil française," *Le Monde,* 11 June 1983.

76. Equity in Intelautomatisme was shared by Bank of Suez (51%), the IDI, through its subsidiary SOPARI (30%), and CIT-Alcatel (19%).

77. Dacier et al., *Dossiers noirs,* 368; "Le Dernier Carré du dernier plan," *Nouvel Economiste,* 21 May 1984, 75; *Wall Street Journal/Europe,* 5 February 1985; *Financial Times,* 3 February 1987.

78. *Echos,* 28 April 1983, 10; 10 January 1984, 8; and 23 January 1984, 10; *Nouvel Economiste,* 21 May 1984, 75.

79. Interview, Ministry of Industry, Paris, July 1986.

80. Dacier et al., *Dossiers noirs,* 343.

81. Interviews, Ministry of Industry, Paris, July 1986, and former ministry official, Paris, December 1988.

82. Dacier et al., *Dossiers noirs,* 342.

83. "Apprentissage, un bon moyen d'apprendre un metier?" *L'Usine nouvelle,* monthly ed., June 1982.

84. Interview, Ministry of Industry, Paris, July 1986.

85. Interview, Société NUM, December 1988.

86. "Les Bacheliers du technique assis entre deux chaises," *Le Monde,* 5 August 1987, 5.

87. Interview, professor at University of Grenoble, Cambridge, Mass., April 1989.

88. NUM acquired the CNC operations of SNECMA in January 1982 and of Manuméric (the CNC operations of Manurhin) in 1986. *Echos,* 20 January 1982; *L'Usine nouvelle,* 20 March 1986.

89. *L'Usine nouvelle,* 10 June 1982, 153, and 26 March 1981; and information supplied by NUM. For NUM's acquisition of the Swiss NC producer Guttinger and its affiliate in Stuttgart, see *Echos,* 14 December 1981, and *NC-Fertigung,* July 1988, 70.

90. Interviews, NUM, Nanterre December, 1988. This figure compares favorably with the legal minimum (1.1%) and the average for mechanical engineering (1.26%), as well as the average for all French business (1.83%), as reported in "De la mécanique traditionalle à la productique," 46.

91. *Echos,* 23 September 1986, 7.

92. *Nouvel Economiste,* 7 June 1985, 75; *Echos,* 11 September 1986, 10.

93. *Echos,* 17 October 1986.

94. *Financial Times,* 3 February 1987.

95. Ibid.; *Tribune économique,* 5 May 1988.

96. *Echos,* 17 January 1983, 10; "Machine-outil: On efface et on recommence," *Nouvel Economiste,* 5 February 1988, 76–77.

97. *Le Monde,* 4 September 1992 and 30 May 1995.

98. This discussion is based on interviews at German business associations (the BDI, Cologne, and the VDMA, Frankfurt) and the Ministry for Research and Technology, Bonn, 1986. For the implications of these two economic perspectives for technology policy, see also Susanne Lütz, *Die Steuerung industrieller Forschungskooperation: Funktionsweise und Erfolgsbedingungen des staatlichen Förderinstrumentes Verbundforschung* (Frankfurt: Campus, 1993), and Andreas Stucke, *Institutionalisierung der Forschungspolitik: Entstehung, Entwicklung und Steuerungsprobleme des Bundesforschungsministeriums* (Frankfurt: Campus, 1993), esp. 171, 173. The significance of Ordnungspolitik remains underappreciated in the English-language literature. For correctives, see Chris Allen, "The Underdevelopment of Keynesianism in the Federal Republic of Germany," in Peter Hall, ed., *The Political Power of Economic Ideas: Keynesianism across Nations* (Princeton: Princeton University Press, 1989), and Razeen Sally, "The Social Market and Liberal Order: Theory and Policy Implications," *Government and Opposition* 29 (Autumn 1994): 461–476. For the SPD's anticipatory Strukturpolitik, the semi-official statement is Volker Hauff and Fritz Scharpf, *Technologiepolitik als Strukturpolitik* (Frankfurt: Europäische Verlagsanstalt, 1975). See also K. H. F. Dyson, "The Politics of Economic Management in West Germany," in William E. Paterson and Gordon Smith, eds., *The West German Model: Perspectives on a Stable State* (London: Frank Cass, 1981), esp. 35–36, 41.

99. The requirement that the major interest groups be consulted during the drafting of legislation is the so-called GGO (Gemeinsame Geschäftsordnung)—an administrative regulation that is generally adhered to.

100. Kurt Biedenkopf, *Freiheit im Fortschritt,* quoted in Hauff and Scharpf, *Technologiepolitik,* 126.

101. Figures from *Statistisches Handbuch für den Maschinenbau, 1974,* cited in Kommission für wirtschaftlichen und sozialen Wandel, *Technologische Entwicklung,* vol. 3, *Ausgewählte Sektoren* (Göttingen: Schwartz, 1976), 89, 90; and Industriegewerkschaft Metall, *Strukturwandel in der Metallindustrie* (Frankfurt: IG Metall, 1977), 63.

102. Kommission für wirtschaftlichen und sozialen Wandel, *Technologische Entwicklung,* 3:104, 109; Industriegewerkschaft Metall, *Strukturwandel,* 66.

103. *BMFT Förderungskatalog 1975,* entries 3797, 3819, 3820, 3828, 3836, 3814 (Bonn, 1976). Grants ranged from DM2.4 to 4.3 million over five years.

104. Ibid., entries 3910 and 3921. Grants of DM1.18 and 0.75 million over four years.

105. See, for example, *BMFT Förderungskatalog 1981,* which reports grants to such firms as Boehringer, Diedesheim, Gildemeister, Gühring, Gebr. Heller, Hahn & Kolb, Maho, Fritz-Werner, Traub, and Wohlenberg, ranging in magnitude from DM36,050 (Wohlenberg, two years) to over DM1,500,000 (Diedesheim, three years).

106. *Die Zeit,* 31 May 1974.

107. Interviews, former officials of the BMFT, Bonn, and IG Metall staff members, Frankfurt, fall 1988. For the advisory bodies, see BMFT, *Das Programm "Forschung zur Humanisierung des Arbeitslebens"* (Frankfurt: Campus, 1981), 27. For union views of this program and related efforts, see Walter Didicher, *Die umstrittene Humanisierung der Arbeit: Gesellschaftspolitische u. betriebliche Strategien v. Staat, Gewerkschaften, Privatwirtschaft* (Frankfurt: Campus, 1981), 144, 149; and Bernd Kaßebaum, *Betriebliche Technologiepolitik: Arbeitsgestaultung in der Politik der IG Metall* (Frankfurt: Campus, 1990), 185.

108. *Frankfurter Allgemeine Zeitung,* 25 January 1979; *Die Welt,* 27 September 1979; *Wirtschaftswoche,* 14 March 1980; Otto Wolff von Amerongen, quoted in *Nürnberger Nachrichten,* 9 April 1980; and *Frankfurter Allgemeine Zeitung,* 14 June 1980.

109. "Nicht nur Wind," *Der Spiegel,* 20 December 1976, 36–38.

110. *Forschungs- und technologiepolitisches Gesamtkonzept der Bundesregierung für kleine und mittlere Unternehmen* (Bonn: 1978). The government's position on R&D promotion among small and medium-sized firms is traced in Karl A. Stroetmann and Wolfgang J. Stienle, "Kleine und mittlere Unternehmungen als Adressaten staatlicher Forschungs- und Innovationsförderungspolitik," in W. Bruder et al., *Forschungs- und Technologiepolitik in der Bundesrepublik Deutschland* (Opladen, 1985).

111. This program is evaluated in Frieder Meyer-Krahmer, Gisela Gielow, and Uwe Kuntze, "Impacts of Government Incentives Towards Industrial Innovation," *Research Policy* 12 (1983): 153–169.

112. Interviews, BMFT, Bonn, and Forschungskuratorium, VDMA, Frankfurt, November 1988. See also Meyer-Krahmer et al., "Impacts of Government Incentives," 153–169.

113. *Bundesbericht Forschung* (Bonn: BMFT 1979), 15–16.

114. See *Wirtschaftswoche,* 14 March 1980, for critiques of the Gießkannprinzip.

115. Interviews, BMFT, Bonn; *Sonderprogramm Anwendung der Mikroelektronik* (BMFT brochure) (Bonn, 1981). For the implications of Strukturpolitik and Ordnungspolitik for this program, see also Stucke, *Institutionalisierung der Forschungspolitik.*

116. "Geschäftsbericht 1974 bis 1976 des Vorstandes der IG Metall" (biannual report, IG Metall, 1976).

117. *European Industrial Relations Review* 74 (January 1980): 10–11 and 85 (February 1981): 15–16. General reviews of IG Metall's position on technology policy are given in Horst Hinz, "Innovationsberatungsstellen: Instrumente der Strukturpolitik," *Der Gewekschafter,* September 1976, 34ff.; and "Innovationspolitik aus gewerkschaftlicher Sicht," *Der Gewekschafter,* June 1979, 36ff.

118. Interview, Forschungskuratorium Maschinenbau, VDMA, Frankfurt, November 1988.

119. Bernhard Kapp quoted in *Industriemagazin,* July 1980, 24.

120. Günther Vettermann quoted ibid., 24.

121. Hans-Jurgen Marczinski quoted ibid., May 1977, 22.

122. Ibid.

123. Managers from the firm Joh. Friedrichs Behrens, a specialist in fasteners and pneumatic hammers, are quoted in *Industriemagazin,* July 1980, 26.

124. Interview with former BMFT official, Bonn, Summer 1986.

125. Interview, BMFT, Bonn, summer 1986. Complaints about the paperwork and time lag involved in BMFT grants had been voiced by small firms in the 14 March 1980 issue of *Wirtschaftswoche.*

126. See the article by the VDI's president, Karl Eugen Becker, "Umschlagplatz von technischem Wissen," *VDI Nachrichten,* 12 October 1984.

127. The VDI counted 90,000 individual members and 38 active regional chapters by the 1980s.

128. The Sachverständigenkreis Mikroelektronik im Maschinenbau included the principal representatives of IG Metall and the Forschungskuratorium of the VDMA. Its report, "Anwendung der Mikroelektronik im Maschinenbau," was issued in September 1980.

129. Heinrich Revermann, ed., *Wirkungsanalyse zum "Sonderprogramm Anwendung der Mikroelektronik"* (n.p.: Markt & Technik, 1986), 22, 70; *Fertigungstechnik: Programm der Bundesregierung* (BMFT brochure) (Bonn, 1983), 18.

130. For the relevant Fraunhofer Institutes and other institutes, see *Fertigungstechnik,* 17; *BMFT Förderungskatalog 1985.*

131. *Bundesbericht Forschung* (Bonn: May, 1984), 26.

132. Ibid., 13.

133. *Osnabrücker Zeitung,* 22 October 1982; *Neuorientierung der Forschungs- und Technologiepolitik* (BMFT brochure) (Bonn, 1984); "Forschungspolitik: Keine Wende," *Die Zeit,* 23 September 1983.

134. Interview, location and date withheld by request.

135. *Neuorientierung,* 73–74; *Bundesbericht Forschung* (1984), 125.

136. *Bundesbericht Forschung* (1984), 126. For a detailed account of this policy instrument, see Lütz, *Steuerung industrieller Forschungskooperationen.*

137. *Bundesbericht Forsching* (1984), 125.

138. Revermann, *Wirkungsanalyse,* 117ff.

139. *Förderschwerpunkt Mikroperipherik, 1985–1989* (BMFT brochure) (Bonn, 1985), 20.

140. Interview, BMFT, Bonn, date withheld by request.

141. Ernst-Jürgen Horn, Henning Klodt, and Christopher Saunders, "Advanced Machine Tools: Production, Diffusion and Trade," in Margaret Sharp, ed., *Europe and*

the New Technologies (Ithaca: Cornell University Press, 1986), 46–86; Gary Herrigel, "Industry as a Form of Order: A Comparison of the Historical Development of the Machine Tool Industries in the United States and Germany" (paper presented at a conference on the governance of sectors, Wingspread, Wis., May 1988).

142. Examples were Iko Software Service (Stuttgart) and T-Programm (Reutlingen). BMFT, Förderungskatalog 1981, entries 3784–3787, 4475, 4478. Other sources on the development of CNC technology include interview, IG Metall, Frankfurt, November 1988; Horn et al., "Advanced Machine Tools"; 53; *AIF Handbook 1980*, (Cologne: AIF), 189.

143. See *BMFT Förderungskatalog 1981* for numerous examples.

144. Figures from the Verein Deutscher Werkzeugmaschinen.

145. These characterizations, along with relevant citations, are provided in Hartmut Hirsch-Kreinsen, "Technische Entwicklungslinien und ihre Konsequenzen für die Arbeitsgestaltung," in Hartmut Hirsch-Kreinsen and Rainer Schultz-Wild, eds., *Rechnerintegrierte Produktion: Zur Entwicklung von Technik und Arbeit in der Metallindustrie* (Frankfurt: Campus, 1986), 13–47.

146. Warnecke's views can be traced in H.-J. Warnecke, "Taylor und die Fertigungstechnik von morgen" (address before the Fertigungstechnischen Kolloquium, Stuttgart, 10–11 October 1985); T. Martin, E. Ulich, and H.-J. Warnecke, "Angemessene Automation für flexible Fertigung," *Werkstatttechnik* 78 (1988): 17–23, 119–122.

147. The status of these problems in the German case is given in Hirsch-Kreinsen, "Technische Entwicklung," 21.

148. Interview, location and date withheld by request of interviewee.

149. Rainer Schultz-Wild, "An der Schwelle zur Rechnerintegration," *VDI-Z* 130, no. 9 (September 1988): 40–45.

150. For a summary of the debate and relevant evidence, see Schumann et al., *Trendreport*, esp. 371–389.

151. Horst Kern and Michael Schumann, "New Concepts of Production in West German Plants," in Katzenstein, *Industry and Politics in West Germany*, 95.

152. On the *dual System* and the revision of the metalworking and electrical trades, see Wolfgang Streeck et al., *The Role of the Social Partners in Vocational Training and Further Training in the Federal Republic of Germany* (Berlin: CEDEFOP, 1987); Karlwilhelm Stratmann, "Curricular and Organizational Problems in Modernizing the Educational Systems in West Germany, with Emphasis on the Needs of Small and Medium-Sized Enterprises in the Metal and Electronics Sectors" (Conference on Worker Skills in the U.S. and the FRG, Goethe Institute, Boston, 28 May 1987); and *Die neuen Metall- und Elektroberufe* (brochure of the DIHT, the ZVEI, and the employers' bargaining association, Gesamtmetall) (Deutscher Instituts Verlag, 1986).

153. *Diebold Management Report* (Frankfurt) 1 (1986).

154. Harley Shaiken, *Work Transformed: Automation and Labor in the Computer Age* (New York: Holt, Rinehart & Winston, 1984), 98ff.

155. Interview, IG Metall, Frankfurt, November 1988; and Wolfgang Weber, "CNC Steuerungen für qualifizeirte Facharbeit," *Technische Rundschau* 28 (1988): 14–18.

156. Examples cited in T. Martin, E. Ulich, and H.-J. Warnecke, "Angemessene Automation für flexible Fertigung," *Werkstattstechnik* 78 (1988): esp. 19. See also Hans-Jürgen Warnecke, "Integration of Information and Material Flow in a Pilot Plant," in J. Ranta, ed., *Trends and Impacts of Computer Integrated Manufacturing* (Proceedings of the IIASA Workshops on Computer-Integrated Manufacturing, Stuttgart,

18–20 July 1988, and the IIASA Workshop on Technological Factors in the Diffusion of CIM Technologies, Prague, 24–27 May 1988).

157. These included IBH Bernhard Hilpert Ingenieurgesellschaft (Schwieberdingen), the Institut für angewandte Organisationasforschung (Karlsruhe), RWT Rechnersysteme für Wissenschaft und Technik (Krailling), and Softing (Munich).

158. *BMFT Förderungskatalog 1985,* entries 3401/1–3401/16. Total funding, 1984–87, was approximately DM9 million. Grants ranged from DM78,500 for work on sheet-metal operations (Behrens) to over DM2 million for work on milling operations and data bank architecture (Robert Bosch).

159. Interview, IG Metall, Frankfurt, November 1988, and cases cited in *Technische Rundschau* 11 (1988): 8; *Der Spiegel* 15 (6 April 1987): 98–110.

160. Burkhardt Lutz and P. Veltz, "Maschinenbauer versus Informatiker," in K. Düll and B. Lutz, eds., *Technikentwicklung und Arbeitsteilung im internationalen Vergleich* (Frankfurt/New York, 1990); Maurice et al., *Social Foundations.*

161. See, for example, Karl Pitz, "Ein Ruck nach vorne: Qualifizeirungs- und Humanisierungsoffensive im Schiffbau," *Der Gewekschafter,* January 1986, 44–45; and special feature on the factory of the future in *VDI-Nachrichten,* 9 October 1989, 18ff.

162. Quoted in *Wirtschaftswoche* 35 (23 August 1985): 32.

163. *Fertigungstechnik Programm, 1988–1992* (BMF brochure), 6.

164. Personal communication, Darmstadt, November 1988.

165. *Management Wissen,* November 1988, 84. Executives at Trumpf, Traub, and Gildemeister are quoted at length in the same article. Similar remarks from other individuals at Traub, Trumpf, Deckel, and Maho are reported in *Der Spiegel* 15 (1987): 98ff.

166. "Maschinenbau fühlt sich personell ausgeblütet," *Süddeutsche Zeitung,* 7 January 1995.

167. "Industrie und IG Metall für Investitionsförderung," *Süddeutsche Zeitung,* 16 December 1993. For production figures and other information on the crisis in the sector, see also *Süddeutsche Zeitung,* 24 March and 23 September 1994, and *Financial Times,* 10 September 1996.

168. "Le Gouvernement prépare la réforme de l'apprentissage: Filière française et modèle allemand," *Le Monde,* 4 June 1991; Lucie Tanguy, *Quelle formation pour les ouvriers et les employés en France* (Paris: Documentation française, 1991).

169. "La professionalisation des études—Les IUP vont former les nouveaux 'ingénieurs-maîtres,'" *Le Monde,* 12 May 1992; "IUT, STS, IUP, l'impossible remise à plat des filières technologiques; 400,000 étudiants reçoivent des formations mal articulées et concurrentes," *Le Monde,* 13 February 1995.

170. In the specialist press, see "Der Neue Facharbeiter muß autonom sein: Folgen des Taylorismus und Ansprüche heutiger Arbeitnehmer im Innovationsprozeß," *VDI-Nachrichten,* 9 October 1987, 18. In the general press, see the special feature "Ein Seelchen, aber extrem flexibel: SPIEGEL Redacteur Lutz Spenneberg über die Erfolge der deutschen Werkzeugmaschinenbauer," *Der Spiegel* 15 (1987): 98ff.

5. Searching for Industrial Sovereignty: Semiconductors

1. For the early history of the semiconductor industry, see Ernst Braun and Stuart Macdonald, *Revolution in Miniature: The History and Impact of Semiconductor*

Electronics (New York: Cambridge University Press, 1978), and Robert Noyce, "Micro-electronics," *Scientific American*, 237, no. 3 (September 1977).

Additional sources that were particularly helpful to my work on this sector include Michael Borrus, *Competing for Control: America's Stake in Microelectronics* (Cambridge, Mass.: Ballinger, 1988); Giovanni Dosi, *Technical Change and Industrial Transformation* (New York: St. Martin's Press, 1984); Edgar Grande and Jürgen Häusler, *Industrieforschung und Forschungspolitik: Staatliche Steuerungspotentiale in der Informationstechnik* (Frankfurt: Campus, 1994); Franco Malerba, *The Semiconductor Business: The Economics of Rapid Growth and Decline* (London: Frances Pinter, 1985); Daniel Okimoto, Takuo Sugano, and Franklin B. Weinstein, eds., *Competitive Edge: The Semiconductor Industry in the U.S. and Japan* (Stanford: Stanford University Press, 1984); Laura D'Andrea Tyson and David B. Yoffie, "Semiconductors: From Manipulated to Managed Trade," in David B. Yoffie, ed., *Beyond Free Trade: Firms, Governments, and Global Competition* (Boston: Harvard Business School Press, 1993); and John Zysman, *Political Strategies for Industrial Order: State, Market, and Industry in France* (Berkeley: University of California Press, 1977).

2. Noyce, "Microelectronics."

3. The changes that accompanied LSI are nicely summarized in Malerba, *Semiconductor Business*.

4. Rebecca M. Henderson and Kim B. Clark, "Architectural Innovation: the Reconfiguration of Existing Product Technologies and the Failure of Established Firms," *Administrative Science Quarterly* 35 (March 1990): 9–31.

5. See, for example, Eric von Hippel, "The Dominant Role of Users in Semiconductors and Electronic Subassembly Process Innovation," *IEEE Transactions on Engineering Management*, EM 24 (May 1977): 60–71; and, by the same author, "A Customer Active Paradigm for Industrial Product Idea Generation," Research Policy 7, no. 2 (1978): 240–266.

6. On the changing processes in semiconductor manufacturing, see Kazuhira Mashina, "Essays on Technological Evolution" (Ph.D. diss., Harvard University, Graduate School of Business Administration, 1989), and Ross A. Young, "Silicon Sumo: U.S.-Japan Competition and Industrial Policy in the Semiconductor Equipment Industry" (report of the IC2 Institute, University of Texas, Austin, 1994).

7. The standard source for the early structure in the industry is John E. Tilton, *International Diffusion of Technology: The Case of Semiconductors* (Washington, D.C.: Brookings, 1971). The following discussion draws also on J. Nicholas Ziegler, "Semiconductors," in Raymond Vernon and Ethan Kapstein, eds., *Searching for Security in a Global Economy*, special issue of *Daedalus*, Fall 1991.

8. Malerba, *Semiconductor Business*, 65.

9. For production and consumption figures, see Dosi, *Technical Change*, 150.

10. *Electronics*, 4 April 1966, 26; *Financial Times*, 20 May 1969.

11. Pierre Thuillier, "Science et pouvoir social: La Formation des 'élites' en France," *La Recherche* 17, no. 173 (January 1986): 120–127, which includes Thuillier's review of Terry Shinn, "Enseignement, epistemologie et stratification," in *Le Personnel de l'enseignement supérieur en France aux XIXème et XXème siècles*, proceedings of a colloquium held in June 1984 (Paris: CNRS, 1985), 229–246.

12. Pierre Bonelli and Alain Fillion, *L'Impact de la microélectronique* (Paris: Commissariat Général du Plan, 1981), 89–91, 93.

13. A series of valuable studies on the LETI and the CNS were conducted by Bernard Cuneo, Annie Dona-Gimenez, and Jean-Claude Thénard of the Centre de Recherche sur les Mutations des Sociétés Industrielles (CRMSI) in 1985 and 1986.

14. "Bericht der Queisser-Kommission an das Bundesministerium für Forschung und Technologie" (report to the BMFT, Bonn, 1985).

15. Estimates based on interviews and grant records of the BMFT, selected years.

16. Hermann Bössenecker, "Der Süd-Süd-Konflikt: Baden-Württemberg und Bayern wetteifern miteinander als Industriestandorte," *Die Zeit*, 3 May 1985, 23; Bavarian State Ministry of Economic Affairs and Transport, *Forging Ahead in Bavaria* (brochure) (Munich, March 1986), 19; and from the same ministry, *Analysis of the Electronic Components Industry and Its Significance for the Bavarian Economy: Report on Findings* (brochure) (Munich: October 1984).

17. *Electronics*, 22 January 1987, 16; *Handelsblatt*, 13 October 1983.

18. For descriptions of the Max Planck and Fraunhofer Societies, see Volker Hauff and Hans-Hilger Haunschild, *Forschung in der Bundesrepublik Deutschland*, 2d ed. (Stuttgart: Kohlhammer, 1976), and Hans-Willy Hohn and Uwe Schimank, *Konflikte und Gleichgewichte im Forschungssystem: Akteurkonstellationen und Entwicklungspfade in der staatlich finanzierten außeruniversitären Forschung* (Frankfurt: Campus, 1990).

19. Interviews, Bosch, Stuttgart; and Siemens, Munich, July 1986.

20. As one industry spokesman remarked in 1967, "The French have succeeded every time they've tried something like this." Quoted in *Electronics*, 3 April 1967, 164.

21. Pierre Gadonneix, "The Plan Calcul: An Attempt to Meet the U.S. Challenge in the French Computer Industry" (Ph.D., Harvard Business School, 1974), 2-13, 2-14. Unless otherwise noted, material on the Plan Calcul is drawn from Gadonneix's dissertation; Zysman, *Political Strategies for Industrial Order;* and Elie Cohen and Michel Bauer, *Les Grandes Manoeuvres industrielles* (Paris: Belfon, 1985).

22. Gadonneix, "Plan Calcul," 3-4.

23. The political dynamics of the national champion model are analyzed systematically in Zysman, *Political Strategies for Industrial Order*.

24. *Electronics*, 3 April 1967, 164.

25. *Financial Times*, 15 May 1972, 22; Gadonneix, "Plan Calcul," 3-75.

26. These machinations are summarized in Cohen and Bauer, *Grandes Manoeuvres*.

27. Malerba, *Semiconductor Business*, 159.

28. Dosi, *Technical Change and Industrial Transformation*, 158, Table 3.9. Malerba, *Semiconductor Business*, 59, cites a decline from 23 percent of the French market to 16.3 percent in 1974.

29. Editorial, *Frankfurter Allgemeine Zeitung*, 24 March 1965.

30. The Diebold study is cited in *Der Volkswirt*, 26 March 1965.

31. The main sources for the German program in data processing are Tom Sommerlatte et al., "Die Entwicklung der Datenverarbeitung in der Bundesrepublik Deutschland—Programmbewertung der DV-Förderung des BMFT, 1967 bis 1979" (report by A. D. Little to the Federal Ministry of Research and Technology, Wiesbaden, 1979); and Klaus Mainzer, "Entwicklungsfaktoren der Informatik in der Bundesrepublik Deutschland," in Wolfgang van den Daele, Wolfgang Krohn, and Peter Weingart, *Geplannte Forschung* (Frankfurt: Suhrkamp, 1979). For the Siemens-AEG memorandum, see Sommerlatte et al., "Entwicklung der Datenverarbeitung," 121.

32. *Die Welt*, 6 December 1966.

33. Sommerlatte, "Entwicklung der Datenverarbeitung," 121.

34. Ibid., 98.

35. Gerd Junne, "Multinationale Konzerne in 'High-Technology'-Sektoren, oder: Wie gut is die Strategie vom guten Zweiten?" in Peter Mettler, ed., *Wohin expandieren Multinationale Konzerne?* (Frankfurt: Haag & Herchen, 1985).

36. This assessment is also given by French observers; see Gadonneix, "Plan Calcul," 3–64, who also cites Jean-Michel Treille, *L'Economie mondiale de l'ordinateur* (Paris: Seuil, 1973), 60. See also Kenneth Flamm, *Targeting the Computer: Government Support and International Competition* (Washington, D.C.: Brookings, 1987), 158.

37. Metal oxide silicon (MOS) technology, was soon to become the preferred approach for LSI. Producers experimented with several variants, including negative MOS (NMOS), positive MOS (PMOS), and complementary MOS (CMOS), the last of which eventually became the preferred technology for very large-scale integration (VLSI).

38. Sommerlate, "Entwicklung der Datenverarbeitung," 88, 90.

39. *BMFT Förderungskatalog, 1974.*

40. Specific purposes and amounts are listed in Malerba, *Semiconductor Business,* 191.

41. *BMFT Förderungskatalog, 1975.* Gallium arsenide began to attract intensive study because it conducted electrons at considerably higher speeds than silicon and was expected to have important military applications.

42. Not including an additional $45 million in "captive" production, which Siemens sold to its own operating divisions. *Financial Times,* 4 December 1974.

43. *BMFT Förderungskatalog, 1975; Electronics,* 15 May 1975, 69; *Elektronik,* 17 October 1975, 1; *Electronic News,* 6 October 1975, 21.

44. See Dimitri Ypsilanti, *The Semiconductor Industry: Trade Related Issues* (Paris: OECD, 1985), 125, Table 28, for a list of acquisitions and equity investment in U.S. semiconductor firms.

45. *Wall Street Journal,* 7 June 1977, 7; *New York Times,* 8 June 1977, 53; *Elektronik,* 31 October 1977, 1; *Electronic Business,* August 1981, 41.

46. Simon Nora and Alain Minc, *L'Informatisation de la société* (Paris: Documentation Française, 1978).

47. *Handelsblatt,* 4 February 1981; *Der Spiegel,* 9 February 1981; *Müncher Merkur,* 16 April 1981.

48. *Le Monde,* 19 April 1977; *Figaro,* 7 April 1976; *Echos,* 8 November 1978.

49. This view was expressed vehemently by interview subjects at Thomson and other firms.

50. This opinion, voiced in interviews with former defense officials, was not disputed by others.

51. For interministerial bargaining, see especially *Le Monde,* 18 January and 24 December 1977.

52. Unless otherwise noted, information on the various agreements financed by the Plan Composants is drawn from *Le Monde,* 9 November 1978; *Echos,* 8 November 1978; *Journal des Finances,* 11 January 1979; *Financial Times,* 18 June 1979; *Le Monde,* 1 February 1979, 30, and15 April 1980, 21.

53. *Le Monde,* 19 April 1977; Malerba, *Semiconductor Business,* 194.

54. Since the CEA was a military research facility, it was hardly surprising that the specific processes were not divulged, but they were thought to include Motorola's

standard NMOS and CMOS processes as well as silicon-on-sapphire (SOS), which was commonly used for ruggedized components.

55. *Journal des Finances,* 11 January 1979. On the interest of CII-Honeywell-Bull and CGE in such an arrangement, see also *Echos,* 8 November 1978.

56. CMOS, as opposed to NMOS and other variants, carried electrical signals more slowly than bipolar technologies, but because it used much less power and therefore generated much less heat, it was expected to become the technology of choice for VSLI designs, which were clearly going to dominate the next ten or fifteen years.

57. This paragraph is based on interviews and the press accounts cited above. Similar dynamics have been documented in a study by Joycelyne Barreau and Abdelaziz, *L'Industrie électronique française: 29 ans de relations Etat–groupes industriels, 1958–1986* (Paris: Librarie Générale de Droit et de Jurisprudence, 1987).

58. *Le Monde,* 10 April 1981, 31 August 1982, and 22 January 1983.

59. Christian Stoffaes, *Politique industrielle* (Paris: Cours de Droit), 485–486.

60. *Electronic News,* 23 February 1981, 1; *Financial Times,* 3 April 1981; *Figaro,* 3 April 1981; *Le Monde,* 10 April 1981; *Electronic Business,* June 1982.

61. For the concerns about Matra's agreements with Intel, see J.-M. Quatrepoint, "Un Deuxième 'Plan Composants,'" *Le Monde,* 10 April 1981, 32.

62. *Quotidien de Paris,* 20 October 1984; *Le Monde,* 22 September 1983.

63. Stoffaes, *Politique industrielle,* 490.

64. Quoted in *Le Monde,* 30 July 1982. See also *Le Monde,* 31 August 1982.

65. "Rapport Schwartz," *L'Express,* 17–23 January 1986.

66. Pierre Dussauge, *L'Industrie française de l'armement: Intervention de l'Etat et stratégies des entreprises* (Paris: Economica, 1987); Stoffaes, *Politique industrielle,* 490; *Le Monde,* 4 October 1985, 28.

67. The deficit of Fr400 million in 1982 included 150 million from Eurotechnique, and declined to about Fr300 million in 1983. See *Echos,* 7 November 1983, and *Financial Times,* 6 February 1986.

68. *Le Monde,* 15 November 1985; Thomson Annual Reports for 1980 and 1983; *Nouvel Economiste,* 3 April 1987; *L'Express,* 17–23 January 1986, 33.

69. *Le Monde,* 30 April 1987.

70. See the articles on Siemens in *Die Zeit,* 6 November 1981 and 30 March 1984.

71. Interview, Siemens, Unternehmensbereich Bauelemente, Munich, May 1986. For earlier changes in the board members responsible for components, see *Die Zeit,* 6 November 1981, and *Der Spiegel,* 9 November 1981.

72. Uli Decker, "Der Megachip," *Bild der Wissenschaft,* November 1985.

73. Material on the Megachip Project is drawn from interviews at Siemens, Munich, and BMFT, Bonn, summer 1986. See also *Handelsblatt,* 17 December 1985, 15; *Wall Street Journal/Europe,* 7 January 1985; and *Konzeption der Bundesregierung zur Förderung der . . . Informationstechnik* (Bonn: BMFT, 1984).

74. A DRAM, or dynamic random access memory, is the simplest kind of chip in the sense that its design is the most regular. Consequently, competition in the DRAM markets hinges on production costs, which are more clearly characterized by learning curve effects than the costs of other, more complex chips. DRAMs differ from static random access memories (called SRAMS) in that they must be frequently recharged. SRAMs hold their charge, but only through more complex design features.

75. *Financial Times,* 16 July 1985; *Wall Street Journal/Europe,* 7 January 1985; *Financial Times,* 14 March 1986.

76. Interview, CDU member of the Bundestag, Bonn, May 1986.

77. *Financial Times,* 16 July 1985; *VDI-Nachrichten,* 14 February 1986, 7.

78. For more detailed examination of the information asymmetries involved in public technology promotion, see especially Frieder Meyer-Krahmer, *Der Einfluß staatlicher Technologiepolitik auf industrielle Innovationen* (Baden-Baden: Nomos, 1989), 222–44.

79. *Handelsblatt,* 16–17 May 1986.

80. K.-H. Kaske, CEO of Siemens, interviewed in *Der Spiegel,* 14 April 1986, 70.

81. Hermann Franz, quoted in *New York Times,* 11 May 1987, D8.

82. For a good statement of that strategy, see the interview with K.-H. Kaske in *Financial Times,* 19 July 1987.

83. *VDI-Nachrichten,* 26 June 1987, 1; *Electronics,* 9 July 1987; *Süddeutsche Zeitung,* 18 March 1987, 30; *Electronics,* 19 March 1987; *Financial Times,* 18 November 1987.

84. See *Financial Times,* 4 February 1986 and 14 February 1986 (Frankfurt ed.), 20, for reports on Siemen's progress in the United States. For the firm's activities in ISDN chip sets, *Electronics,* 23 July 1987.

85. *Electronics,* 5 February 1987, 78. For the founding of the Fraunhofer Institut für Mikrostruktur, see *Frankfurter Allgemeine Zeitung,* 24 October 1985.

86. For the industry's supply infrastructure and the difficulty of maintaining it, see Kazuhira Mishina, "Essays on Technological Evolution" (Ph.D. diss., Harvard University, Graduate School of Business Administration, 1989), and other sources cited in Ziegler, "Semiconductors," on which parts of the following discussion rest.

87. For such fears in the U.S. case, see Defense Science Board Task Force, *Defense Semiconductor Dependency* (Washington, D.C.: Department of Defense, 1987); and "U.S. Semi Equipment Makers Must Move the Earth to Survive," *Electronic Business,* May 14, 1990, 44. For similar anxieties in Europe, sources include author interview at Siemens, Components division, Munich, July 1991, and Kenneth Flamm, "Semiconductors," in Gary C. Hufbauer, ed., *Europe 1992: An American Perspective* (Washington, D.C.: Brookings, 1990).

88. *New York Times,* 6 January 1987, D7.

89. For the semiconductor trade agreement, see especially Laura D'Andrea Tyson and David B. Yoffie, "Semiconductors: From Manipulated to Managed Trade," in David B. Yoffie, ed., *Beyond Free Trade: Firms, Governments, and Global Competition* (Boston: Harvard Business School Press, 1993). For the agreement's consequences on Europe, see Flamm, "Semiconductors."

90. For Sematech, see Ziegler, "Semiconductors," and U.S. General Accounting Office, "Federal Research: Sematech's Efforts to Strengthen the U.S. Semiconductor Industry," no. RCED-90-236 (Washington, D.C., September 1990).

91. For this view of Silicon Valley's development, see Annalee Saxenian, *Regional Advantage: Culture and Competition in Silicon Valley and Route 128* (Cambridge: Harvard University Press, 1994), and, by the same author, "Regional Networks and the Resurgence of Silicon Valley," *California Management Review,* Fall 1990.

92. Interview, location withheld at interviewee's request, summer 1990.

93. Nixdorf's involvement in JESSI is described in *Dialog Wissenschaft: Magazin der Nixdorf Computer AG* 1989, no. 1, 36.

94. Interviews, BMFT, Bonn, July 1990. See also "JESSI Green Book" (Planning document, BMFT, December 1988) and "JESSI soll mittelständische Wirtschaft an die Mikroelektronik heranführen," *BMFT Journal,* June 1990.

95. Interviews, BMFT, July 1990; Commission of the European Community, DG 13, Brussels, November 1992; and Ministry of Industry, Paris, November 1992. The EUREKA framework included twenty governments: the twelve member governments of the European Community, the six member governments of the European Free Trade Association, Turkey, and the Commission of the European Community.

96. "European Chips Plan Clouded by Siemens, SGS-Thomson Dispute," *Financial Times,* 15 April 1988.

97. Interview, BMFT, Bonn, July 1991.

98. Sources include interviews, BMFT, Bonn, July 1991, and JESSI office, Munich, March 1993. For interorganizationial networks as a form of governance, see Walter Powell, "Neither Market nor Hierarchy: Network Forms of Organization," *Research in Organizational Behavior* 12 (1990), and John L. Campbell and Leon N. Lindberg, "The Evolution of Governance Regimes," in John L. Campbell, J. Rogers Hollingsworth, and Leon N. Lindberg, eds., *Governance of the American Economy* (New York: Cambridge University Press, 1991).

99. For this view, and examples, see Grande and Häusler, *Industrieforschung und Forschungspolitik,* 289n, 311n.

100. Interviews, Ministry of Industry, Paris, and Thomson-CSF, La Défense, July 1992.

101. "Siemens and Philips Dismiss Thomson's Chip Merger Idea," *Financial Times,* 11 June 1991; "Up or Out for the Chip-Makers," *Financial Times,* 19 June 1991.

102. Interview, cabinet of Jacques Delors, Brussels, November 1992. See also George Ross, *Jacques Delors and European Integration* (New York: Oxford University Press, 1995).

103. *Financial Times,* 5 July 1991; "Paris dringt auf Staats-Projekte für Chips," *Frankfurter Allgemeine Zeitung,* 22 July 1991.

104. Interview, Siemens, Munich, March 1993; *Financial Times,* 17 July 1992.

105. Interviews, Siemens Components Division and JESSI office, Munich, March 1993.

106. Interview, JESSI office, Munich, March 1993.

107. One example was the so-called Petersberg Paper, drafted jointly by Siemens, Daimler, Bosch, AEG, and the BMFT, in 1993. For additional examples, see Christine Margerum, "German Policy towards the Microelectronics Industry," paper presented at the Conference of Europeanists, Chicago, 15 March 1994.

108. Interviews, BMFT, Bonn, July 1994.

109. Bundesministerium für Forschung und Technologie, "Bericht des Bundesministeriums für Forschung und Technologie an den FTTA-Ausschuß des Deutschen Bundestages zum Thema Hochleistungs-und Innovationszszentrum Dresden der Siemens AG," Bonn, 23 February 1994.

110. Tyson and Yoffie, "Semiconductors."

111. *Le Monde,* 11 September 1992.

112. Interviews, Thomson-CSF, La Défense, and Ministry of Industry, Paris, July 1992.

113. *Financial Times,* 9 December 1994; *Le Monde,* 27 July 1995; *Electronic Engineering Times,* 20 May 1996; *New York Times,* 9 December 1996.

114. For evidence of Europe's improving technological capabilities, see Mike Hobday, "The European Semiconductor Industry: Resurgence and Rationalization," *Journal of Common Market Studies* 28, no. 2 (December 1989): 155–86; and L'Industrie microélectronique européenne fait bloc dans la recherche," *Le Monde*, 29 November 1996.

6. Conclusion

1. Rebecca M. Henderson and Kim B. Clark, "Architectural Innovation: The Reconfiguration of Existing Product Technologies and the Failure of Established Firms," *Administrative Science Quarterly* 35, no. 1 (March 1990): 9–31.

2. Ezra Suleiman, "Change and Stability in French Elites," in Gregory Flynn, ed., *Remaking the Hexagon: The New France in the New Europe* (Boulder, Colo.: Westview, 1995); interview, Alcatel, N.V., Division of Research and Technology, Paris, July 1992. See also Razeen Sally, "Alcatel's Relations with the French State: The Political Economy of a Multinational Enterprise," *Communications et stratégies* 9 (1993).

3. Interview, France Telecom, Service des Télécommunications de l'Image, Paris, July 1992.

4. The following paragraphs draw in part on my article "Institutions, Elites, and Technological Change in France and Germany," *World Politics* 47, no. 3 (April 1995): 341–72.

5. Ernst B. Haas, *When Knowledge Is Power: Three Models of Change in International Organizations* (Berkeley: University of California Press, 1990). See also Paul Pierson, "When Effect Becomes Cause: Policy Feedback and Political Change," *World Politics* 45 (July 1993).

6. Peter A. Hall, "Policy Paradigms, Social Learning, and the State: The Case of Economic Policymaking in Britain," *Comparative Politics* 25 (April 1993); Margaret Weir, *Politics and Jobs: The Boundaries of Employment Policy in the United States* (Princeton: Princeton University Press, 1992). For somewhat different approaches to the ideas of state officials and private-sector elites, see John Zysman, "How Institutions Create Historically Rooted Trajectories of Growth," *Industrial and Corporate Change* 3 (1994), and Peter B. Evans, *Embedded Autonomy: States and Industrial Transformation* (Princeton: Princeton University Press, 1995), 39–42, 235.

7. Frank Dobbin, *Forging Industrial Policy: The United States, Britain, and France in the Railway Age* (New York: Cambridge University Press, 1994), 230.

8. For a systematic analysis of these difficulties, see Jonah Levy, "Tocqueville's Revenge: Dilemmas of Institutional Reform in Post-*Dirigiste* France" (Ph.D. diss. MIT, 1994).

9. See, for example, Clyde Prestowitz, *Trading Places: How We Are Giving Our Future to Japan and How to Reclaim It* (New York: Basic Books, 1989).

10. See especially Peter J. Katzenstein, *Small States in World Markets* (Ithaca: Cornell University Press, 1985).

11. See especially Gary Herrigel, *Industrial Constructions: The Sources of German Industrial Power* (New York: Cambridge University Press, 1996); Richard M. Locke, *Rebuilding the Italian Economy* (Ithaca: Cornell University Press, 1995); AnnaLee Saxenian, *Regional Advantage: Culture and Competition in Silicon Valley and Route 128* (Cambridge: Harvard University Press, 1994).

12. For an analysis of different views on convergence, see especially Suzanne Berger, "Introduction," in Suzanne Berger and Ronald Dore, eds., *National Diversity and Global Capitalism* (Ithaca: Cornell University Press, 1996).

13. See, for example, John Cantwell, *Technological Innovation and Multinational Corporations* (Oxford: Blackwell, 1989), and Anthony S. Frost, "The Location of Technical Innovation in the Multinational Enterprise: A Longitudinal Analysis Using Patent Data" (paper presented at the 1994 annual meeting of the Academy of Management, Dallas).

14. Interviews, Commission of the European Community, Brussels, November 1992, and Verein Deutscher Ingenieure, Düsseldorf, March 1993.

Index

Abbot, Andrew, 22, 24, 216n18, 217n28
Académie des Sciences, 28, 107
ADEPA (Agence pour le Développement de la Productivité et de l'Automatisme), 111
Administrative elite. *See* Knowledge-bearing elite
AEG, 51, 80, 84, 157, 172
AIF (Arbeitsgemeinschaft industrieller Forschungsvereinigungen), 131, 133
AIT (Association des Ingénieurs des Télécommunications), 59
Alcatel, 75–79, 85, 86, 89, 192, 199. *See also* CGE; CIT; CIT-Alcatel
Anticipatory policy. *See Strukturpolitik*
AOIP (Association des Ouvriers en Instruments de Précision), 46, 47
Apprenticeship, 33, 97, 121, 142, 149. *See also Dual System*
ASIC (application-specific integrated circuits), 161, 187, 190, 191
Autarky, 157, 170, 171–174, 176, 180, 181, 193, 202. *See also* Autonomy
Automation, 101, 105–109, 112, 115–119, 129, 138–144, 150–151
Autonomy, 22, 32–33, 141, 180. *See also* Autarky

Barre, Raymond, 106
BCG (Boston Consulting Group), 110
BDI (Bundesverband der Deutschen Industrie), 130
Beamter (official), 63–64
Beliefs. *See* Cultural explanation
Ben-David, Joseph, 28, 217n39, 220n66
Berger, Suzanne, 214nn34–35, 229n21, 232n65, 244n12

Bipolar technology, 177, 178, 241n56
BMFT (Bundesministerium für Forschung und Technologie), 50, 81, 83, 127, 129–131, 133, 135, 137, 140, 141, 143–144, 147, 150, 156, 167, 168, 172, 173, 182, 183, 188, 190, 191, 194, 201
Bosch, 77, 129, 139, 144, 169, 173, 174, 192
Boublil, Alain, 75, 114
Bull. *See* Compagnie des Machines Bull
Bundespost. *See* DBP; DT; Reichspost

CAD (computer-aided design), 135–141, 160, 173
CAM (computer-aided manufacturing), 136–139
CEA (Commissariat à l'Energie Atomique), 31, 165, 170, 177
Centralization, 12, 13, 92–93, 110, 141–143, 145–146, 178, 200, 201, 205
CERMO (Centre d'Etudes et de Recherches de la Machine-Outil), 103, 111, 122, 201, 205
Certificat d'Aptitude Professionelle, 97
CETIM (Centre Technique des Industries Mécaniques), 103, 111, 122, 201, 205
CFDT (Confédération Française Démocratique du Travail), 78, 108, 110, 116, 117
CGCT (Compagnie Générale des Constructions Téléphoniques), 46, 48, 71, 75, 77
CGE (Compagnie Générale d'Electricité), 60–61, 70–72, 74–77, 176–178
CGT (Confédération Générale du Travail), 78, 108, 110, 117

247

Chevènement, Jean-Pierre, 118, 119, 180
Chirac, Jacques, 77, 78
Christian Democratic Party (CDU), 85, 127, 136–138
CIASI (Comité Interministériel pour l'Aménagement des Structures Industrielles), 105, 108
CII (Compagnie Internationale pour l'Informatique), 170
CII-Honeywell-Bull, 177, 178
CIM (computer-integrated manufacturing), 140–141
CIMATEL, 179
CIT (Compagnie Industrielle des Téléphones), 47, 58, 69–71. See also Alcatel; CGE; CIT-Alcatel
CIT-Alcatel, 60, 74, 114, 115, 120
Civil service, 25, 33, 38, 41, 42, 63, 64, 90, 92, 93, 95, 103–104. See also Government; Politics; State
CMOS technology, 177–180, 241n56
CNC (computer numerical control), 200; in France, 103, 105, 108, 110–112, 119–122, 125, 140; in Germany, 130, 133, 139–140, 142–144, 147
CNET (Centre National d'Études des Télécommunications), 57, 58, 66–71, 74, 76, 78–80, 89, 165
CNRS (Centre National de Recherche Scientifique), 30–31
CNS (Centre Norbert Segard), 165, 166, 192
CODIS (Comité d'Orientation des Industries Stratégiques), 106–107
Collaboration, 63, 159, 172. See also Consultation; Cooperation; Joint development; Mixed enterprise
Commissariat Général du Plan, 45, 70, 101, 102
Compagnie des Machines Bull, 170, 171, 179
Competence, politics of, 2, 14–16, 203, 204
Competition: and European Community, 76–77; and French machine tools, 112, 115, 116; and French semiconductors, 176, 178, 194; and French telecommunications, 46, 60–61, 70, 71, 73–76, 78, 88, 199–200; and German machine tools, 134, 136; and German semiconductors, 167, 182–183; and German telecommunications, 67, 83–85; and knowledge, viii, 4–7, 24, 197, 206, 208–209; regulation of, 199–200; and semiconductors, 159, 193; for status, 22; and telecommunications, 52, 54, 55, 90

Computer programming, 83, 118, 139–140, 143, 144, 147
Computer technology, 53, 92, 160, 169–170, 193, 200; French, 68, 106, 118, 119, 157, 170–171, 177; German, 42, 66, 80, 82, 83, 135–136, 140, 171–175. See also Electronics; Microprocessors; Semiconductors
Conservatoire National des Arts et Métiers, 28
Consultation, 126–127, 150, 162, 168–169. See also Collaboration; Cooperation; Verbundprojekte; Mixed enterprise
Cooperation, 47, 182–83, 184–85, 187–91, 198, 206. See also Collaboration; Consultation; Joint development; Mixed enterprise; Verbundprojekte
Corps d'Armements, 29
Corps des Ingénieurs des Télécommunications, 59, 77, 79, 88. See also Ingénieurs des télécommunications
Corps des Mines, 29, 96
Corps des Ponts et Chaussées, 29, 96
Council of Ministers (France), 111
CP400, 47, 48, 68
Craft/craft group, 14, 28–29, 32, 33, 96, 99, 214n37
CREDIMO (Caisse de Crédit pour l'Achat de Machines-Outils), 101
Cresson, Edith, 149
Crossbar technology, 46, 53, 58, 68, 80
Crozier, Michel, 35, 97
CSF (Compagnie Générale de Télégraphie sans Fils), 74, 170
Cultural explanation, 15–16, 21, 23, 25–26, 37–38, 150, 205, 217n36. See also Symbol; Worldview

DAII (Direction des Affaires Industrielles et Internationales), 70
DATAR (Délégation à l'Aménagement du Territoire et à l'Action Régionale), 176, 177
DBP (Deutsche Bundespost), 40, 43–44, 48–52, 65–66, 80–83, 87, 200
Deckel, 139, 147
Deductive reasoning, 29–31, 34, 36, 92, 96, 117, 159, 164, 175, 195, 205
Delors, Jacques, 189
Demand, 102–103, 105–106, 111, 116, 123, 147. See also Market
DGT (Direction Générale des Télécommunications), 45–46, 58–60, 67–78, 80, 85–89, 199
Diebold, John, 171–172

DIELE (Direction des Industries Electroniques et de l'Informatique), 106, 176

Diffusion-oriented policy, 4, 36, 91–93, 126, 151; and German machine tools, 200, 201; and German programs, 198; and semiconductors, 159, 188, 194, 195; and telecommunications, 41, 61

Digital technology, 42, 54, 68, 90

DIHT (Deutscher Industrie- und Handelstag), 50

DIME. *See* DIMME

DIMME (Direction des Industries Métallurgiques, Mécaniques et Electroniques), 101, 106, 110, 115, 120, 121, 124

Dobbin, Frank, 205, 212n18, 216n9

Dondoux, Jacques, 75

DRAM (dynamic random access memory), 183, 184, 189–191, 241n74

Dreyfus, Pierre, 100, 112

DRG (Direction de la Réglementation Générale), 78

DT (Deutsche Telekom), 86–87, 89, 90, 200

Dual System, 33, 35, 98, 142

Dufour, 105, 108, 114, 120, 125

Durkheim, Emile, 214n37

DÜV (Dampfkessel-Überwachungs-Vereine), 93–94

Dyson, Kenneth, 220n72

Ecole Centrale des Arts et Manufactures, 96

Ecole des Mines, 28, 30

Ecole des Ponts et Chaussées, 28, 30

Ecole du Génie Militaire et Mézières, 28

Ecole Nationale Supérieure des Arts et Métiers, 111

Ecole Normale Supérieure, 28

Ecole Polytechnique, 28–30, 33, 60, 76, 79, 96, 97

Ecole Professionelle Supérieure des PTTs, 58

Ecoles des arts et métiers, 96

Ecole Supérieure des PTTs, 56, 58

Ecole Supérieure de Télégraphie, 56

Economics Ministry (Germany), 50, 131, 132, 135, 137–138

Education: and machine tools, 92; and semiconductors, 162, 164–165; vocational, 29, 31, 35, 98, 121–122. *See also* Knowledge; *specific institutions*
—French, 28–36, 99, 218n48, 218n50; and machine tools, 96–97, 110–112, 116, 118–121, 123, 149–150, 201; and

semiconductors, 165–167, 169, 180; and telecommunications, 56, 58–60, 79
—German, 32–36; and machine tools, 98, 130, 133, 142, 145, 148; and semiconductors, 166–168

Ehmke, Horst, 81, 130

Einheitstechnik, 67, 80, 83, 86, 89

Electronics, 52–54, 82, 91, 92, 121, 129, 132, 135, 138, 157, 159–162, 202. *See also* Computer technology; Microprocessors; Semiconductors

Electrotechnical industry association. *See* ZVEI

Elite, 21–33, 36, 98, 159, 164. *See also* Knowledge-bearing elite

EMD (Edelmetall-Motor-Drehwähler), 80

Employment, 13, 109, 115, 116, 123, 145–148, 151, 153, 154, 171–175, 207–208. *See also* Human resources

ENA (Ecole Nationale d'Administration), 29, 60

Engineers/engineering, 23, 25, 64; and semiconductors, 164–166, 193
—French, 24, 96–97, 218n48, 218n50; vs. German, 33–35, 93–94; and machine tools, 121; and semiconductors, 166, 168–169, 176, 179–181; and telecommunications, 41–42, 55–61, 70, 76, 77, 79, 88, 199
—German, 34–35, 63, 64; and machine tools, 98–99; and semiconductors, 167–169; and telecommunications, 65–66

ENSPTT (Ecole Nationale Supérieure des PTTs), 60

ENST (Ecole Nationale Supérieure des Télécommunications), 58–59, 79

Ericsson, 46–48, 51, 58, 62, 66, 68, 71–73, 77

Ernault-Somua, 108–109, 114, 120, 124

Ernaut-Toyoda-Automation, 124, 125

Europe, 23, 162–164, 187–190, 195, 203, 207–208

European Community, 76–77, 132, 188, 189, 209

Eurotechnique, 177, 179, 180

EWS (Elektronisches Wählsystem), 71, 72, 80, 82–83, 227n126

EWSD (Elektronisches Wählsystem Digital), 82, 84

Expertise. *See* Knowledge

Export, 54, 94, 102, 104, 122, 129, 148, 180, 230n26

FDP (Freie Demokratische Partei), 81, 131, 185

FGM (Féderation Générale de la
  Métallurgie), 116
Filière électronique, 75–77
Finance: and JESSI, 189; and
  semiconductors, 185, 188; and
  telecommunications, 54–55
—in France: and machine tools, 92,
  101–102, 104, 107, 111–115, 119, 125,
  148–149, 181; and semiconductors,
  165, 169, 171, 176, 177, 179–181; and
  telecommunications, 45, 56, 59–60, 71
—in Germany: and computers, 172, 173;
  and machine tools, 93, 126, 129–133,
  135, 137, 138, 140, 147, 156, 201; and
  semiconductors, 168, 173, 182; and
  telecommunications, 50, 86–87
Firm, 22, 124, 198; and machine tools,
  92, 95, 153; and semiconductors, 188,
  202; and technology policy, 197; and
  telecommunications, 41, 43. *See also*
  Suppliers
—French: and machine tools, 97–98,
  102–104, 110, 112, 116, 121–122,
  200–201; and semiconductors, 166,
  176, 194, 195; and
  telecommunications, 199
—German: and education, 35; and
  machine tools, 134, 138, 168–169; and
  semiconductors, 168–169, 194, 195;
  and telecommunications, 50
Firm size, 151, 153; and French machine
  tools, 95, 103–104, 106, 112, 113, 118,
  123, 129, 146, 148, 149; and German
  machine tools, 113, 126, 129–133,
  135, 136, 139, 141, 143, 146–148, 150.
  See also Scale
FKM (Forschungskuratorium
  Machinenbau), 133, 134, 150, 201, 205
Flexibility, 101, 107, 119, 129–130, 132,
  140, 188
FO (Force Ouvrière), 78, 110
Foreign technology, 173, 174, 181–183.
  See also Technology transfer
France Telecom, 78–79, 86, 87, 89–90,
  192, 199
Franke, Adolf, 64
Fraunhofer Society, 137, 143, 151, 168,
  201
FTZ (Fernmeldetechnisches Zentralamt),
  65, 66, 83, 87, 89, 200

Gadzart, 96
Geertz, Clifford, 18, 215n3, 220n72
General Electric, 108, 139, 170, 171
Gerschenkron, Alexander, 11–12
Gildemeister, 130, 139, 144, 147, 148

Giscard d'Estaing, Valéry, 70, 72, 88,
  100–102, 109, 171, 175, 178, 194, 199
Gomez, Alain, 181
Government, 1–4, 8–14, 197–198. *See
  also* Civil service; Politics; State
Graffenstaden, 109, 114, 115, 120, 125
Grandes écoles, 28–31, 35, 121, 164, 167,
  169, 218n48
Guild, 28, 32–33, 215n37

Hall, Peter, 12, 37, 214n30, 216n7,
  217nn31–32, 221n80, 244n6
Hardenberg, Karl August, Fürst von, 32
Hauff, Volker, 81, 131–134, 239n18
Herrigel, Gary, 216n9, 244n7
Hierarchy: occupational, 15, 24, 27, 36,
  94, 97–100, 103–104, 121–122,
  125–126, 145, 204, 213n22;
  organizational, 20, 208
Historical institutionalists, 19–20, 35
Hoffmann, Stanley, 26, 217n35, 218n44,
  231n43
Hughes, Everett, 23–24
Human resources, 168, 169; and French
  machine tools, 97, 112, 115–116,
  119–121, 123, 125, 149, 201; and
  German machine tools, 126, 128, 134,
  139, 141–145, 147, 150, 201. *See also*
  Employment; Knowledge-bearing elite
Humboldt, Wilhelm von, 32
Huré, 114, 115, 120

IBM (International Business Machines),
  66, 85, 162, 170–172, 186, 189–191
IC. *See* Integrated circuit
Identity, viii, ix, 14, 20, 76, 205, 207, 209
Ideology. *See* Cultural explanation
IDI (Institut de Développement
  Industriel), 103–105, 108, 113–114,
  120, 124
IG Metall, 94, 129, 133–135, 144, 145,
  148
Indirect-specific policy, 93, 126, 128, 132,
  134–138, 150, 201
Industrial concentration, 102–104, 109,
  112, 113, 129, 148, 149. *See also Pôle*
Ingénieurs des télécommunications,
  41–42, 55–61, 66, 73, 76, 77, 79, 88,
  199
Innovation, vii–ix, 2, 3, 5, 17, 151; and
  French machine tools, 103, 104, 109,
  115, 148, 200–201; and German
  machine tools, 132–134, 137; and
  German telecommunications, 88, 200;
  and knowledge-bearing elites, 207; and
  machine tools, 95; and semiconductors,
  159–161, 192–195; and technology

Innovation *(cont.)*
  policy, 203–206; and
    telecommunications, 41, 52–54; types
    of, 198
Institut National des
  Télécommunications, 79
Institution, viii, 8, 11–13, 18–19, 25–26
Institutionalist perspective, 14, 15, 19–21,
  25–26, 35, 214n26
Integrated circuit, 159, 163, 165, 167,
  173, 175–177, 180
Intel, 164, 171, 174, 178, 179
Interest group, viii, 10, 13–15, 17, 26,
  28–29, 82, 128, 135, 150, 197, 204
International economy, ix, 4–8, 40, 208;
  and machine tools, 106–107, 109, 112,
  122, 128, 146, 155; and
  semiconductors, 176, 181, 185–196;
  and telecommunications, 40, 42, 54,
  82, 84, 85
ISDN (integrated services digital
  network), 54
Italy, 94, 110, 111, 181, 187, 192, 195,
  202
ITT (International Telephone &
  Telegraph), 46–47, 51, 58, 68, 71–73,
  75, 77, 80, 84
IUT *(instituts universitaires de technologie),*
  31

Japan, 4, 12, 94, 105, 107, 110, 111, 119,
  147, 162–163, 182–186, 207
JESSI (Joint European Silicon Structures
  Initiative), 187–189, 192, 203
Jeumont-Schneider, 77, 109, 114, 120
Joint development, 200. *See also*
  Collaboration; Consultation;
  Cooperation; Mixed enterprise;
  Verbundprojekte

Katzenstein, Peter, 12, 211n2, 217n32,
  220n68, 220n73, 228n1
Knowledge, vii, 12, 17–19, 215n1; and
  competition, viii, 4–5, 208–209; and
  French machine tools, 100, 116, 149,
  201; and French semiconductors,
  164–166, 168–169, 181; and German
  machine tools, 137–139, 145, 201; and
  German semiconductors, 166–169,
  181–184; vs. scale, viii, 2, 4–5, 7, 197,
  206, 209; and semiconductors, 158,
  159, 162–164, 185, 186, 188, 193; and
  state, 27; and technology policy, 203;
  and telecommunications, 44. *See also*
  Education
Knowledge-bearing elite, vii–ix, 2, 11, 12,
  19, 24; and culture, 15–16; and

identity, 14, 207, 209; and machine
  tools, 93; and semiconductors, 162,
  193; and technology policy, 38, 197,
  204; and telecommunications, 40,
  87–89. *See also* Engineers/engineering;
  Professional order
—French, 205; vs. German, 4; and
  machine tools, 96–98, 100, 106,
  109–110, 116, 121–122, 125, 148–149;
  and semiconductors, 164–166,
  168–169, 181; and
  telecommunications, 41–42, 55–61,
  199
—German: and computers, 172; and
  machine tools, 98–99, 125–126, 128,
  145; and semiconductors, 166–169,
  181–184; and telecommunications,
  61–67, 200
Kocka, Jürgen, 63, 224n65
Kohl, Helmut, 86, 190
Krieger, Leonard, 32
KtK (Kommission für den Ausbau des
  technischen Kommunikationssystems),
  81–82, 88

Labor unions, 13, 77, 78, 85–86,
  108–110, 115–117, 126, 128, 130, 142,
  145
Lagardère, Jean-Luc, 179
Lambsdorff, Otto von, 131
Larson, Magali, 22, 216n19
LCR (Laboratoire National de
  Radioélectricité), 57
LETI (Laboratoire d'Electronique et de
  Technologie de l'Informatique), 165,
  166, 192
Liberalism, 6–11, 13, 14, 33, 127, 209,
  213n22; and Germany, 33
Libois, Joseph, 70
Liné, 105, 109, 113, 114, 120, 125
Liné, Henri, 113, 114
LMT (Le Matériel Téléphonique), 46–48,
  68, 71–73
Locke, Richard, 216n9, 244n11
Longuet, Gérard, 77
LSI (large-scale integration), 160, 171,
  173, 227n126
Lüschen, Fritz, 64–65

Machine Tool Plan, 109–125
Machine tools, 3, 39, 91; French, 4, 13,
  91–94, 96–126, 202; French vs.
  German, 4, 91–99, 125–127, 130, 139,
  140, 146, 148–151, 200–201, 204–206;
  German, 4, 14, 91–94, 125–148,
  201–202

Manufacture, 121, 159, 160–162, 185, 186. *See also* Production
March, James, 21, 213n24, 216n10, 216n13
Market, 10, 20, 197, 207; and French machine tools, 105–106; and French semiconductors, 171, 179, 181; and French telecommunications, 41, 46, 48, 71, 199; and German machine tools, 134; and German semiconductors, 195; and German telecommunications, 84; vs. government, 1–3, 197–198; internal, 54, 109, 112, 119, 124, 147, 180; and machine tools, 152, 155; and technology policy, 197; and telecommunications, 43, 54. *See also* Demand; International economy
Matra, 177–180, 202. *See also* MHS
Matthöfer, Hans, 130
Maurice, Marc, 31, 219n57, 219n75, 219n77, 228nn7–8
Max Planck Society, 168
Mayntz, Renate, 222n20, 222n23, 228n2
MECA (Materiéls et Équipements de Conception Avancée), 103, 111
Mechanical engineers, 93–94, 96–99, 119
Megaproject, 158, 183
Merton, Robert, 213n22
Meyer-Krahmer, Frieder, 234nn111–112, 242n78
MFL (Machines Françaises Lourdes), 114, 115, 119, 125
MHS (Matra-Harris-Semiconducteurs), 178, 179
Microprocessors, 52, 161, 171, 174, 175. *See also* Computer technology; Electronics
Military, 45, 157, 158, 170, 171, 176, 179, 180
Ministry of Defense (France), 45, 57, 176, 179, 180
Ministry of Employment (France), 110
Ministry of Finance (France), 45, 60, 110
Ministry of Industry (France), 45, 77, 102, 110, 119, 121, 176, 189, 201
Ministry of National Education (France), 102–103, 111, 119–121
Ministry of Posts and Telegraphs (France), 56. *See also* PTT
Ministry of Research and Industry (France), 179, 180
Ministry of Research and Technology (Germany). *See* BMFT
Mission, 19, 20, 26, 31
Mission-oriented policy, 4, 36, 198; and machine tools, 100, 116, 118, 148, 151; and semiconductors, 159, 180,

193, 195–196, 202; and telecommunications, 41, 91, 199, 204
Mitterrand, François, 109, 190
Mixed enterprise, 47, 51, 52, 65, 67
Monnet, Jean, 10
Motorola, 162–164, 171, 177, 180, 191

National champion strategy, 172, 174, 178, 189, 192
Nelson, Richard, 212n19, 213n1
Neocorporatist perspective, 13–14
Network: industrial, 5, 96, 108, 111, 194, 207; organizational, 4, 7, 13, 23, 167, 188–189, 195–196; professional, 17, 38, 100, 103, 126, 136, 198, 203, 207–209; technological, 38, 40–47, 49, 51, 52, 54, 58–60, 62–67, 70, 72, 77–78, 80–82, 84, 86, 88, 106, 140, 141, 151, 200
Nixdorf, 66, 85, 172, 174, 187
NUM. *See* Société NUM
Numerical control, 130. *See also* CNC

Occupational group, 2, 14, 15, 19, 23, 32–36, 38, 99, 116, 133, 159. *See also* Guild; Organization, intermediary; Professional order
Olsen, Johan, 21
Ordnungspolitik, 127, 130–133, 137, 150
Organization, 16, 18–19; intermediary, 126, 136, 148, 200, 201, 205–206. *See also* Guild
Organizational structure, for industry, 25–26, 41–52, 87, 94–95, 100, 139, 158–162, 201
Ornano, Michel d', 100, 108, 110, 112

PERICLES, 68–69
Perrow, Charles, 20
Philips, 71, 84, 86, 139, 158, 163, 172, 174, 176, 177, 182–183, 187–188
Pistorio, Pasquale, 191
Plan Calcul, 157, 170–172, 176, 193
Plan Composant, 157, 175–176, 180
Plan Filière, 178, 179. *See also* Filière électronique
Plan Machine-Outil, 109–125
Plan Productique, 118–123, 126, 140
PLATON, 68–69, 71, 74
Pluralism. *See* Liberalism
Pôle, 103, 111, 114, 124–125
Policy. *See* Technology policy
Politics, vii, 2, 12, 14–17, 25–27, 30, 69, 203, 204. *See also* Civil service; Government; State
Polyani, Karl, 6
Polyani, Michael, 31, 215n1

Polytechnicien, 58–59, 164
Polyvalence, 30, 34, 59, 93
Postal Ministry (Germany), 48–50. *See also* DBP
Prestige, viii, 18, 22–24, 30, 33
Prévot, Hubert, 78
Price, Don, 10–11
Private sector, 2, 42, 61, 63–64, 207
Privatization, 78, 79, 86, 90, 199, 200
Procurement, 43, 60–61, 69, 70, 83–86, 88, 166
Production, 113, 134, 141, 148; and French machine tools, 101, 112, 117, 121, 129; and French semiconductors, 166; and German machine tools, 128–130, 134, 136, 145, 146, 169; and semiconductors, 190, 193. *See also* Manufacture
Profession, 17–39
Professional order, 18–19, 27–38, 41, 87–89. *See also* Knowledge-bearing elite
Programm Fertigungstechnik, 135–138, 141, 147, 156
Programming. *See* Computer programming
Property rights, 20, 43
PTT (Postes, Télégraphes et Téléphones), 40, 42–45, 49, 50, 52, 57, 69, 71, 76, 87, 89, 175, 176, 221n8
Public policy. *See* Technology policy

Qualification, ethos of, 36, 159, 195, 206, 220n72
Quilès, Paul, 78

Radical innovation, 105–106
Reichspost, 51, 62–64, 222n21. *See also* DBP
Renault, 107, 108, 114, 115, 120
Renault Machine-Outil, 107
Research, ix; corporate, 5; and Deutsche Telekom, 200; and European semiconductors, 188; and JESSI, 189; and liberalism, 10; and machine tools, 92; and telecommunications, 52–54, 63
—in France, 30–31; and machine tools, 92–93, 103, 104, 111–112, 116, 117, 120, 122; and semiconductors, 165, 169, 171, 181; and telecommunications, 41–42, 47, 56–58, 69, 71, 75, 78, 89–90
—in Germany: and machine tools, 130–134, 136, 138, 143–144, 169; and semiconductor industry, 181–183; and semiconductors, 167–168, 191, 203; and telecommunications, 80, 86–87, 89, 90

Restructuring, 55, 92–93, 119–120, 123, 134, 140, 200–201
Riesenhuber, Heinz, 136
Robotics, 101, 105–109, 119, 138, 144
Rotary exchange, 46, 51, 53, 57
Royal Society, 28
RTC (Radiotechnique-Compelec), 176–179
Ruge, Ingolf, 182
Ruggie, John, 6, 209

Sabel, Charles F., 215n3, 229nn14, 17
Samuels, Richard J., 214nn32–33, 217n32
SAT (Société Anonyme de Télécommunications), 71
Saxenian, AnnaLee, 216n9, 242n90, 244n7
Scale, 106, 110, 112–113, 118, 181; vs. knowledge, viii, 2, 4–5, 7, 197, 206, 209. *See also* Firm size
SCFMO (Syndicats des Constructeurs Français de la Machine-Outil), 100
Scharpf, Fritz, 119, 214n35, 226n19
Schonfield, Andrew, 102
Science, 9, 10–11, 24–25, 27, 28, 32, 34, 164–167. *See also* Knowledge
Scientists, 2, 15
Sector, 2, 9, 13, 26, 37–38. *See also* Machine tools; Semiconductors; Technology policy; Telecommunications; *specific programs*
SEL (Standard Elektrik Lorenz), 51, 77, 79, 80, 84–86, 172
Self-governance/regulation, 32, 93, 95, 123, 134, 143, 158
Self-image, viii, 21, 93, 94
Self-sufficiency. *See* Autarky; Autonomy
Sellier, François, 31, 219n57, 219n75, 219n77, 228nn7–8
Selznick, Philip, 18, 21, 215n2, 215n4, 216n11
Semiconductors, 3, 39, 52, 159–164; European, 162–164, 187–190, 195, 203; French, 13, 168, 170–171, 173, 175–181, 187–195, 202; French vs. German, 4, 157–159, 161, 202; German, 166–169, 171–176, 181–185, 187–189, 193–195, 203; and international economy, 185–196
SERT (Service d'Études et de Recherches Techniques), 56, 57
SESCOSEM, 170, 171, 177, 178
SGS (Società Generale Semiconduttori), 181, 191, 195, 202
SGS-Thomson Microelectronics (STM), 187–189

Shinn, Terry, 30, 218n41

Siemens, 157; and computers, 172; and machine tools, 108, 139, 169; and semiconductors, 158, 163, 173–175, 181–184, 187–192, 194, 195, 203; and telecommunications, 40, 42, 50–52, 61–67, 71, 77, 80, 82–86, 88–89, 200

Siemens, Georg von, 63, 224n61

Siemens, Werner von, 62

Simon, Herbert, 21

Skilled worker, 97, 99, 126, 128, 134, 141, 143–144, 148, 150

Skocpol, Theda, 12, 213n25, 214nn28–29, 214n31

Social Democratic party. See SPD

Socialist party (France), 74, 77, 78, 88, 109, 110, 121, 178, 179, 202

Société de Téléphone Ericsson, 46

Société d'Ingénieurs Civils, 96

Société d'Innovations Mécaniques, 114

Société Française de Téléphone-Ericsson, 72

Société Industrielle des Téléphones, 46, 47, 57

Société NUM, 108, 112, 122–125, 140

Society, 8, 12, 23–24

Sociological institutionalists, 19–21

SOCOTEL (Société Mixte pour le Développement de la Technique de la Commutation dans le Domaine des Télécommunications), 47

SOCRATE, 68–69

Software. See Computer Programming

SOTELEC (Société Mixte pour le Développement de la Technique des Télécommunications sur Câbles), 47

Souviron, Jean-Pierre, 70–72, 107, 108, 112, 119

Soviet Union, 207–208

SPD (Sozialdemokratische Partei Deutschland), 81, 86, 88, 127, 131, 134–136

Specialization, 100, 111–112

Special Program for the Application of Microelectronics, 132, 137–138

State, 14, 206–208; and French engineers, 30, 35; and innovation, 151; and institutionalist perspective, 19–20; and knowledge-bearing elite, 19; and liberalism, 10; vs. market, 197–198; and professions, 22, 23; and semiconductors, 187–188; vs. society, 8, 12; and technology policy, 27, 36–39; and telecommunications, 54–55, 199. See also Civil service; Government; Politics

—French: and machine tools, 92–93, 101, 105–106, 109–110, 117–118, 122, 123, 148–149; and research, 30–31; and semiconductors, 176, 193–194, 196; and telecommunications, 41, 44–45, 57

—German: and engineers, 35; and machine tools, 127–128; and occupations, 33; and telecommunications, 48–50, 81

State-certified occupations, 32–36, 99, 159

Statist perspective, 11–13, 127

Stein, Friedrich Karl, Freiherr von und zum, 32

Streeck, Wolfgang, 220nn76–77, 226n120, 236n152

STM (SGS-Thomson Microelectronics), 187–189

Strowger technology, 51, 62, 63, 80

Strukturpolitik, 127, 129–133, 136, 137, 150

Suleiman, Ezra, 217n38, 218n46, 218n48, 218n51, 223n49, 244n2

Suppliers: and Deutsche Telekom, 200; and French machine tools, 95, 100, 117–118; and French telecommunications, 46–47, 57–58, 60–61, 67–79; and German telecommunications, 50–52, 80, 82–85; and semiconductors, 160–161, 185, 187–188, 191, 192; and telecommunications, 43–44, 52, 54, 89. See also specific firms

Supplier-user link, 117–118

Swidler, Ann, 217n33, 217n36

Switching technology, 42, 53, 68–69, 71–73, 75–77, 80, 82–84, 200, 227n126

Sylvestre, Jean-Jacques, 31, 219n57, 219n75, 219n77, 228nn7–8

Symbol, 18, 19, 21, 22, 24, 25, 220n72. See also Cultural explanation

T&N (Telefonbau und Normalzeit), 51, 80, 84

Technical elite. See Knowledge-bearing elite

Technical university, 34, 168

Technician, 2, 33, 97, 98, 111, 112, 118, 122

Technology policy, vii–ix, 1–2, 8–14, 27, 28, 204–206; approaches to, 36–39, 197–198. See also Diffusion-oriented policy; Indirect-specific policy; Mission-oriented policy; National champion strategy; entries beginning Plan

NATIONAL UNIVERSITY
LIBRARY   SAN DIEGO

—French: and computers, 170–171; and
machine tools, 99–125, 148–150; and
semiconductors, 175–181; and
telecommunications, 67–79
—German: and computers, 171–175; and
machine tools, 125–148, 150–151; and
semiconductors, 181–185; and
telecommunications, 80–90
Technology transfer, 157, 158, 165, 176,
181. *See also* Foreign technology
Telecommunications, 3, 4, 39, 199;
French, 13, 44–48, 54–61, 67–79, 199,
204, 206; French vs. German, 40–44,
52, 86–90; German, 40–42, 48–52,
54–55, 61–67, 80–90, 183, 200
Théry, Gerard, 70, 71, 72, 75, 76
Thomas, Uwe, 182
Thomson, 69–76, 88, 108, 170, 176, 179,
181, 187–189, 191, 192, 202
Thomson-Composants, 179, 191, 195
Thomson-CSF, 124, 170, 171, 177, 178,
189, 191, 192
Toshiba, 183, 190, 191
Toyoda, 109, 120, 124, 125
Toyota, 109
Trägerorganisation, 126, 136, 148, 200,
201, 205–206
Training. *See* Education
Transaction-cost analysis, 20, 43–44
Traub, 139, 144, 147
Trumpf, 144, 147, 148
TÜV (Technische-Überwachungs-
Vereine), 93–94

United Kingdom, 11, 12, 22, 23, 28, 94,
181, 187
United States, 2–3, 11, 12, 22–24, 63,
111, 127, 157, 207; and

semiconductors, 162, 163, 170, 174,
176, 184, 186–187, 193, 203
University, 33–35, 137, 168–169

Values. *See* Cultural explanation
VANS (Value-added-network service), 77
VDI (Verein Deutscher Ingenieure), 33,
64, 98, 135, 138, 142, 150, 201, 205
VDI-Technologiezentrum, 135, 138, 150,
205
VDMA (Verband Deutscher Maschinen-
und Anlagenbau), 66, 133. *See also* FKM
VDPI (Verband Deutscher
Postingenieure), 65–66
VDW (Verein Deutscher
Werkzeugmaschinenfabriken), 148
Verbundprojekte, 137, 150
Vernon, Raymond, 6, 10
Vichy government, 44–45, 58, 101
VLSI (very-large-scale integration), 184,
186, 241n56

Walzer, Michael, 213n22
Warnecke, Hans-Jürgen, 141, 236nn146,
156
Weber, Max, 11–12, 18, 214n26
Weir, Margaret, 12, 214n29, 244n6
Williamson, Oliver, 20
Witte, Eberhard, 85
Worldview, 19, 24–27, 55, 61, 220n72. *See
also* Cultural explanation; Symbol

Yamazaki, 124

Zentrum für angewandte
Mikroelektronik, 167
Zuse, Konrad, 171
ZVEI (Zentralverband der
elektrotechnischen Industrie), 66, 83
Zysman, John, 12, 211n2, 214n17,
230n25, 238n1, 239n23

Cornell Studies in Political Economy

EDITED BY PETER J. KATZENSTEIN

National Diversity and Global Capitalism, edited by Suzanne Berger and Ronald Dore
Collapse of an Industry: Nuclear Power and the Contradictions of U.S. Policy,
    by John L. Campbell
The Price of Wealth: Economies and Institutions in the Middle East,
    by Kiren Aziz Chaudhry
Power, Purpose, and Collective Choice: Economic Strategy in Socialist States,
    edited by Ellen Comisso and Laura D'Andrea Tyson
The Political Economy of the New Asian Industrialism,
    edited by Frederic C. Deyo
Dislodging Multinationals: India's Strategy in Comparative Perspective,
    by Dennis J. Encarnation
Rivals beyond Trade: America versus Japan in Global Competition,
    by Dennis J. Encarnation
Enterprise and the State in Korea and Taiwan, by Karl J. Fields
National Interests in International Society, by Martha Finnemore
Democracy and Markets: The Politics of Mixed Economies, by John R. Freeman
The Misunderstood Miracle: Industrial Development and Political Change in Japan,
    by David Friedman
Ideas, Interests, and American Trade Policy, by Judith Goldstein
Ideas and Foreign Policy: Beliefs, Institutions, and Political Change,
    edited by Judith Goldstein and Robert O. Keohane
Monetary Sovereignty: The Politics of Central Banking in Western Europe,
    by John B. Goodman
Politics in Hard Times: Comparative Responses to International Economic Crises,
    by Peter Gourevitch
Closing the Gold Window: Domestic Politics and the End of Bretton Woods, by Joanne Gowa
Cooperation among Nations: Europe, America, and Non-tariff Barriers to Trade,
    by Joseph M. Grieco
Nationalism, Liberalism, and Progress, volume 1, by Ernst B. Haas
Pathways from the Periphery: The Politics of Growth in the Newly Industrializing Countries,
    by Stephan Haggard
The Politics of Finance in Developing Countries, edited by Stephan Haggard,
    Chung H. Lee, and Sylvia Maxfield
*Rival Capitalists: International Competitiveness in the United States, Japan, and Western
    Europe,* by Jeffrey A. Hart
The Philippine State and the Marcos Regime: The Politics of Export,
    by Gary Hawes
Reasons of State: Oil Politics and the Capacities of American Government,
    by G. John Ikenberry
The State and American Foreign Economic Policy, edited by G. John Ikenberry,
    David A. Lake, and Michael Mastanduno
The Paradox of Continental Production: National Investment Policies in North America,
    by Barbara Jenkins
Pipeline Politics: The Complex Political Economy of East-West Energy Trade,
    by Bruce W. Jentleson
The Politics of International Debt, edited by Miles Kahler
Corporatism and Change: Austria, Switzerland, and the Politics of Industry,
    by Peter J. Katzenstein
Cultural Norms and National Security: Police and Military in Postwar Japan,
    by Peter J. Katzenstein
Industry and Politics in West Germany: Toward the Third Republic,
    edited by Peter J. Katzenstein
Small States in World Markets: Industrial Policy in Europe, by Peter J. Katzenstein
*The Sovereign Entrepreneur: Oil Policies in Advanced and Less Developed Capitalist
    Countries,* by Merrie Gilbert Klapp

Norms in International Relations: The Struggle against Apartheid, by Audie Klotz

International Regimes, edited by Stephen D. Krasner

Business and Banking: Political Change and Economic Integration in Western Europe, by Paulette Kurzer

Power, Protection, and Free Trade: International Sources of U.S. Commercial Strategy, 1887–1939, by David A. Lake

State Capitalism: Public Enterprise in Canada, by Jeanne Kirk Laux and Maureen Appel Molot

Why Syria Goes to War: Thirty Years of Confrontation, by Fred H. Lawson

Remaking the Italian Economy, by Richard M. Locke

France after Hegemony: International Change and Financial Reform, by Michael Loriaux

Economic Containment: CoCom and the Politics of East-West Trade, by Michael Mastanduno

Business and the State in Developing Countries, edited by Sylvia Maxfield and Ben Ross Schneider

Mercantile States and the World Oil Cartel, 1900–1939, by Gregory P. Nowell

Opening Financial Markets: Banking Politics on the Pacific Rim, by Louis W. Pauly

Who Elected the Bankers? Surveillance and Control in the World Economy, by Louis W. Pauly

The Limits of Social Democracy: Investment Politics in Sweden, by Jonas Pontusson

The Fruits of Fascism: Postwar Prosperity in Historical Perspective, by Simon Reich

The Business of the Japanese State: Energy Markets in Comparative and Historical Perspective, by Richard J. Samuels

"Rich Nation, Strong Army": National Security and the Technological Transformation of Japan, by Richard J. Samuels

Crisis and Choice in European Social Democracy, by Fritz W. Scharpf, translated by Ruth Crowley

In the Dominions of Debt: Historical Perspectives on Dependent Development, by Herman M. Schwartz

Winners and Losers: How Sectors Shape the Developmental Prospects of States, by D. Michael Shafer

Europe and the New Technologies, edited by Margaret Sharp

Europe's Industries: Public and Private Strategies for Change, edited by Geoffrey Shepherd, François Duchêne, and Christopher Saunders

Ideas and Institutions: Developmentalism in Brazil and Argentina, by Kathryn Sikkink

The Cooperative Edge: The Internal Politics of International Cartels, by Debora L. Spar

Fair Shares: Unions, Pay, and Politics in Sweden and West Germany, by Peter Swenson

Union of Parts: Labor Politics in Postwar Germany, by Kathleen A. Thelen

Democracy at Work: Changing World Markets and the Future of Labor Unions, by Lowell Turner

Troubled Industries: Confronting Economic Change in Japan, by Robert M. Uriu

National Styles of Regulation: Environmental Policy in Great Britain and the United States, by David Vogel

Freer Markets, More Rules: Regulatory Reform in Advanced Industrial Countries, by Steven K. Vogel

The Political Economy of Policy Coordination: International Adjustment since 1945, by Michael C. Webb

International Cooperation: Building Regimes for Natural Resources and the Environment, by Oran R. Young

International Governance: Protecting the Environment in a Stateless Society, by Oran R. Young

Polar Politics: Creating International Environmental Regimes, edited by Oran R. Young and Gail Osherenko

Governing Ideas: Strategies for Innovation in France and Germany, by J. Nicholas Ziegler

Governments, Markets, and Growth: Financial Systems and the Politics of Industrial Change, by John Zysman

American Industry in International Competition: Government Policies and Corporate Strategies, edited by John Zysman and Laura Tyson

J. Nicholas Ziegler is Associate Professor at MIT's Sloan School of Management and Faculty Associate at the Center for European Studies at Harvard University.